MARKETING AND COMMUNICATIONS ON THE JOB

How to Establish a Marketing and Corporate Communications Department from Scratch

Understanding Marketing, PR, Media, Events, Sponsorships, and Marcomms Strategies

Marwa Kaabour, BSMIS, MBA

PASSIONPRENEUR®
P U B L I S H I N G

Marketing and Communications on the Job
Copyright © 2022 Marwa Kaabour, BSMIS, MBA
First published in 2022

Print: 978-1-76124-073-7
E-book: 978-1-76124-074-4
Hardback: 978-1-76124-075-1

Because of the dynamic nature of the Internet, any web addresses or links contained in this book may have changed since publication and may no longer be valid. The information in this book is based on the author's experiences and opinions. The views expressed in this book are solely those of the author and do not necessarily reflect the views of the publisher; the publisher hereby disclaims any responsibility for them.

The author of this book does not dispense any form of medical, legal, financial, or technical advice either directly or indirectly. The intent of the author is solely to provide information of a general nature to help you in your quest for personal development and growth. In the event you use any of the information in this book, the author and the publisher assume no responsibility for your actions. If any form of expert assistance is required, the services of a competent professional should be sought.

Publishing information
Publishing and design facilitated by Passionpreneur Publishing
A division of Passionpreneur Organization Pty Ltd
ABN: 48640637529

Melbourne, VIC | Australia
www.passionpreneurpublishing.com

To my mother, who has always been a tower of strength and commitment. I grew up watching you work without a shadow of a doubt or a complaint, and you have continued to do so for forty years to date.

To my dad, thank you for introducing me to the world of books at such a young age. In my best memory of you, there is a book in your hand.

Table of Contents

Acknowledgments

What I love most about Elizabeth Gilbert's book *Big Magic* is the way it confronts the world with the fact that ideas are rarely original. She makes the point that the best innovations are ideas that sought fruition before others.

I must insist on acknowledging that the body of work presented in this book did not all originate with me. My intention was to pick the theories I applied throughout my career and rearrange them into frameworks that are easy to use.

In this exercise, I made sure to honour the originators of the theories and the authors of the content that I have borrowed those ideas from.

These authors have my full respect and admiration. Nothing is more warming to the heart than to see industry veterans and scholars putting aside time from their busy schedules to supplement the industry with their knowledge through books.

I did hit a wall of fatigue a couple of times while writing this book. The chapters were written in the long hours of the night or the early mornings of the weekend days. My days are usually spent answering to pressing work demands and the duties of a single parent looking after two little children – all amidst a once-in-a-century pandemic.

What kept me going was the pile of great books stacked up on my desk. They inspired me to read more and write more.

My children's nanny, Cherito, was as excited about the book as I was. She took it to heart to help me get some quiet time at home and looked after my kids as if they were her own. For this, Cherito deserves my biggest thanks.

Foreword

Are you looking to establish your marketing and communications department from scratch? Are you an entrepreneur or small business owner? Perhaps you have a background in sales or advertising and are making your way to a marcomms job on the client-side?

Maybe you are still an aspiring student who is new to the marcomms field altogether. Possibly you do work for a marcomms department and know that some things need to change but you can't quite put your finger on where to start... Regardless of your background or aspirations, as long as you dream of working in marketing and communications, this book is for you.

There are many books on marketing filling every library and bookstore in the world, and all of them have one thing in common: they are landed with theories that sound good on paper but not all of us have the means to execute them. A lot of these books are either written by university professors or CMOs of the world's largest and most impressive brands. They derive learnings from the best-in-class companies in a wonderful way, but their points might simply not be applicable to the other 90% of companies, which do not have the bandwidth nor the budgets to make golden case studies on award-winning work. This book does not have any case studies; it only carries frameworks, processes, and tangible steps that make marketing and communications on the job practical and easy to implement. You can start your own department from scratch by following the first ten chapters of the book.

I have accumulated over two decades' worth of learnings to provide you with practical tools that will enable you to take on the rewarding mission of leading impactful marcomms teams, growing and establishing brands, and ensuring profitability to contribute to the overall welfare of your company.

During my last 25 years of work, I have established marketing and corporate communications departments from scratch for both homegrown companies and major corporations, each with varying nuances and different kinds of challenges. My work experience spans across sectors and industries that include power and utilities, renewable energy, food and beverage, airlines, banking, manufacturing, logistics, electronics, and automotive.

Any marketer can take on a marcomms role with their knowledge of the market, but only a skilful marketer can truly excel at it. This requires the ability to take small steps every day in an analytical and strategic manner while keeping your messaging focused and your department's grand vision intact.

If you follow the guidelines in this book step by step, I guarantee you will build an efficient and successful marcomms department. Before we begin, here is a thought-starter to what you need to keep in mind while navigating the marcomms field.

Manage the pipeline jungle!

Establishing a marcomms function is like playing a game of Whack-A-Mole. An extensive list of tedious ongoing projects will pop up as one mole. Suggested initiatives that may be beneficial in the short term but not necessary for solving the company's most pressing issues will pop up as a second mole. Your own thoughts on where to start will pop up as a third mole, and a fourth one, and a fifth one. It can get overwhelming.

As you hammer down each popping mole, keep your composure and don't lose sight of the bigger picture. Building a successful marcomms department is not an overnight achievement. You can't just hit every popping matter unless it is necessary. Winning means a slow evolution that occurs when small but correct steps are taken every day. Priority is key.

Hit the mole on the head where it matters with nimbleness and confidence. The marcomms field branches out into several domains, making it inevitable that you will get carried away with too many projects while smaller tasks, which may seem menial but are essential, begin slipping through the cracks. Add to that the pressure of an under-resourced team and tight budgets, and you'll feel like you've started to lose perspective.

In establishing a marcomms department, a minimalist and balanced approach is the most effective. Yes, that project sounds promising, and that one too, but perhaps the solution at first is to opt for a process of elimination rather than addition. That means putting some projects to sleep – especially the ones that have been tried again and again but plateau when it comes to their results. Accept that, at least in the foundation-building stage, which can last for many months, you need to follow an 'if it ain't broken, don't fix it' approach so you can spend your time and energy on the work that will bring in the real change.

When joining a new company, marcomms executives are always expected to bring to the table a visible change; one that can be seen. You can still make your presence felt in your company by mapping out a series of tasks that will create 'small wins' without overstretching your resources or impacting the overall vision of the department. These may be milestone projects or any requests that, although you may not deem them necessary, management wants and will enjoy witnessing their birth. You'll need to exercise your own judgment when striking that balance.

When I joined one of the fastest-growing banks in the United Arab Emirates, I was part of the strategic team finalising the launch of the brand and its go-to-market strategy. After that, I was asked to help them establish their marketing function and then their communication and public affairs function. Although it was an exciting time in my career, it was daunting. I had to juggle several hot potatoes at once: the bank's website and internet banking portal and a 360-marketing campaign to create intrigue and awareness in the local market as well as a complete communication plan for building an impeccable reputation for this newly birthed bank. Everything was moving faster than the speed at which we could deliver. We were still in the process of hiring the team and the suite of agencies to bring all these projects to life. I knew I had to prioritise and get back to the management with what projects need to be done, one at a time.

Although the department was growing new branches at lightning speed, with the team responsible for launching almost all the bank's personal and wholesale banking products, launching their retail banking assets, credit cards, network of branches as well as their internet portals and mobile apps, I realised I had fallen into the ultimate trap: I was trying to do too much too early, and I wanted to be everything for everyone when what I should have really done was focus on setting the building blocks of the department.

In this book, I hope to fill all the gaps the academic field has no interest in and give you that hands on knowledge and guidance that is normally hidden between the lines and beneath the lines, so that all your marcomms dreams can come true on both a personal and professional level.

In universities, students in the communications field are taught how to promote a brand, how to function in the realms of the digital and social, how to navigate the global and local media scenes, and how to develop skills in visual design, and audio and video production. It is necessary to learn about all these mediums, but the reality of the matter is this:

The world is changing at a rapid speed, and the lines between marketing and communications are blurring.

What pleases customers and succeeds in markets today might stop working tomorrow. Budgets are shrinking but expectations are expanding, and marcomms folks need to make more bang for their bucks.

Here are all the practical learnings from the experiences I've had working in the field. I hope they help you in one way or another.

Happy reading.

1

A LITTLE ABOUT ME

*'The future belongs to the curious. The ones who
are not afraid to try it, explore it, poke at it,
question it and turn it inside out.'*

— Anonymous

Hello. I am Marwa, and I am a 'curious' marketer. Let me tell
you a little bit about my journey in the world of marketing and
communications.

During the years of my childhood, in war-torn Beirut, I spent a
large chunk of my days watching TV and skimming through magazines and newspapers. Apart from the heart-wrenching news about
the civil war in Lebanon that my family watched every night, I was
mesmerised by TV commercials. They were my window to the outside world. I then fell in love with talk shows and the work of journalism. The best part of my day was sitting next to my father in the
morning as he flipped through the daily newspaper. Being hidden
behind the large spread of papers made me feel safe and warm. The

world was inches away from our eyes. I read headlines and never bothered with more than a couple of sentences from the articles. I'd take those nuggets of news to school and show off my knowledge to my classmates and teachers.

My family fled the Lebanese civil war to seek a new chance at life in the United Arab Emirates in the 80s. I grew up in a country that has witnessed the fastest and most positive economic transformation in the region.

Having access to electricity all day long, a blessing that most Lebanese still appreciate until today, meant a lot of TV binge watching. I was fascinated with the production work of TV commercials and the promotional sampling activities that took place in supermarkets and malls. In the early 80s, door-to-door selling was very common and gaining popularity. I remember the infamous sound of a 'Laylam', a travelling merchant who passed through neighbourhoods and approached your door with an opera-like sonata, *'La La La LayLaam'*. They often carried close to 50 kilos of merchandise wrapped in large fabric bags over one shoulder and arched their way to people's houses. They would knock doors and sell their merchandise to families all the while keeping up with the unwavering haggling of housewives in the sunny temperatures of the day.

I remember a saleslady who used to knock on our door gently and then sell me a pink translucent peeling facemask that stuck to my face like the glue found on the flap of envelopes. She sold me the promise of a miracle that will wipe away my teenage acne. I also remember how I would flutter with excitement when my mother brought home perfume samples in tiny one-millilitre dropper bottles packaged with nicely designed paper jackets from the mall.

I graduated high school in 1997. Talk shows were starting to pick up in the Middle East. A lot of taboos were not yet addressed, and

Oprah Winfrey was on a roll. The youth tuned in to her show as she was so relatable and uncovered the secrecy of people's pains and agonies. It felt like she was a new media saint, sent to bring a lot more awareness on societal stigmas and mental health to the lives of the masses.

My mother worked as a local journalist and a translator, and my father, although a banker, wrote a weekly column on the economic and financial matters in the leading Arabic newspaper of Sharjah. It was my dream to become a content creator of some sort. I had a desire to study journalism and mass communication. I wanted to go back to Lebanon after graduating high school and study in my home country, but the political instability discouraged my parents from sending me back there.

Luckily, I managed to gain admission to the American University of Sharjah in its very first year of opening in the UAE. Affiliated by the American University of Washington, the university was set to open its doors and receive new students in October. The university didn't have a journalism or mass communication course yet, so I signed up for a degree in Marketing and Management.

Here is how I fell in love with marketing

I remember my very first marketing class with great fondness. It was around noon and the classroom felt so warm and bright from the beaming sun rays crossing through the glass windows. The walls were exceptionally white and clean since the building was freshly painted. The teacher walked in and greeted the students cheerfully. As this was the students' first introduction to the world of marketing, the professor started the class by asking the students a question: 'If you were given a choice to market a specific product or service, what would you choose?' Naturally, each one of the students replied with a type of business or product that they obviously liked.

Some suggested ice-cream shops, sportswear, real-estate developments, NGOs and cat cafes. The professor listened to everyone and then shook her head sideways and gave out a long gaze of disappointment. A moment of awkward silence hovered over the classroom, which was full of puzzled faces. The teacher then replied, 'A good marketer can market just about anything! Just like a great salesperson can sell anything, a great marketer can market just about anything too!'

She then went on to explain that the secret to great marketing anything lies in applying the right marketing formulas. She started by referencing the STP tool and others as well. **STP** stands for **Segmentation, Targeting,** and **Positioning**, and it has a formula too.

STP examines your products or services as well as the way you communicate their benefits to specific customer segments. This book will cover the usage of STP in strategies in later chapters. I didn't realise that such a simple tool could stick with me throughout my career.

All right. Back to my story. From that day onwards, I made a promise to myself that I would be a curious marketer. One who can market just about anything.

After my graduation, I ventured into the field of marketing and communications, which I will frequently refer to as 'marcomms' in this book. I navigated my way through its many different disciplines including branding and PR. I realised that once you have the right understanding of the business, and the willingness to keep learning, you become a great marcomms professional.

Working with the best of agencies

Life presented me with a wonderful opportunity to start my first job at one of the world's best advertising agencies. I worked there for a year while completing my master's degree studies. In the beginning of my stunt, I interned at the agency's different departments, from account handling to advertising design and video production. I was mesmerised and, at the same time, intimidated by the characters of the creative directors. They were inspiring but unnerving. They kept to themselves for long hours and then they would suddenly gush into loud forms of animated expressions, from laughter to speeches, to jokes and political debates.

After completing my internship, I was offered a full-time job at the agency. I was so happy walking into the HR manager's office knowing that I would be receiving an offer to work as a full-time in account handler or as a junior copywriter. I honestly believed I was good at writing headlines and scripts. But the job offered was in the media planning department. Media planning is the process of deciding which media channels are best suited for delivering an advertising campaign. Was I happy? Not really. The disappointment lasted a few minutes as the HR manager pitched the excitement of a career in media planning to me. I accepted the job with a grateful mind and a disappointed heart.

Sometimes you go through agonising tasks in your career to learn a thing or two that will come in handy in your future. I really thought I was not a numbers person, but I later learnt that the ability to work with numbers is imperative to the success of a marcomms professional. As far as I remember, I spent my days in the media department by the photocopy and fax machines. My hours were spent dispatching and filing away media booking forms. Back in the day, booking orders were paper-based tabular-style forms used to reserve advertising spots or spaces over a specified period of time for a campaign. My job was to transmit those booking orders to the common media outlets of our time – newspapers, magazines, and TV stations over a fax machine. A mundane admin job at best.

If you don't know what a fax machine is, I don't blame you. Fax machines scan a document and then send it electronically to another machine over a telephone line. Now try to imagine the closest simulation of an enlarged dial-like telephone blown out of proposition with a wide keyboard supplemented with buttons of unequal sizes. Yup, that's a fax machine.

After I spent an endless number of hours standing by those loud machines learning about every type of media outlet out there, I was finally promoted to role of a media planner; one where you get to sit behind a desk and rest your legs. I indulged in filling complicated Excel sheets. I had to input the measurements of advertising spaces, calculate the price of that space in different currencies and show off large numbers for a grand total. I also learned how to apply formulas to forecast viewership for every buck the client paid. Back in the days, Excel was considered a very progressive piece of software, and I treated it like my creative canvas. Apart from numbers and formulas I applied, I enjoyed colour coding those tiny rectangular fields on my sheets. My media plans were nothing short of a cheerful unicorn-coloured display.

With the passing of time, I was confident that media planning was not what I wanted for my career. Yet, I understood how much it widened my understanding of the industry. I knew the cost of every second on TV, Radio, and every column in a newspaper. I still envied the account handlers, the graphic designers, and the copywriters. I wrote a few emails to HR in the hope that I would be transferred to the account management or planning side of the business. 'You are doing great in media; the clients love you,' HR would reply. 'But I don't love spending my days on booking systems and formulas,' I would reply back – only silently and to myself.

After graduating with an MBA, I knew it was time for me to venture further into the field of marcomms. I was particularly interested in strategy and planning, and I decided to start looking for a new job.

Establishing a business from scratch

The universe answered my prayers, and I was called by a family acquaintance who was launching his own advertising agency. He asked me to help him establish the agency from scratch. The notion of starting a company from scratch thrilled me. We launched the agency as a team of three. One in charge of new business development, one in charge of account handling and one in charge of creative development and production. None of us stuck to their agreed roles. Each of us had to do a bit of everything to help the business grow. I spent days and nights in that tiny office. I was not embarrassed to fill in as a secretary, a receptionist, a general manager, and the lunch and, almost always, dinner order volunteer. I do not recall any other time in life when I've worked that hard. The office was my lounge, and my home minus a restful bed for a good night's sleep.

In the early 2000s, the economy of Dubai was on fire! The advertising industry was in some sort of paranormal romance with the market, and businesses flocked to us in large and small sizes. We landed amazing clients, both global and homegrown. I worked on brand activations for international brands such as Siemens, Honda, Nestle, and Panasonic. I also worked extensively on events management and creating brands from scratch for small business owners and entrepreneurs. We conducted strategy sessions and launched amazing local brands in real estate, insurance, healthcare, and fast-moving consumer goods.

In a short period of time, the agency's team grew to over fifty members, and we expanded our offices and specialities. In addition to marketing and design, we assembled specialised teams in branding, packaging, and public relations.

I fell in love with the art of pitching for new businesses. I loved knocking on company's doors, pitching creative services, writing business briefs and watching them morph into real-life campaigns. I ran massive events and roadshows. I worked alongside celebrities, artists, documentary filmmakers, and award-winning advertising directors. I spent hours in studios and recording sessions feeling that I was just in the right place at the right time.

Despite missing out on a lot of fun that I was meant to have as a young woman in her twenties, I felt happy and satisfied. I discovered how entrepreneurial I could be. My work has taken up a large chunk of my life, but every day, every client and every project I'd take affirmed to me how passionate I am about the field.

Back to why you may want to read this book or find me the right person to share my knowledge with you. Our indigenous agency caught the attention of the international agency community in Asia, and after four years of great work, the founder was approached by one of Japan's largest agency networks. They were looking to incept a new operation in the promising market of the UAE to serve the Middle East region.

Our agency soon partnered with them, and I took over the entire recreation of the agency and its rebranding exercise. The base of our clientele was soon upgraded by the addition of global Japanese automotive brands. My work experience took on new horizons as I learnt the Japanese way of doing business. Methodology and precision were key critical elements in the planning processes. Perfection was at the core of every little process. I learnt a whole new outlook to quality and excellence. I was then taught the art of reporting and understood the wealth of insights a brand adopts from accurate and articulate analytics.

Although I was considered a hardworking advertising executive, and my family consistently complained of my deep involvement with work, the commitment to a job in the Japanese culture was a leap ahead of mine. At times, the demands of meticulousness exhausted me. I was scared that the process of creativity and spontaneity that I thoroughly enjoyed were at the risk of jeopardy with all the exhaustive checklists and audit reports requested. To me, it felt like the Japanese methodology of predicting every outcome could leave no room for instantaneous sparks of witty ideas.

During business meetings, and while I enthusiastically pitched campaign ideas, my Japanese client would draw an oval shape that resembled a human brain on the white board in the meeting room and then draw a straight line across the shape from top to bottom as if he is trying to split the brain shape into half vertically. He would then point to the right side of the shape with his marker and say 'You are thinking with your right brain. I want you to think with your left one,' dragging his pointed marker to the left side. Those years were tough, and now I know, there is no better teacher than hardship itself.

Sales and marketing in the air

A decade or so into my agency life, I was presented with the opportunity to join an international advertising network that was ranked the best in billings worldwide. I was going to be an Account Director on the leading airline brand Emirates Airline and Yum's International brand Pizza Hut as well. The role was a combination of pitching new campaigns and navigating the relationship between the sales offices in the MENA and African region. I was curious, and I said yes to the job.

Apart from the enjoyment of luxury travel in business class for many years, I was responsible for gathering the business requirements of every sales office in every country in the region and translating them into local marketing plans that were specific to every market individually. How I loved this role, and how I enjoyed it! I felt like the middleman who will decipher sales talk to marketing actions.

I was the messenger who was going to transcribe the struggles of each sales office into marketing campaigns and promotions. I was working both my operational business acumen and my creative flair. I had to come up with efficient ways to understand the dynamics of every sales office in a country and derive a local sales and marketing calendar tailored to its needs. Each country had its own unique set of challenges – some were political and some were geographical; others were economical and driven by price competition from other players.

Moving to the client-side

After years of service in the creative and glamourous field of advertising, with the longest of hours I've ever served, the highest number of cities I've ever visited, supervising the most complicated of video shoots in beautiful corners of the planet, my curiosity kicked in again, and I was feeling very interested in moving to the client-side. I wanted to understand what marketers do on the client-side. And why is the

PR department so quiet on the inside when it creates so much noise on the outside?

'Aren't we doing all the Client's work?' this is a phrase you hear from many agency veterans, and one that was always on my mind. What I saw being on the agency side was that the teams plan, strategize, execute, evaluate, and even present work to the management of the Client. We look out for competition, scan the markets, understand the dynamics of the economy, put in propositions, sharpen the expression of brands, and then implement all that. If you are a client, please don't shoot the messenger. I'm now working on this side, and I understand that there is more to your role.

I knew all the disciplines of marketing from my studies and devoured readings of Porter and Godin. I had a library of business books, which I read over weekends and listened to as audio companions on my long trips. I continued to keep my know-how up to date by attending advertising and marketing shows. I frequently read industry publications such as the *AdAge*, *Communicate* and *Campaign ME*. I then became laser-focused on finding myself a job on the client-side. The creative and advertising field had thrilled me for over a decade, but it was time for me to broaden my experience, and I felt ready!

Hello from the other side

My search for a job at the client-side was not a walk in the park, as I imagined it would be. I did start to count the number of interviews I conducted with no success, but at some point, I decided it was best not to keep count. Despite numerous rejections, including some particularly impolite ones, I knew that every 'No' was bringing me closer to the 'Yes'. For many companies, not having the experience at the client-side may mean you are not an eligible candidate for a senior role in a company. To date, I fully dismiss this idea. I believe that starting your career at the agency side is a great foundation builder to your future in the field of marcomms.

Many admired my enthusiasm and listened intently to my perfected two-minute pitch on why they should hire me. I must have practised that argument over a hundred times. My wardrobe mirror would testify to that. 'You would make a great asset,' they'd say. 'But there is so much about what we do that you don't have experience in,' and the interview ends there. I refused to believe it. If you have the will, you can learn anything. One thing life at an agency teaches you is that you can learn the dynamics of any brand faster than you'd learn how to make a faultless sourdough loaf at home. Practice makes perfect, and life at an agency prepares you to do what my first teacher in marketing said – *a good marketer can market just about anything.*

Luckily, life has its magic dust saved for you when you least expect it. I was later headhunted for a family business operating in the retail and casual dining sectors. A large investment capital firm granted the company enormous funding, and they were up for an aggressive expansion in the region. The company planned to open over thirty outlets in the UAE, Kuwait, Oman, and Saudi Arabia. They needed someone to establish the marcomms department and get them ready for an unprecedented regional expansion.

Leading up to the day of the interview, I decided not to leave any room for speculation. I was going to be the person they chose. I plotted a plan to study their brands well, visited many of their flagship stores, spoke to their staff and shop managers, reviewed their online ratings, and experienced their customer journeys myself.

Since they had over 18 concepts in casual dining retail, I showed up to the interview dressed like a chef. I custom-made an outfit with their logo on it and whipped up an impressive pitch on how I am going to provide them the ultimate recipe for success.

Little did I know that the owner of the company was a young and handsome gentleman who was probably just a few years older than I. He must have thought I was one of the kitchen staff acting casual!

The good omen of it all is that I got the job. I finally made it to the Client side.

Establishing a department from scratch

The excitement of finally landing a job on the client side instantly faded away as I walked into the office on the first day. After I was introduced to my new colleagues and was shown my office, I sat down at my desk contemplating the hard-hitting reality that has bestowed itself upon me. I am now expected to establish an entire marcomms department from scratch -all by myself. Questions arose in my head like hot kernels popping from the kettle of a popcorn machine.

- Where do I start?
- How will I oversee the opening of 30 stores in 48 months?
- How do I budget for what I was planning to do?
- How do I brand the company?
- How many employees do I need on my team to get started?
- What agencies do I need to hire?
- How do I distribute the budget across marketing, branding, and PR?

I was hoping I would find a book that would give me a step-by-step guide on how to organise my thoughts and achieve what I wanted in a structured way. I found many books on marketing and PR strategies.

There were plenty of others on business management and leadership. There were more books on digital marketing than the world needs. But there were no books on how to build a marketing and communications department from scratch.

That was when I had one of those 'a-ha' moments of my life. And so, I had to learn this all by myself, and I am sure many of you are in that same position or have been there too.

Looking back, all I can say is that I learnt so much on the job. I had a fully functioning team within six months, and we had a suite of agencies as well. The expansion plans went smoothly, and I successfully launched many outlets in six countries. My department delivered branding, public relations, marketing, and promotional campaigns. Everything was built from scratch!

From global to homegrown

In 2009, the government of Abu Dhabi was set to launch its first progressive Islamic bank. I had a stunt at a branding agency and was working closely with the management of the bank on launching the brand. I came to learn that they were on the lookout for a professional that could establish the brand and its marcomms department from scratch. And there I was again, working on one of the most amazing homegrown brands in the UAE.

A few years later, Abu Dhabi's largest family business, which carried a rich diversity of companies was on the look for an expert that can establish their marcomms from scratch. The company was going through a huge transformation and needed to relaunch its brand, build its corporate communication strategy brought me on board to take on the same mission.

From there on, establishing marcomms departments from scratch became my thing. I found myself to be the type of executive who is passionate about this very particular challenge. Working with companies to create a trailblazing department that not only markets products but also helps companies transform and company cultures

Although I've done this several times again with large family businesses in many fields, industrial, manufacturing, energy and automotive, every time I go through it feels like the first time.

A book for you

And because I never found that book that can help me establish a marcomms department from scratch, I decided to write one.

2

HOW TO USE THIS BOOK

'A guru is like a live roadmap. If you want to walk uncharted terrain, I think it is sensible to walk with a roadmap.'

— JAGGI VASUDEV,
MORE FAMOUSLY KNOWN AS SADHGURU

At last, a company with a long business history realises that their marketing needs to be done right. They are looking for that passionate and fired-up individual to establish their presence department and build a team of wizards that will take their business to the next level.

You believe yourself to be that wizard! You press that 'Apply' button, go through an excruciating interview process, and then – *ta-da* – you land your dream job.

Mabrook!! Felicitations! Congratulations!

You are excited, happy, and vivacious.

But what's next from here? Where do you start?

The beginning could often be more difficult than you think. It is not how to do the job that makes it difficult. It is knowing where to start and by when to deliver what that could be a slippery slope. There is much to learn about the company, its people, and its brand, markets, and customers and the challenges facing its future.

This book will offer you practical frameworks to establish your department from scratch.

Two books in one

Consider this book a two-in-one bundle. The first part of the book will help you in establishing your department from scratch and the second part will assist you in navigating the world of branding, corporate communication, and putting together a comprehensive strategy deck.

Part One

This part runs from Chapter 3 to Chapter 10. These chapters will offer different frameworks of discovery and planning that will help you establish a roadmap for your department.

Chapter 3 offers The **First Impressions Framework**. In this framework, you will be guided on how to draw observations on three key areas in the business prior to joining or as soon as you join the company.

Chapter 4 introduces **The View From The Top Framework**. Here, you are guided on how best to explore the status of the business as the founders or management see it. It then allows you to understand the company's vision and future orientation.

Chapter 5 introduces **The View From The Bottom Framework**, where you complete your exploration from the bottom of the company and its customers.

Chapter 6 introduces **The View in Numbers Framework** and shows you how to understand the company's financial structure and marketing budgets.

Chapter 7 is about **Envisioning Your Department**. This chapter will help you identify challenges on hand and how to match the right marcomms solution to them.

Chapter 8 looks at **The Team That Will Get You There** and will guide you on how to build a winning marcomms team.

Chapter 9 shows you how to design annual **Budgets and Calendars**.

Chapter 10 touches upon legal matters and processes that you need to know to make your department's work efficient and ethical.

By the end of **Chapter 10**, you should be able to have a clear vision of how your department and will be functioning.

Part Two

The second section of the book offers multiple crash courses on branding building and corporate communication. These will come in handy to those who have not yet experienced public relations, media relations, branding, sponsorships, and events.

Chapter 11 offers my very own **Brand Persona Framework**.

Chapter 12 continues the branding discussion to cover brand storytelling and creating a brand identity guide.

Chapter 13 introduces the disciplines of **Public Relations and Media Relations**.

Chapter 14 introduces **Internal Communication** and how it gets planned and executed.

Chapter 15 talks about **Sponsorships** and briefly touches upon **CSR (Corporate Social Responsibility)**.

Chapter 16 explains the different types of **Corporate Events,** and how these get executed.

Putting it all together into a strategy deck

Chapters 17, 18 and 19 will provide you with a flow of body-work that, if applied, can help you arrive at a detailed **Marcomms Strategy Deck**.

Chapter 20 touches upon skills that can help you excel in the field of marcomms.

Before you get started

Prior to getting started with this book, I wish to offer my five cents on how to keep focused on the path to great work. There are a few pitfalls one can fall into when taking over a new function or building one from scratch.

These pitfalls can be:

- Getting tempted to do what you know best.
- Not understanding what is best for the company at the present time.
- Jumping on the rebranding bandwagon.
- Changing teams too soon.
- Not making sure the company's brand has what it needs.

Getting tempted to do what you know best

When you start establishing a new marcomms department, you might get tempted to start implementing what you know best from previous job experiences. This is a natural human tendency and an instant type of human temptation. I've seen instances where a professional with a strong PR track record runs a great PR campaign for a brand that is in dire need of a pricing strategy.

You could be a great marketer who comes from a retail background, and you are joining a B2B (Business to Business) role. You decide to launch a massive seasonal advertising campaign when what the brand really needed was a targeted trade roadshow campaign.

The point I am trying to make here is that your many years of experience may not always be the first and best ammunition on this job. With every new job comes a breakup with the old and an affair with unchartered territories. The point is, don't get tempted to start flexing your strongest muscle. Immerse yourself in the brand and what it requires in terms of marcomms before launching something too quick, too soon. Applying the weightage approach in Chapter 7 will come in very handy.

Not understanding what is best for the company at the present time

Immerse yourself fully with the business before kicking off any new ideas. Make a list of what you think is best for the company first and then sit on it and contemplate it. If you join from an advertising background, you may rush into hiring a creative agency when the brand requires a PR (Public Relations) agency or a CRM (Customer Relationship Management) platform. The company could be doing well in communication and what it needs is an automated sales marketing solution with an advanced tracker for digital leads.

If you are moving from a B2C (Business to Consumer) to a B2G (Business to Government) business, you may be tempted to use consumer marketing tactics when what the brand needs is communication speciality tactics. Bottom line – don't rush to apply what you think is best. Learn what is best for the business first. Chapter 3 and 4 will help you get all the answers you need.

In my present job, I overlook the marcomms department for one of Abu Dhabi's leading family businesses which has a successful car dealership for global brands. The dealership has a phenomenal marketing team and has been overachieving in lead generation, sales actualisation and, in terms of PR, has the hit the highest SOV (Share of Voice) in town. In planning for the dealership's future, my approach was to revisit the product mix, and work with the management to supplement the existing portfolio of brands with new ones that will answer to the future customer demand. The strategy was also going to focus on omni-channel marketing and rethinking the customer journey. In Chapter 17, I will introduce you to the PESTLE approach which can help you in mapping the outer ecosystem of the company and identify solutions to help its business thrive in the future.

Applying the learning from Chapters 3, 4 and 5 can help you get the right understanding of the future outlook for the business.

Jumping on the rebranding bandwagon

I've been around this block long enough to hear of the horror stories of new marketing or communication heads joining companies and rushing to execute a rebranding exercise. They change logos and slogans too soon and launch new colours soon after they join. Rebranding is great fun; it allows you to quickly make a visible change and have your presence felt. But rebranding is a double-edge sword.

I once interviewed a young executive who worked for a prestigious private jet brand. The brand was well-established and was witnessing healthy growth in the region. She explained to me that the management decided to promote one of their senior pilots to CEO position. As soon as the pilot got landed the new role, he asked for a complete rebranding exercise because he simply didn't like the how the logo looked. The brand had absolutely no reason for this change.

If not done during the time it is required, rebranding may create a fundamental backlash to a business. Although a new logo is a great way to show change, try to stay focused on the change that is reflected in the company's operations and profitability. Rebranding should be done to reflect a strategic change in the company's structure or way of doing business. What a brand may need is a new pricing strategy, a new customer success team, or perhaps an image and reputation management plan.

Chapters 11 and 12 of the book will offer you tools by which you can diagnose what your company needs in terms of branding and storytelling.

Changing teams too soon

I am one of those who worked for a lot of companies in different sectors. Yes, I've been called a corporate nomad. Once you arrive, you are expected to bring in new schools of thought and the latest best practices. Poor performance or stagnancy is often blamed on your predecessors or the existing teams. I have come to realise that, often, the circumstances around performance are not solely in the hands of the employees at work. It could be poor management decisions, a challenge with the brand's Unique Selling Propositions (USPs), incomplete briefing, scarcity of budgets, wrong hiring or unfair pay structures. As and when you take on a new role, I would urge you not to change existing team members until you have a full assessment of their capabilities and their willingness to improve.

Chapter 5 offers you a list of questions that you can follow to help you assess any existing marketing teams. Additionally, Chapter 8 of the book is dedicated to building marcomms teams.

Making sure the company brand has what it needs

Every brand needs a solid foundation. This foundation includes a clear USP, a compelling story, a pricing and placement strategy, and a campaign management plan. Brands also require other important enablers such as archives, identity guides and an annual strategy deck. You may be commissioned to work on an expansion of a brand, but the brand development is still in its infancy.

You could be joining a company that wants to go public in a year's time. Before you engage in the equity story, you will need to make sure the brand story is available on the required touchpoints, you have a dedicated and well-trained spokesperson, you have a brand history or timeline communicated, and you have already grabbed the interest of the media in the company.

Chapters 17, 18 and 19 will assist you in making sure the company's brand or brands have what it needs to move into its desired future.

3

FIRST IMPRESSIONS FRAMEWORK

'A good first impression can work wonders.'

— JK ROWLING

What you observe at the very beginning of your journey with a company could be stunningly true.

Much like humans, brands don't get another chance to make a very good first impression. The **First Impressions Framework** is the beginning of your discovery of the company and brands it represents. This framework is easy to use and consists of a set of questions you'll need to answer.

In this phase, you will draw very general observations without the influence of anyone inside the company yet. It is also executed based on your very own research and should ideally be done before you start working for the company or in your very early days on the job.

The **First Impressions Framework** is broken down into three areas of observations. These three areas are: Brand, Digital Footprint, and Customer Experience.

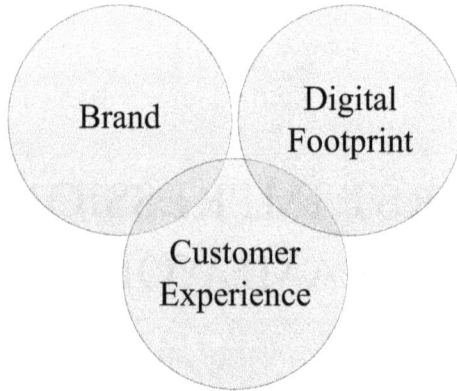

Brand

Digital Footprint

Customer Experience

Pillar 1: Brand

The terms 'brand' and 'branding' are used with many different interpretations. For the sake of simplicity, the below diagram will depict how the word 'Brand' is interpreted for this exercise. These include the brand purpose, values, personality, USP, story, architecture, identity, taglines, and tone of voice.

Brand

Brand Purpose	Brand Values	Brand Personality	USP (Unique Selling Proposition)	Brand Story

Brand Architecture	Identity Guide	Tagline(s)	Tonality

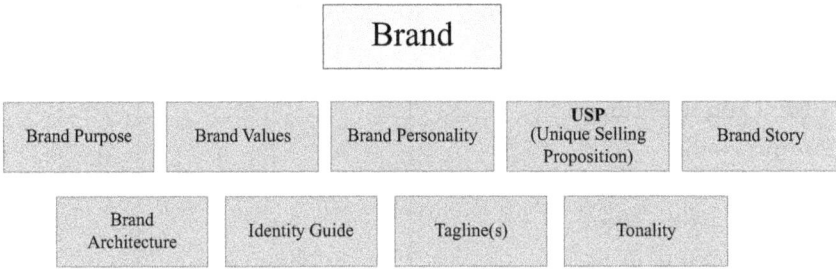

Identify those elements and try to rate them. The below table suggests four categories of ratings: Not-Available, Generic, Different, and Inspiring.

The Brand	Not-Available	Generic	Different	Inspiring
Brand Purpose. The reasons why the brand exists were easy to articulate through a vision and a mission statement.				
Brand Values. The company's beliefs and set of principles were clearly reflected in it's actions towards stakeholders and the planet.				
Brand Personality. The brand can be described as a person with clear and distinctive traits and values.				

The Brand	Not-Available	Generic	Different	Inspiring
USP (Unique Selling Proposition). The reason(s) why the company is different to its competition is available.				
Brand Story. The dream or legacy of the company is communicated through a series of micro and macro stories. The corporate narrative is both explicit and subliminal. It explains how the company benefits customers and communities.				
Brand Architecture. The structure of the company in terms of brands, divisions and subsidiaries is clearly identified.				
Brand Identity. The company and its brands carry a noticeable look and feel in its visual and animated assets across different media channels.				
Brand Taglines. The company's brand(s) have memorable slogans.				

The Brand	Not-Available	Generic	Different	Inspiring
Tonality. The tone of voice of the company is unique and uniform in its different types of communication.				

In addition to the above summary, try to answer all or some of the below questions:

- Was the company brand or brands confused with any other brands? If yes, mention the brands and the similarities you found.
- Did the brand inspire you?
- Did you get an insider's peek into the culture of the company?
- Were you able to converse easily with the company? For example, did the website offer an instant chat option?
- Has the company and its brand(s) proven to be responsible corporate citizen(s)?

The brand story

In the world of business, the story you tell the world time and again is a sign of what type of company you are on the inside. While many marketers and communicators live the hype of brand storytelling, it would be nice to take this a step further and see what sequels the brand story holds.

Here is a checklist that helps you assess the effectiveness of a company's brand story:

- Did you easily find the story?
- Can you re-tell the story?

- Does the story answer a human need?
- Did you find evidence that bring the story to life?
- Was the story told by influential members of the company?
- Did you find the story beyond the 'About Us' section of the company's website?
- Was the press interested in the story?

USP (Unique Selling Proposition)

Donald Miller is famous for telling the business world that every day, businesses make a mistake that costs them a lot of money. They do not explain clearly what their company does or what they're very good at. They lack a USP.

A USP helps your company uphold an accurate image about its offering. The book will offer detail on understanding the concept of USPs in Chapter 11.

Here is a checklist of questions that helps you assess the effectiveness of the company's USP:

- Has the brand differentiated itself from others in the same segment?
- Is the proposition authentic, overpromising, or under promising?
- Is this proposition good enough for the company to succeed in present market conditions?
- Will it help the company thrive in the future?

Write down the company's USP in your own words and then later discuss it with the seniors of the company. This will be part of the exercise you will conduct in Chapter 4, **The View From Top Framework**.

Pillar 2: Digital Footprint

A digital footprint is, as the name suggests, the trail of information a brand leaves behind online. A good digital footprint reflects the progressiveness of a company in adopting beneficial technology. Your first impression of a brand's digital footprint could be focused on the following five areas:

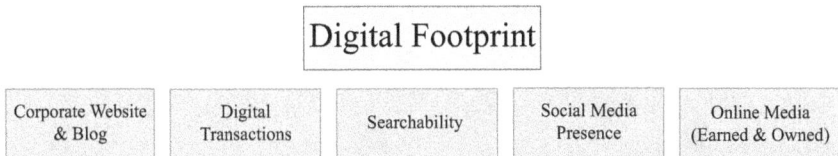

Digital Footprint				
Corporate Website & Blog	Digital Transactions	Searchability	Social Media Presence	Online Media (Earned & Owned)

The concept of a digital footprint can diverge into multiple fields. At this stage, you are only trying to get a sense of how well rooted the company is in the digital space.

Digital Footprint	Not-Available	Weak	Poor	Advanced
Corporate Website. The company's website is up-to-date, well designed, fully functional, and offers a seamless customer journey. It is easy to navigate and has a friendly mobile version.				

Digital Footprint	Not-Available	Weak	Poor	Advanced
Corporate Blog. The company has a dedicated corporate blog. It publishes interesting industry content such as opinion pieces and market updates on regular basis.				
Digital Transactions. The ease with which a customer can purchase or research the company's products and services online.				
Searchability: The company is optimizing its online presence on the search platforms. The company is undertaking SEO and SEM strategies.				
Social Media. The company is present and active on social media platforms. It manages social engagements in a timely and professional manner.				
Earned Online Media. The public and the press have generated positive and favourable online content about the company.				

Corporate websites

Despite all the debate out there about websites, I believe we are not yet ready to bid them farewell. Auditing a website is a long process, but what you would need to look at are the following essential features for a corporate website.

Corporate Website Evaluation Checklist	Not-Available	Weak	Poor	Advanced
What we do. The website clearly has an introduction to the business and what it does in a concise, engaging, and easy to find manner.				
Message from the CEO. Includes a message from the founder, chairperson or CEO of the company. The message touches upon the company's strategies and future business plans.				
Vision, Mission, Values. Contains a tab that introduces the company's vision, mission and corporate values.				

Corporate Website Evaluation Checklist	Not-Available	Weak	Poor	Advanced
Easy Navigation. The website banners and drop-down menus are simple to browse, and users can go where they want to go. Usually on the top and the bottom of the page.				
Contact Information. You are given a Chat option or an easy to find Contact Us tab.				
Availability of a Sitemap. A navigation through a Sitemap is made available to direct users to the pages of the website.				
Seamless user journey. The website is easy to browse, and users can get to where they want to go easily and intuitively.				
Loading speed. The website is easy to load on computers and mobile phones.				
Visually engaging. The website is dynamic and contains impressive static and moving images.				

Corporate Website Evaluation Checklist	Not-Available	Weak	Poor	Advanced
Media and News. The website provides enough access to its media assets and latest news.				
Careers. The website has enough information what job opportunities it has and how to apply to them.				

If your company is an online business, there will be a host of other features to assess. Here is an additional list of questions to consider:

Commerce Website	Not-Available	Weak	Poor	Advanced
Safe and secure. The site provides accreditation and certifications to establish its safety and security.				
Visual merchandising. The products or services are represented visually using high resolution photos in a way that makes them very appealing. Different views of the same product are also available.				

Commerce Website	Not-Available	Weak	Poor	Advanced
Clear Product Information. Whatever it is the company is selling, the website offers all the necessary details required to make a purchase.				
Call to Actions. The website has enough retail hooks or clear prompts that encourage customers to make a purchase.				
Payment Options. Offers flexible and easy payment options such as interest-free instalment plans.				
Shipping and delivery information. Deploys the best practices in delivery such as a step-by-step update on the status of orders. Also offers free shipping or clear shipping fees, free returns or a clear policy on returns and refunds.				
Customer testimonials. Authentic customer reviews are available on the site.				

Commerce Website	Not-Available	Weak	Poor	Advanced
Ease of registration and sign-in. The site offers an easy way to register an account and build a profile.				
Customer information. The website has the right forms to retain customer information and enable future customer interactions.				
Personalisation. Allows customers to personalize their experience by creating their own wish list and filters.				
Mobile optimized. The website design on mobile screens is efficient and easy to navigate.				

Searchability

Searchability or visibility in search is where you check how visible the company's website and content are on the search platforms. In other words, try to find how effective the company's SEO (Search Engine Optimisation) strategy is. You can detect that by making sure the content related to the company is leading you to the company's website.

Similarly, try to detect if the company is deploying effective SEM (Search Engine Marketing), which means it has advertisements displayed online once you search for content related to its offerings.

To learn more about SEO and SEM, you can visit Chapter 18 of the book.

Social media

With the world living online and people and brands joining social media platforms every day, many customers now prefer to interact with companies on social media. They expect companies to be available to engage with and address their concerns. There is not a 'one size fits all' approach to a social media strategy. In assessing the company's social media strengths, you can investigate the following:

Social Media Effectiveness Checklist	Not-Available	Weak	Poor	Advanced
Available on the right social platforms. The company is active on social media platforms it benefits from. The company's content is tailored to each channel.				
Frequent Posting. Channels are updated and have a regular and always-on content generation strategy.				

Social Media Effectiveness Checklist	Not-Available	Weak	Poor	Advanced
Healthy Engagement. You can detect a healthy level of engagement on the channels. Engagement is the collective measure of Likes, Shares, Comments, and other interactions.				
Reaching the right audience. The content strategy has succeeded in attracting the right type of audiences on the channels.				
Generate Leads. The social media channels are being used as a lead generation tool for the brand.				
Product and service enquiries. A successful social media presence means that companies are also attracting the right type of product and service enquiries and are generating genuine interest.				
Channels are equally up-to-date. All the social channels of the company carry the latest information about the company without any discrepancy between them.				

Where is the company on LinkedIn's barometer?

LinkedIn is the world's largest and fastest-growing online platform for professionals and businesses. The platform started as an avenue for job seekers to land jobs, but in less than a decade, LinkedIn has grown to be a hub of insights for companies and professionals. LinkedIn is a medium where you can showcase your company's culture and achievements as well as build an 'employer brand' along the way.

LinkedIn revolutionized recruitment and opened a channel for dialogue between companies and individuals. I lived in the times when recruitment happened through physical networking and traditional recruitment houses. A decision to join a company was purely based on a one-sided stream of information, which came from the company's website, the recruitment firm, or the information the HR personnel offered you as a candidate. The employer had the upper hand. But the new generation no longer subscribes to this model.

Not only did LinkedIn change how companies recruit talent, it also changed the way a company builds its 'employer brand'. The old ways of building an employer brand were dictated through formal media announcements. Today, if a company keeps its employees happy, they will turn into brand ambassadors sharing positive work experiences online. Companies with well-looked-after LinkedIn pages send out a message that they are progressive and forward-thinking. They proudly display their work culture online. The analytics of the platform allows you to see how many of your employees are engaging with your page and resharing your content.

Today, LinkedIn has become an avenue for companies to promote their products and services as well. Progressive and forward-looking companies are now expected to be present on LinkedIn. Building a digital trail on LinkedIn is highly beneficial to companies of all sizes, regardless of whether they are start-ups or conglomerates.

Online media presence

The expansion in digital communication gave way to three types of media: paid, owned, and earned. The three constantly feed into each other. Here is how Oxford College of Marketing defined each of these three categories.

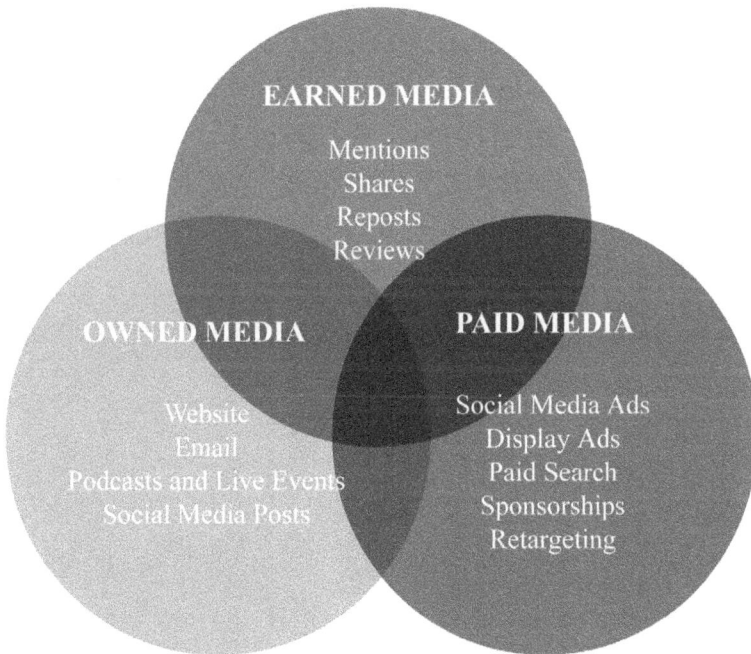

As the name implies, paid media is media that the company has paid for. That would include SEO, SEM, digital advertisements and promoted content.

Owned media is the content that a company owns and usually resides on its digital assets such as websites and blogs. Earned media is usually considered the most credible category when assessing brands because it is generated by a third party such as the press or a customer. Earned media is composed of news generated about your company, the mentions of your brands in online conversations, and reviews. Your next step in this framework is to identify how much the company is utilising each of those three categories and mark it with a rating.

The media industry is changing. With the widening of social media networks, earned media now takes up a large chunk of new-age publicity and is worth looking into. We will work on assessing that first. Earned media also includes customer reviews, product or service trials from bloggers, and coverage from social media influencers. It also incorporates the content generated by its own employees.

Online Presence Effectiveness Checklist	Not-Available	Weak	Poor	Advanced
Earned media. Promotion of the company and its brands through organic means such as mentions, shares, reposts and reviews.				

Online Presence Effectiveness Checklist	Not-Available	Weak	Poor	Advanced
Owned media. Company controls the content and dictates it such as content on website, email communication, social media posts and online news.				
Paid media. Marketing the company's products and services through paid channels such as social media ads, video ads, sponsored content and re-targeting.				

Earned media

To understand the value of a brand's earned media, you need to determine what portion of its news is soft news and what portion is hard news. Soft news is announcement-stye news about a company's new appointments or new store openings.

Hard news is more compelling and is generated by a story that attracts the press and online communities. Take, for example, the story of a company disrupting an industry with a new innovation. Multimodal mobility platforms have recently changed the way people perceive ownership of a vehicle in the automotive sector.

When I joined the food retail company, I realised the company only issued announcements of new store openings. The company was very active on many other fronts. The restaurants were constantly launching new regional speciality dished and menu items. They had talented chefs who brought in new locally inspired dishes to global brands.

The company had an inclusive hiring strategy that was ahead of its time in the region. The workforce was of over 38 nationalities with equal opportunities despite race and gender. Part of the inclusivity was equal chances given to small vendors such as organic farms that produce artisanal products. I soon realised I had to put together a PR strategy that brought to the press captivating stories about the brand.

Press-related earned media

You can study the online press coverage of the company to understand what PR strategies it has adopted. Here are a few questions to contemplate.

Press-related earned media analysis	Questions to ask
Types of titles the company publishes with.	• Is the company news published regularly in daily newspapers? • Is the news disseminated to different media like newspapers, podcasts, online portals, magazine, radio and TV stations? • Does the company publish stories in annual business magazines and economy reports?
Frequency of publishing.	• How often is the company speaking to the press? • Is there a seasonality to the news of the company? • If the company has cover stories, how often are these published? • Are there exclusive interviews with the company leaders in high profile media outlets?

Press-related earned media analysis	Questions to ask
Nature of the company's relationship with the media.	• How would you describe the company's relationship with the media? • Is the company media savvy or media shy?
Spokesperson(s).	• Does the company have a prominent spokesperson or multiple spokespersons? • How would you describe the company's spokesperson(s)? Are they mature, young, inspiring, reserved, or progressive? • Does the spokesperson have what it takes to go on new-age media channels such as podcasts and YouTube videos? • Are the company's spokespersons actively engaged online and with the community? • Have the company's spokespersons received credible industry accolades?
Thought leadership.	• Are there thought leaders at the company generating their own content? • Are they publishing opinion pieces, predictions, and industry updates with the media? • Are they being sought out by the media for commentary on industry matters? • Do they attend roundtables and industry panel discussions? • Do they genuinely possess the right knowledge about their industries? • Does the company publish reports and white papers ?

Press-related earned media analysis	Questions to ask
Association and sentiment.	• What are the main media themes and topics associated with the company? • What is the overall sentiment of the brand towards the market and the region in operates in?

Pillar 3: Customer experience

Today, customer experience has become a prerequisite to the success of a company. What was once considered part of a marketing strategy is now becoming part of a company's overall business strategy. Customer experience starts at the very beginning of a customer's relationship with a brand. It begins with the consideration phase up until post-purchase phase. ActiveEngage showed in a recent survey on customer experience in the automotive sector that 91% of unhappy customers are non-complainers and simply leave. This is not uncommon in other industries too.

Companies are operating in times when you cannot discount the importance of making your customers happy. This begins with understanding the emotions of your customers and being there for them when they need you. The desired outcome from a successful customer experience is a seamless customer journey.

In drawing a first impression of the company's customer experience, you are trying to see if the company has proved itself committed to serve all the needs of its customers. We will consider the following areas:

Customer Experience				
Customer Journey	Responsiveness	Online Reviews & Social Conversations	Customer Loyalty	Mystery Shopping

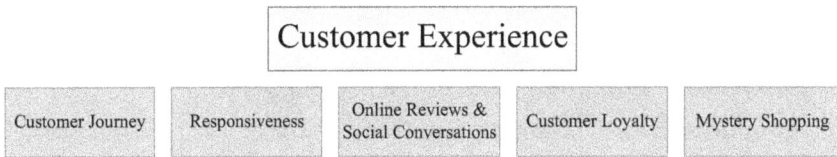

Customer journey

The customer journey is the complete collection of steps a customer takes to purchase a product. As such, it's a huge part of the customer experience as it compromises the actions a customer takes before, during, and after their purchase. The customer journey begins before a customer finds your brand up until after it has interacted with it.

The first job I landed on the client-side was Head of Marketing for an up-and-coming food and beverage company. The company was operating a very exciting portfolio of brands that fall in the QSR (Quick Service Restaurants), Casual Dining, and Café businesses. I made sure I visited their flagship stores with my family and some of my friends. I also checked how they are performing online and how well their delivery service is. I allowed myself to live the brand experience to the fullest. I asked the restaurant manager how the restaurants were doing and what the bestselling dishes were. I had side conversations with the waitresses and tried to see what they had to say about their experiences with customers. I tried the food, paid the bill, and took down my notes.

The duration and length of a customer journey will change depending on your business and customers. Nevertheless, to understand how a seamless customer experience works, it's worth developing an understanding of the customer journey's basic stages.

- **Awareness.** The customer becomes aware that your product or service can serve them and fulfil a present need.
- **Consideration**. Your brand makes it to the top of the short-listed options for your customers.
- **Purchase.** The customer ends up purchasing your product or service.
- **Retention.** The customer finds the product useful or enjoyable and purchases with the business again.
- **Advocacy.** The customer turns loyal and recommends your product or service.

Responsiveness

Stelios Haji-Ioannou, Chairman of EasyGroup and founder of EasyJet said, 'You can spend 15 million pounds on advertising, go bankrupt, and your name still mean nothing to people; your brand is created out of customer contact and the experience your customers have of you.'

The degree of responsiveness to a customer influences their experience. Responsive is an element that the brand frontliners need to adopt, be it the operators, call centre agents, or the sales team of after-sales advisors.

Responsiveness does not pertain to the speed of response only, but to the level of friendliness and helpfulness. This is an indication of how well trained your employees are.

Online reviews and social conversations

We are living in the age of unprecedented customer power. Today, a company's online reviews, regardless of whether they are on Google or other platforms, are powered by people's experiences. The importance of word of mouth is not an old wives' tale. It is there, and much more prevalent online. Word of mouth won't be forgotten and will always be there. The rating of a company, its products, or service has become an avenue to tell you how well a company is doing.

Sadly, online reviews and ratings never tell the story unless the company and brand respond to them in a timely and professional manner. Looking into these reviews and ratings will help you get information on how serious a company is about customer satisfaction.

Social media allows a company to humanise its brand and build a genuine relationship with its communities. Social media will give you a good picture of how a company interacts with its customers. If there are good reviews, you know the company has a solid reputation. If there are too many complaints, you may not want to work for that company.

Loyalty

Customer loyalty is often achieved through the relationship built between the customer and the brand. In your experience, were you given reasons to believe in this brand?

In my long years in banking, market research always came back with these three needs from customers: trust, transparency, and reliability.

Here are a few questions to help you asses the level of loyalty the company has earned:

- Is the company rewarding your loyal and repeat purchases?
- Is the company offering a loyalty scheme?

- Is the company offering exciting redemption options?
- Is the company able to recognise you as a loyal customer?

Mystery shopping

Isaac Marion, bestselling author of fiction novels, said it rightly. 'Every experience, good or bad, is a priceless collector's item.' Experiencing the brand by yourself is going to leave you with impressions that are much needed for your journey ahead.

If you want to make a good judgment, try to live the role of a mystery shopper. It is fun, and you will learn quite a bit about a company, whether it is online or bricks and mortar. Mystery shopping is a great market research tool. Many companies use mystery shopping to measure the quality of job performance and sales and service, or to see what the competition is up to. Here is what you look for when you shop a brand:

- Did you feel satisfied engaging with the brand?
- Was your experience memorable?
- Was there a brand promise? Was it delivered?
- Does the company have a customer excellence centre?
- Were you able to try and test the product or service?
- Was there an attainable level of attention to detail by the staff?
- Did you sense that other customers were enthusiastic?

In the next two chapters, we will rebuild the impression but from the inside. We will hear from the leaders of the company and the employees who interact with the customers and other stakeholders.

4

THE VIEW FROM THE TOP FRAMEWORK

'We are like those who had climbed a mountain
and reached the top. When we looked down,
we still wanted to go higher to realise our goals.
Despite all the achievements, we still have an ambition
for more. That is my way of looking at things.'

— THE LATE SHEIKH ZAYED BIN SULTAN AL NAHYAN

Understanding the vision from the captains on top is like being handed the treasure trove that holds within its four walls the secret to the company's future.

The **View From The Top Framework** is a discovery exercise where you get introduced to the brand through its founders or leaders and hear it right from the lion's mouth. The focal point of the journey starts at the tip of the corporate iceberg.

The **View From The Top Framework** focuses on five areas; the company's future orientation, markets, products and services, customers and capabilities.

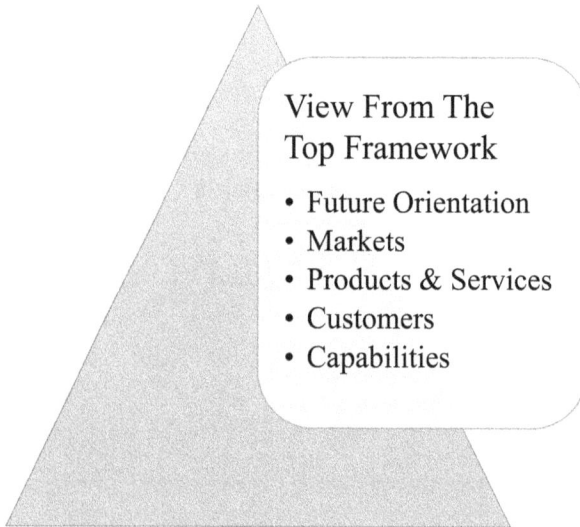

View From The
Top Framework

• Future Orientation
• Markets
• Products & Services
• Customers
• Capabilities

Understanding the company's future orientation

The framework begins with understanding the company's vision and future orientation.

Many companies grow because they operate in a high-growth sector and a booming economy. This could be attributed to a new innovative product or service, or their growth might be attributed to macroeconomic factors such as growing population and urbanisation. Drawing an example from the UAE, Wikipedia declares that the UAE's non-oil sectors have grown 28 folds from 1981 to 2012. During these times, the UAE's real-estate companies along many others in transport, logistics, asset management, leisure, entertainment and retail experienced unrivalled growth. For some, having an articulated strategy or not did not hinder their profitability.

Other companies may have had a vision and stuck to it, but their market was presented with unfavourable conditions such as sanctions, inflation, supply chain challenges, rising cost of raw material or a change in customer sentiment that could have hindered their growth. The recent pandemic has shown the world that abundance does come to an end. Many of the world's prosperous sectors declined miserably in under a year. Yet, at the same time, many companies in other sectors witnessed an exponential spike in business, take for example healthcare, pharmaceuticals, power generation and last-mile services.

Companies experiencing a decline in their business or are faced with fierce competition would be looking to change their overall strategy. They could be on a pursuit of differentiating themselves with higher quality offerings or could be trying to lower their costs and pricing structures. They could be focusing on opening new market spaces for them by introducing new product lines in an attempt to make their competition irrelevant. In recent years, the automotive sector has witnessed a great set back with customers changing their minds about owning a car and opting for alternative means such as leasing and car hailing. Car dealerships changed the course of their work from relying solely on their exclusive brands to introducing multiple brand service centres as well as leasing and subscription options.

In the first part of this framework, you'll be able to have a complete understanding of the company's future orientation and whether the company's strategy or master plan is residing in the head of the leaders only or if it has been cascaded down to the rest of the employee population.

When I joined Al Masaood Group, one of Abu Dhabi's leading family businesses, the company had leading brands in the automotive, transport, logistics, power, construction, and marine industries. They were also venturing into manufacturing and renewables. The company had existed for five decades and was about to celebrate its golden jubilee. I had to understand the company's vision. This vision led me to host inspiring conversations with the sons of the founders and the Chairman. What I heard with every passing story was the theme of the founders wanting to help the people of the UAE get access to a better life.

It was very evident that the true intention behind the diversification of the company was to create sustainable growth for the UAE's economic sectors so it can in turn provide comfortable living conditions to the residents. The company was the first to bring a water desalination plant to the capital followed by the first facility to supply power to the city. They introduced the first Japanese automotive brand in Abu Dhabi in the early 70s when the city's urban infrastructure was not yet fully developed, and stories have it, camels were still a mode of transportation in certain remote areas. Most recently, the company built the UAE's first solar powered electric charging system and was set to be the first to supplement hydrogen to its marine transport. The company often answered to the needs of the economy. With the passing of the years, the company did not take a close look at their vision statement or took the time to communicate it frequently to their growing population of employees. But with the 50th anniversary celebration underway, it was time for the 3000 some employees of the company to get a clear understanding of the vision that will drive the conglomerate forward. After conducting a few brainstorming sessions, we arrived at a beautiful vision statement for the company, which was simple and straight to the point 'Growing with the nation.'

Who to meet

The first step in this framework is to make a list of the top executives whom you will be meeting. The higher you go up the ladder, the shorter and more focused you want the meeting to be. There is a chance you will be meeting a group of senior executives together at the same time. Senior officials and leaders in a company usually fall within this list:

- The Founder, Chairman, or Board of Directors.
- The C-suite executives: CEOs, COOs, CTOs, and CFOs.
- The General Managers of Sales and Operations or those in charge of the company's revenues.
- The managers in charge of the corporate support units. Support units in a company usually do not generate revenue but support operations through their services. Accounting, Finance, Logistics, Human Resources, Procurement, Compliance, IT support, Audit, Treasury and PMO (Project Management Office) are usually support units. If your department is purely focused on internal communications or corporate communications, it will also be considered a support unit.

Seniors are the hardest to reach. They often have very little time and are always in problem-solving mode. Some like to do the talking, leaving very little room for deliberation and questions. In those meetings, it is best to display the best of your listening skills and to show your interest and express your curiosity openly.

Since this framework is built on asking questions but you don't want the meeting to feel like an interview, I provided suggestions on how to ask strategic questions in an open-ended, friendly manner. Keeping the question light at this stage will help you build rapport with the leaders. It will also provide them with the avenue to express themselves openly. The answers to the below questions will give you the power to understand what the company's vision and future orientation.

In the below table, I've listed the questions and what they're trying to uncover.

Question	What you're trying to find out
What change do you want your company to make in the world?	The company's purpose.
What is the promise the company is making to its stakeholders?	The company's vision.
What will it take to get the company there?	The company's mission.
What makes others believe in your dreams?	The customers' reasons to believe in the company.
How do you see the future?	The future growth strategy of the company.
Who are you looking after?	Who the target audiences are?
Who believes in the company the most?	Who the company's most loyal stakeholders?

Question	What you're trying to find out
What would make people work for the company?	What is the most important aspects of the company's culture?
Which companies do you keep an eye on? And why?	Who in the market is the biggest competition and why?
How do you get ready for the future?	How does the company build its areas of strengths?
What do you need to address to get more competitive?	What are the company's threats and weaknesses?
What is your competition saying about you?	What are the weaknesses the competition can use against the company?
What makes others look up to your company?	What are the company's core competencies?
What is the next step from here?	How satisfied are you with the company's present profitability and market share?

Markets, products and services, customers and capabilities

In order to cover the next four areas of the framework, you will need to undergo meetings with the general manager of sales and operations at the company. Here are the basic questions you need to ask for each of the four areas.

Markets

- What is the status of the current market?
- What are the market opportunities you should be considering?
- In which direction is competition going?
- What are the industry trends pointing to?
- How should we approach new markets?

The conversation on markets should provide you with an understanding of your company's market share. Market share is calculated by measuring the percentage of sales or percentage of units sold a company has against the total sales of the market.

Companies with a high market share are usually competitive. They have great operations, great negotiating power with vendors, and may not need to keep a close eye on their pricing strategies.

Companies with a small market share may be looking at more aggressive marketing plans. They often look at innovation and disruptive technologies to gain an advantage over their competition. They also investigate product diversification and product line extension. They often work hard at their publicity and image building to build up affinity towards their brands. They amplify their sustainability and environmental positions to the communities at accelerated rates.

Other key business matters related to growing or maintaining a company's market share include customer success and higher customer retention, expansion in geographical territory, and greater brand awareness.

Here are some more questions to guide your discovery on the remaining areas of this Framework.

Products and services

- In the company product lines, what are the product demand dynamics?
- How does the company plan to grow its sales? Is it through new products? Product extensions? After-market services? New territory? Diversification? Acquisition?
- How are the company services linked to the product offerings?
- What more can be done to increase the share of wallet or ticket items?
- What can be done to elongate the customer lifecycle?

Customers

- What are the customer segments the company focuses on?
- How are the needs of the customers evolving with time?
- What products or services do the existing customers value the most? Speed, quality, reliability, service, partnership, price, location convenience?
- What actions are needed to improve customer acquisition?
- What actions are needed to raise customer satisfaction?

Capabilities

The last step in this framework is to assess the company's capabilities. A company's capabilities are the qualities that span its operations and people. Having the right capabilities makes a company ready to improve through growth tactics and innovation. Capabilities keep a company aligned with the upcoming trends of the marketplace. You can break these down into the following areas:

- Customer success.
- Competitiveness.
- Organisational structure.
- Skillset.
- Technology adoption.

Customer success. Companies cannot exist without their customers. A company's greatest asset is its ability to grow its customer satisfaction and loyalty while it continues to attract new ones. This happens when a company takes on a proactive approach towards its customers. This is usually manifested through customer data analytics, having a clearly defined customer journey, and a clear customer acquisition and retention strategy. Companies today are placing emphasis on their customer experiences. You will need to see how innovative your company has been in launching new and improved customer experiences.

Competitiveness. In his book *The Infinite Game*, Simon Sinek explains that thriving companies are not the ones that obsess over their competition but rather learn and take inspiration from competition as well as other players in the market. Even when a company is the best in its sector, it needs to continue building its competitiveness.

Competitive companies continuously keep an eye on emerging disruptions. These companies invest in market scanning tools and research. Additionally, these companies have a full understanding of the capabilities of their competitors.

Organisational structure. To understand how well-established a company's organisational structure is, you can start by exploring what functions and roles are highly effective in the company but are not yet fully deployed. These could be Research and Development, PMO (Project Management Office), Innovation or Data Analytics. Another key to success is how the organisational structure facilitates synergy between its business lines. Finally, you will need to analyse if the company's present structure is future-ready and enables empowered decision making.

Skillset. The first factor in a company's skillset is the element of leadership. Does the company have the right leadership in place? Are the leaders of the company fostering a performance-driven culture? Do they inspire great work and keep employees motivated? Other factors that contribute to skillset are the present talent pool and how well versed it is to take the company to a better future. Finally, how good is the company in hiring and retaining competent employees?

Post the COVID-19 pandemic, the corporate world witnessed the great resignation era. According to a Harvard Business Review paper, nearly 57 million Americans quit their jobs between January 2021 and February 2022 for better working opportunities that stipulate flexible hours and remote work. Companies who were rigid in their response to change lost many of their very best employees. The pandemic also brought to life the underground hustle economy and glorified it. Employees today openly brag about their side hustles and hobbies. Smart companies are able to embrace this change and create work environments that satisfy both the employer and the employee.

Technology adoption. This relates to the company's capacity to innovate, adapt to change, and create disruptions that benefit the customer and put the company ahead of its competition. Over the course of the years, we've seen industries dwindle down with disruptions, the first to mention is the print media industry, publishing, recruitment, travel and tourism, and most recently the financial sector.

Today, technology adoption is a main prerequisite to the success of any business. According to McKinsey & Company, their companies increased the adoption of digitization of customer journeys, supply-chain management, and internal operations too. That same study showed that globally, the percentage of products and services that were undergoing a partial or full digitization increased from 35% to 55% in just under two years.

Technology adoption enables better customer engagement, faster turnaround of internal tasks, retained customer data and most noticeably increased team collaboration.

By breaking down the capabilities into certain areas, you can start to define the company's strengths and weaknesses. These can be later used in a SWOT analysis. Most importantly, you can identify how the marketing and communications function is going to supplement those capabilities or bring them to life.

Narrowing the conversation to the marcomms functions

The next type of feedback you will be seeking will be related to the marcomms department.

Sometimes one of the most desired objectives of your marcomms department is to streamline communication between existing marketing teams across the company. Perhaps the company has just received its largest amount of funding ever and has a quest to exponentially expand into a wider region within a small window of time. Other times, your role is to simply upgrade an existing delivery that has hit a plateau. On other occasions, you could be taking over a department that is doing just fine but is unable to properly time manage its deliverables.

Here are questions that can prompt a better understanding of what is expected from the marcomms department:

- What, in your own words, would be the benefit of marcomms department in the company?
- What would you like to see the marcomms team bring to the table?
- What skillsets are you interested to see in the marcomms team?
- From a communication perspective, who do you see as the most fit to be a spokesperson for the company? And why?
- What business media narratives excite you the most?
- What companies do you follow on social media?
- What creative campaigns do you recall, or have you enjoyed recently? And why?
- How would you rate the marketing and communication delivery of your competition?

Presenting your findings

At the end of the series of meetings with the seniors, you should be able to formulate a very clear understanding of the company's vision and long-term plans.

You should understand what business strategies the company is following to achieve its vision, what the state of the market is, and what the customer sentiment is.

You should also understand what the present capabilities of the company are and what other skills, technologies, and capabilities are required to move the company forward.

SWOT Analysis

You may use the SWOT (Strength, Weakness, Opportunities and Threats) Analysis. A SWOT Framework was created by business management consultant Albert Humphrey in the 1960s.

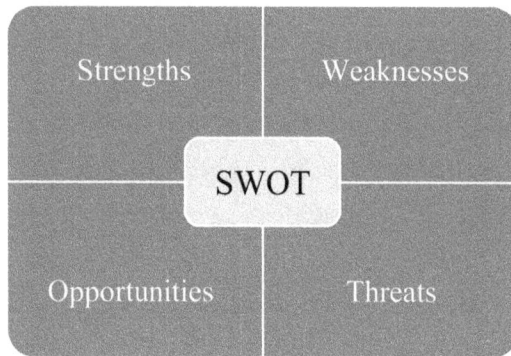

Strengths – these are often internal factors that provide a positive influence on the company. Anything that makes a company best at something becomes a strength. This could be an innovation unique to it, a time advantage to specific services, a legacy that enables trust, a first-mover's advantage, access to capital, certain connections, or alliances, and probably access to source material or back-end services at great value. A company's strength also lies in its capable employees and their ability to continue inventing and bringing new ideas to life.

Weaknesses – these are also often internal to a company. Weaknesses are disadvantages that make your competition ahead of you. There could be a lack of up-to-date technology, the customer service might not be up to the mark, or the company may lack the capability of big data or data documentation that enables better marketing. It could be a wrong pricing, an under proposition, or an over proposition.

Opportunities – these are often external to the company and are representations of changing markets. It could be that the competitors are not serving their solutions up to the mark, or a changing customer sentiment favours your product. Take, for example, a hand sanitisation brand during a pandemic. It could be a new technology or intellectual property that the company owns.

Threats – these are external to the company and could be something like a change in the legislation system. Take, for example, an industry that is a monopoly, and the country's laws change and allow new entrants. It could be a spike in the cost of raw materials that affects the pricing. It also could be embargos or new competitor offerings.

Remember my story on STP from Chapter 1?

You may also apply the STP method that I mentioned briefly at the beginning of the book.

- **Segmentation**: dividing your target market into groups of distinct traits and behaviours.
- **Targeting**: taking an insightful deep dive into the lifestyle of every group of customers identified and deciding which to focus on.
- **Positioning:** using the marketing mix model and insights discovered to create an edge for your product that makes it most appealing among its competition.

The **View From The Top Framework** is about getting up close and personal with the founders or senior leaders of the company as well as its revenue generators. These are the owners of the company's vision and long-term strategy. They can guide you on where the company wants to be and how it is going to get there.

The exercise will enable you to provide a well-rounded SWOT and STP understanding of the company as well as forecast priorities for your department.

This concludes how to best understand the view from the top seniors of your company. In the next chapter, you will validate this view by learning about the view from the front-liners of the company and those who are interacting very closely and intimately with the company's customers.

5

THE VIEW FROM THE BOTTOM FRAMEWORK

'Listen to the people on the ground.
They have all the solutions in the world.'

— BUNKER ROY.

The next phase of your discovery is the **View From The Bottom Framework**. In this view, you will stand in the shoes of the customer and those who deliver the brand experience to them.

You will discover the road to a customer's heart. You will understand if excellent service standards are working or if improvements are needed. You will get ideas on how best to improve certain processes, why a competing product is preferred, what price points lure the customers in, and what cultural insights can help you make your campaigns more attractive.

In this framework exercise, you will be speaking to three groups:

- Customer insights.
- Customer-facing staff.
- Support teams.

View From The Bottom

- Customer insights
- Customer-facing staff
- Support teams

Customer insights

Walking in the customer's footsteps is going to bring about enlightening insights for your business. You will arrive at ideas that have not been brought to life before, and you will cross-check whether they can be done operationally.

During my time as a Senior Communication and Marketing Officer at a leading bank, I felt the need to be very close to the customers since the bank was new and had recently launched in the UAE. Knowing that the banking sector was extremely competitive in the UAE, let alone the high switching costs of customers, I decided to spend a few days at the bank's main branch observing customers and talking to the tellers and service officers.

At the end of the exercise, I had one particularly interesting observation. Customers walking in always referred to the bank as the *'orange bank'*. It seemed that most customers from all walks of life were always using the term 'orange' in their conversations with the bank. The fact was the colour scheme of the branches featured a very distinct and bright shade of orange. A very uncommon colour in the banking industry. From the orange leather couches to the orange stylish round lamps, orange was a primary colour in the colour palette of the brand and did wonders in resonating with the customers.

The reason I found this observation interesting is because when I was working closely with the management on bringing the brand to life, the CEO had a brand epiphany and always said: 'We want to be a new breed of Islamic banks. We could have been blue or green, but we chose orange.' The colour orange was very uncommon in the banking sector, yet it was chosen to place emphasis on the progressiveness of the bank. Now, how did that shape our future campaigns? We amplified it. As the saying goes, we took it and ran with it. We used this statement to stand out and get differentiated. We always referred to it when creating campaigns as we realised that our customers sensed that we were different.

After launching the 'we choose orange' internal brand philosophy to the employees, one that called for challenging the conventional and coming up with something new. The bank was able to create a series of innovative retail and investment products in a very short number of years. This contributed significantly to the bank accelerating its ranking from the 56th bank in the market to one of the top 10.

How to get to know unique insights about your customers

Here are a few ways you can get to know the company's customers well.

Immerse yourself with customers by meeting them. Depending on the nature of the business you're in, this could be through online chats, meet-and-greets, official visits, focus groups, or just by being on the business floor observing and engaging with them. Speak to customers in retail environments about their perceptions of the brand, try to understand why they chose the company over other ones, learn what their experiences with it have been like, and what they would like the company to do more of. If you are working for an online business, you can do so through focus groups and by reading through the social engagements.

Get your hands on customer feedback reports. These could range from customer feedback surveys, customer satisfaction ratings, feedback received on the website and the social media channels, and other research conducted by the company.

In an online business, you can get to learn about your customers' behaviour through reports on pre-purchase browsing, purchase browsing and click through-rates on the site, shopping cart data and cart abandonment data and more.

Read community engagement reports and online comments. Get on the company's social media channels and read through the community's feedback. This will also help you assess what the most frequent enquiries and reoccurring complaints are.

At a car dealership, customer engagement reports cover the number of inbound and outbound calls, average speed of answer, average abandoned call rates, customer satisfaction rate, number of online concerns and queries and the average speed of reply and resolve. Dealerships and agencies also have reports that measure the affinity with their brands in the market.

Go through customer complaint reports. Customer complaint reports can give you an insight into the gaps that need filling between the expectations of the customer and the delivery provided by the company.

In making your observations, you will need to analyse the feedback, try to categorise it, identify the root causes, and find out what needs to be addressed immediately.

Customer-facing staff

Marcomms professionals never underestimate the power of the those they speak to, interact with, and observe. One of your most effective ammunitions is hearing insights right from customer-facing employees.

Customer-facing employees can provide a wealth of insights about the overall customer sentiment. Since they carry out the innermost interactions with customers, they surely know what is working and what is not. They often know what challenges come with the marketing mix, be it the product, price, place, or promotion. In terms of promotion, they can tell you which campaigns worked well, which ones generated leads, and which ones had the highest conversions to sales.

Customer-facing employees would be the staff in charge of sales, field technicians, support staff such as call centre agents and administrators. In the B2B field, they include the pre-sales, sales and client support teams. They can fill you in on the nature of the sales cycles, they know well what the barriers to entry into certain markets are, what the triggers are for a client to seal a deal, and how marketing and communications can help them increase their sales. They can also deliver to you the most authentic of testimonials from the customers. They will fill you in on what campaigns and promotions worked and which ones failed.

Let me tell you the story of the business tower that faced major traffic at the ground-floor elevators specifically at the rush hours of the morning and the afternoon. The architects probably did not factor in the actual number of people who would be using the elevators. As this was a prominent office building, it was soon getting a bad reputation because of the elevator situation. Since no more elevators could be added to the tower, the building management assembled a team to come up with a solution. The team deliberated and suggested many ideas, from setting up magazine stands to adding a TV screen between the elevators to even placing more couches at the corners of the reception.

The security guard eavesdropped on the team discussing their ideas. He approached them with enthusiasm and suggested that they add more mirrors – large mirrors – on the walls of the corridors leading up to the lifts. Waiting in a queue with your reflection won't feel this long. 'People love checking themselves out,' he affirmed confidently.

Customer-facing employees are the ones who interact closely with the customers. These constitute:

- Pre-sales and sales teams.
- After-sales teams and service advisors.
- Call centre agents.

These teams can help you gain the following information:

- Which products sell the most, which don't sell, and probably why.
- Which products need a marketing and sales push.
- What price points are most attractive to customers.
- Any tariffs, import fees, taxes or exchange rate fluctuations affecting the company's pricing strategy.
- Any grey markets hindering market growth.
- What the sales channels are, and which ones perform the best.
- What messaging worked in the past and what didn't.
- What value-additions or product extensions are missing and can help to create more sales.
- Why customers chose the competition.
- What would make the customers more loyal.
- What would send a customer away.

Business seasonality and sales cycles

What the sales team can help you understand is the business seasonality and sales cycle at the company. There could be cases where the company may not have seasonality and cycles. Seasonality in this case can be a time when there is a surge in engagement from your customers or any other fluctuations in the demand for your product. If you are into events, your seasonality may depend on the weather, the tourism season, or certain occasions. If you are into service, the brand's seasonality could be highly affected by macroeconomic fluctuations such as pay day, age of customers, and occasions celebrated.

Here are questions you can ask related to the business cycles at the company:

- How long is the business cycle?
- What are the major business seasons?
- What are the root causes of this seasonality?
- What are the fluctuations in the seasonal cycle?
- Have any irregular cycles been noted in the past 12 months?
- What macroeconomic patterns affect your cycles?
- What are industry disruptions affecting the business?
- Prior to the sales season, how long does the curiosity seasonality last?
- How has this seasonality changed over the years?
- What are the team's back-up plans during the low seasons?

If you are dealing with multi-country or regional operations, it is important to understand the differences in the seasonality across the different areas.

Understanding the seasonality is integral to planning your strategy and the work that goes into launching campaigns to combat periods of stagnation.

The relationship between sales and marketing

We all know well that the two teams feed into each other. Take the opportunity to learn from the sales team about their expectations from the marketing and communications team. Here are some conversation prompts.

- Are you satisfied with the business leads generated by the marketing campaigns?
- Are the campaigns meeting your conversion KPIs?
- What campaigns worked well in the past?
- What sponsorships worked well in the past?
- Do the retail and service environments live up to the brand promise?
- How, in your opinion, can conversion rates be improved?
- How do you integrate customer feedback into marketing initiatives?
- How do you document and measure customer satisfaction levels?
- How dynamic is the brand in responding to the changing needs of the customers?
- What would the customer-facing staff like to receive more of from the marcomms team?

Support teams

The last part of your discovery will end with the support functions of the company. These teams usually constitute:

- Operations and distribution.
- Human Resources and Talent Acquisition.
- Procurement.
- Finance.
- R&D (Research & Development) and Technology.
- Legal, Compliance and Internal Audit.

Discovery with operations and distribution

If you are working for a company that produces goods, then do visit the production facility. Try to understand the production process and, most importantly, any limitations such as fluctuations in currency exchange, seasonality of raw material, upgrades in machinery and equipment, increases in labour costs, and improvements in packaging needed.

Similarly, if it is a company that sells online, understanding the value-chain process and the logistics involved.

• What are the key channels of distribution for the company?
• How is the distribution to wholesalers and retailers done?
• What challenges do you face in importing or sourcing raw material?
• Who are the major suppliers and vendors?
• Are there new technologies that can be deployed in the production and distribution channels?
• Are there any quality issues in the production lines?
• Is the production process optimised and allowing for cost differentiation?
• Is there room for improvement in the production process?
• Can the distribution network be optimised?

Discovery with human resources and talent acquisition

• What is the employee retention rate at the company?
• Do you measure employee satisfaction?
• What is the median age of the employee population?

- What other insights do you have related to the ethnicity and religious backgrounds of the workforce?
- What diversity and inclusion plans have been implemented thus far?
- Are there any employees with inspirational stories?
- How is the company perceived as an employer?
- What makes the company an attractive employer?
- What does the company need to hire better skills?
- What challenges does the company face when hiring outstanding talent?
- What are the company's D&I (Diversity & Inclusion) plans and policies?

Familiarise yourself with training programs offered at the company and see if they have placed any focus on communication, media relations, publicity, etc. There could be an opportunity to do so, as this will make engaged employees future brand custodians.

Discovery with procurement

- Get a list of the vendors providing marketing services and see if they have been evaluated or categorised according to the type and quality of services offered.
- If there are any agencies on retainer – and often there are agencies that were selected not by marketers but by other management members – review the pitch briefs and selection processes, meet them, try to assess their capabilities, and get a full understanding of what tasks they are handling.

- The same goes for vendors who deliver work related to your function; could be branding or PR.
- Familiarise yourself with the procurement processes of your company like vendor registration and tendering protocols.
- Understand the onboarding and evaluation processes of vendors and third-party suppliers.

Discovery with finance

- Understand how the company is financially structured, how it financially trades, and what risks are associated with its financial structure.
- Understand the financial KPIs (Key Performance Indicators) of the company, including the profitability and liquidity ones.
- Understand the financial objectives for the company.
- Understand the existing shareholding structure of the company.
- Understand the equity structure of the company and how easily the company has access to cash.
- If the company is publicly listed or planning to go public, then you will need to have clarity on the company's positioning in the market and its financial competitive positioning.
- Understand how the budgeting is done for the company.
- Understand how much the company has allocated for promotions and marketing as a percentage of its total revenues.
- While I will dedicate a whole chapter to finance, when meeting up with the finance team, I would encourage you to explore if your function has had a P&L statement for it and what budgets were set aside or whether they need you to provide these. Although marcomms is a support function, in some companies,

support departments do carry a P&L statement for the purpose of tracking and keeping budgets under control.

- Then I would encourage you to look at all the historical finances related to marketing and communication expenses if those exist. What was the spend for the last three years? How was the spend spread across the marcomms categories?

Discovery with R&D (Research and Development) and technology

- Understand the current research and development capabilities of the company.
- What R&D techniques are used at the company?
- Understand the technology platforms that are used at the company.
- Understand what limitations in technology are there and how are they affecting the progress of operations.
- What platforms are used for e-commerce operations?
- What technologies are there to manage customer data at the company?
- What technologies are used in automating the marcomms deliverables?

Discovery with legal, compliance, and internal audit

- Try to familiarise yourself with the marketing, advertising, media, and consumer rights laws in the region in which you will be working. These are covered in Chapter 10.

- If you are new to the country or region in which your company operates, you can ask the legal team to help you familiarise yourself with the laws governing your field in that region.
- Run a check to ensure the brand names, logos, and taglines of the company are registered and protected.
- Are there any laws related to product claims and truth in advertising?
- What are the regulations on product labels, in-store point-of-sale purchasing, online promotion codes, and other promotions that the company runs?
- What permits are required for social media and brand activations?
- What are the laws related to product endorsements?
- Are there any health-related laws that are relevant to any by-products or effects from the products being sold at your company?
- Are there any rules related to the environmental impact of your company's products and services?
- How sustainable is the company, and to what degree is it abiding by global agreements like the Paris Agreement and net-zero-emission targets.

If there is an existing marcomms department, here are some questions you can ask.

- What is the current marcomms department's structure?
- What are the previous achievements and wins?
- What are the bottlenecks and challenges the present marcomms team face?
- What is the input of the team on the future of the department?

- What types of reports are being generated by the company that can help in making informed marcomms decisions?
- What tracking and measurement tools are being used?
- How is the marcomms budget planned and utilised?
- How satisfied is the team with the third-party vendors and agencies serving the brand?
- Are the different departments sharing customer data, insights, market trends, and planned activity with one another?
- Does the company have brand assets saved and available in an organised fashion?
- What changes and enhancements would they like to see at the marcomms function?

Organising this discovery process will ensure that it was thorough enough to cover all business units that lead into feeding the operations. In a way, it will ease you into resisting the temptation to jump right into campaign launches based on what you heard back in the senior offices or what you concluded on paper.

The **View From The Bottom Framework** is about getting up close and personal with the customer-facing and operations staff. These are the employees that contribute in a major way to helping you understand your customers very well. Bigger ideas will come your way, and you will hit off your marketing strategies with a solid understanding of the customer journey.

6

THE VIEW IN NUMBERS
FRAMEWORK

---

*"If you think your organization needs a bigger marketing
budget, maybe you just need to be less average instead."*

— SETH GODIN

Now that you understand the customer, the brand offering, the sales
cycles, and the market share dynamics, your next step will be understanding the revenue model and the marketing spend of the company.

Whoever said 'the numbers don't lie' spoke the hardcore truth.
No matter how creative your field is and how tempting it is to jump
straight into your branding and communication work at first, digest-
ing and analysing the numbers are going to provide you with many
insights that you may have not picked up from the other stages of
discovery.

The numbers on a company's financial statements tell a story of
what's working and what's not. They will tell you if the company is

striving to protect its market share or if it is on a growth tangent. Financial statements will also tell you if the company considers its marketing spend an investment or if it merely considers it part of the cost of goods sold. You can see that from the amounts spent on brand building and promotions.

The world of numbers is endless, and the intention of this chapter is not to delve into unnecessary explanations and analysis tools of financial study. This chapter will guide you on what financial data to look for to help you run your marcomms operations smoothly. If you'd like to perfect your financial skills, I recommend that you take up a 'finance for non-finance managers' course.

Looking into the broader financial statements of a company will help you see how much the organisation is investing in advancing its marketing and communication practices. For the sake of simplicity, this chapter will only focus on financial spend and P&L statements.

Surveying the marketing spend

As a first step, obtain the marketing spend of the past three to five years at the company. If this is a new company, you can refer to the spend of a company of a similar nature that is public and has its financial statements made available online.

You'll need to get answers to the following questions.

- What is the historic branding, marketing, and advertising spending of the last three years?
- What is the trend in the spend? Is it upwards, downwards, or flat?
- What is the trend of the marketing and communications spending in comparison to the sales?

- What is the same trend in comparison to the market share over the years?
- What is the same trend in comparison to competition or a leading company in the field?
- What is the same trend in comparison to the profitability (revenues) over the years?
- What are the operating marketing costs?

The marketing spend will include but is not limited to the following:

Digital marketing spend usually includes:
- Website creation.
- SEO – Search Engine Optimisation.
- SEM – Search Engine Marketing.
- PPC – Pay Per Click.
- Email marketing.
- SMS marketing.
- Digital display advertising.
- Social media marketing.
- Digital promotions and coupons.
- Remarketing and retargeting.
- Gaming.
- Paid digital advertising such as programmatic, paid media ads, podcast ads, video ads, retargeting, and online promotions.
- Email and near-field marketing.
- Paid content marketing such as promoted social media posts, paid social media influencer collaborations, and paid reviews.
- Digital agency fees.
- Mobile app development and mobile advertising.
- Acquisition or development of any digitised marketing platforms.

Traditional marketing spend would include:

- Advertising such as TV commercials, radio commercials, outdoor billboards, and print ads in newspapers and magazines.
- Roadshows and exhibitions.
- Event sponsorships.
- Product sampling.
- POS (Point of Sale) offers.
  Events such as displays, ceremonies, sampling, and launches.
- Sales promotions.
- Loyalty programs.
- Cost of sponsorships, brand activations, and events.

Marketing production costs:

- Agency retainers – both reoccurring and one-time – PR, design, branding, events.
- Design costs for branding and advertising material.
- Agency retainers for events and other services.
- Packaging.
- Point of sale material.
- Printing.
- Production of digital assets.
- Imagery and video assets.
- Archiving.

Other expenses to look at:

- Staff costs – salaries of your marketing team, administrative and office support team, including other benefits such as housing and transportation.

- Office rent and upkeep.
- Asset fees – such as printers, scanners, software purchases for any in-house designers, cameras and lights for in-house shoots, and computers for the teams.
- Office furniture – in case you are considering a brand revamp for your office, or you are expanding the team and would require more space.
- Other fees such as utilities, mail, and memberships.

When I first joined one of the industrial conglomerates in the region, the initial discovery with the senior team clearly revealed an intention to upgrade any existing marketing practices across the businesses. They had a concern that there were too many marketers in the marketing department. That got me intrigued. When I looked at the numbers of the company and looked at the marketing spend for the past five years, I soon realised that employee salaries as a ratio to the spend and to the overall expansion in the operations remained the same and had not increased. The numbers gave me an immediate indication that there had been no growth in the team despite the growth in the operations.

The marketing budget was growing by an average of 3.5% year on year. The salaries of those commissioned to enact on these budgets were not. And the percentage of marketing salaries was less than 5% of the total marketing spend. While I needed to investigate a lot more, I knew that the percentage of marketing salaries was healthy, to say the least. Of course, to evaluate the number of team members, you'll need to understand the scope of their work, but a quick glance through the numbers helped to offer a convincing answer. Chapter 8 focuses on the aspect of teams.

Financial statement analysis

There are two types of common financial statement analysis. These are often referred to as:

- Horizontal analysis.
- Benchmarking.

Horizontal analysis

The horizontal analysis method is used to review the spend over multiple periods of time. Your conclusions are usually presented in percentages. In this analysis, you will be able to depict a percentage growth or trend over the same line item in the base year. It is very helpful to spot trends using this method. Aim for at least a three-year comparison.

3-Year Marketing Spend

THE VIEW IN NUMBERS FRAMEWORK

In the above example, you can see that the company invests a lot in sponsorships and trade shows. It also has little spend on direct marketing such as email and SMS marketing or digital marketing and social media. You can immediately draw a conclusion that this company is either adopting a very traditional approach to marketing or may be a B2B (Business to Business) or B2G (Business to Government) brand that is highly dependent on sponsorship platforms and trade shows.

3-Year Marketing Spend

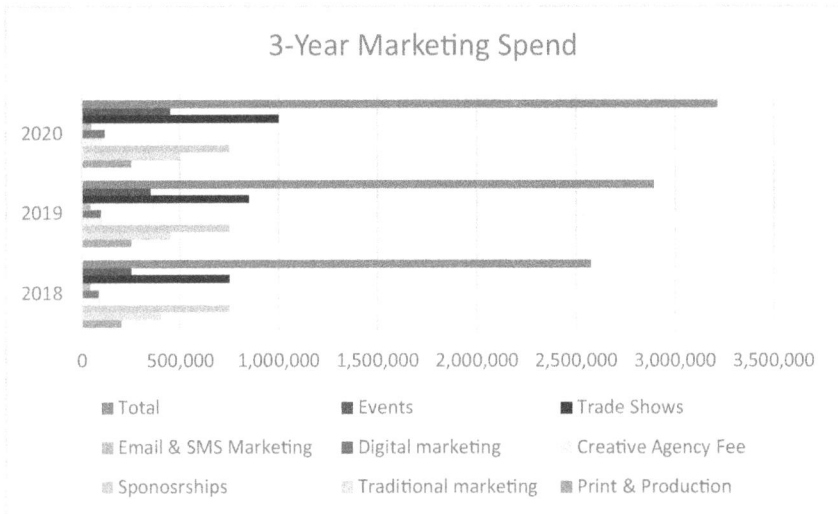

Legend: Total, Events, Trade Shows, Email & SMS Marketing, Digital marketing, Creative Agency Fee, Sponosrships, Traditional marketing, Print & Production

You can also see that the spend did not increase much over the years. This scenario would most likely apply to a stable market, probably a mature one, and a company that is not mass marketing but probably selling to a very distinct market segment.

You can use the horizontal analysis to find out the marketing spend as a percentage of revenue and how that increased or decreased. These figures will help you to understand if the company is carrying a healthy marketing budget to enable growth or is barely safeguarding its position.

This is also going to help you in planning for the right budgets against the business objectives of the company, which you would have understood during the View From The Top Framework in Chapter 4. For example, if the CEO has informed you that it is the vision to be the first in market share, but the marketing spend is just 1.7% as opposed to the market average of 7%, there goes your strong argument.

From what I have read in multiple CMO surveys over the years, I would state industry averages as follows, but these may vary by region, industry, company size, and the leading position of the company in the market.

Type of Company	Industry	Marketing Spend %
B2B Products	Entering goods. These become part of the end product or solution sold. They could be raw materials and spare parts that become part of finished products. For example, the tyres or spare parts of a vehicle. Foundation goods. These are used to make other products. For example, accessory equipment, machinery, and commercial vehicles would also fall into this category. Facilitating goods. These usually help a company achieve its business objectives but are not part of the product formation. For example, sources of energy such as gas, petrol, solar, and wind.	7%-12%

Type of Company	Industry	Marketing Spend %
B2B Services	Marketing services, design, production, banking, investments, financial consulting, facilities management, logistics, insurance, etc.	9.7%-11.5%
B2C Products	Any type of product that is sold to consumers. This includes books, fashion, food, jewellery, luxury items, real estate, cars, etc.	3.5% -10%
B2C Services	Services offered to customers such as dentistry, hair styling, financial advice, banking, and care services.	9%-11.6%

Understanding your marketing spends per category

Through this analysis, you will be able to understand the nature of the marketing activities that marry the brand optimally and what areas of improvement can be introduced.

For example, you may realise that in the past three years, if the market in which you operate is witnessing a 20% increase in digital spend, but the company is still at a flat on digital and still opting to increase sponsorships and traditional advertising spend, you know that in your strategy, you need to increase digital spend to keep up with the competition.

Sometimes, the marketing spend is a healthy percentage, but the distribution of the spend is unhealthy. A company may still be in its infancy and require strong brand awareness and mass marketing but has invested a third of its budget on sponsoring a concert.

There is no right or wrong formula on how marketing spend should be. There are many factors that determine that, including the nature of the product, the personality of the customer, and the effectiveness of the categories in your market or industry. By staying up-to-date with the market trends, you will be able to arrive at a formula that suits your brand best.

A lot of reliable sources from trusted research companies can help you with the data, such as Nielsen, and other websites that can also be of help include marketingcharts.com and komarketing.com.

Vertical Analysis or Benchmarking

In marketing benchmarking, sometimes referred to as vertical analysis, you can zoom in to the marketing categories and spend. This type of analysis is going to help you understand the overall pie chart of your marketing spends. The result is a pie chart showing you the percentage of each spend.

For example, a company is a distributor of an over-the-counter drug, and the majority, 75%, of the sales are generated from the B2B clientele who are pharmacies and hospitals, and only 25% is generated by direct consumers, but the marketing budget shows that 50% of the spend goes on an outdoor campaign. This would certainly be something that you can fix, as 50% of the budget should go on B2B marketing efforts towards the pharmacies and hospitals that are the majority buyers of your product.

During my time in the automotive sector, one of the business divisions was a distributor of a world-class brand of tyres. As an exclusive authorised leader, 80% of the sales were generated by selling to the dealers in the market, and this was a B2B marketing scenario. The company had a very smart and enthusiastic team of junior marketers who had recently graduated. When reviewing the marketing spend, it was immediately noticeable that the marketing spend was designed for a B2C brand. The spend was mostly on social media presence, promoting social media posts and digital ads, although the brand did not yet have an e-commerce site. We re-allocated the funds to cover dealer relations that are usually treated with events and trade shows. We also worked on brand building and introducing an element of PR to the campaigns.

Once this was treated as a B2B product, the following additions and enhancements were then added to the marketing plan:

1. Conduct a thorough customer profiling exercise. This is covered in Chapter 18.
2. Create a highly targeted email strategy, matching messaging and frequency to the identified target groups.
3. Create a dealer's annual awards ceremony.
4. Organise dealer trips with journalists to the factories of the brand.
5. Intensify the signage branding and POS material at the stores.
6. Double the sales promotions calendar shared with the dealers.
7. Branding customer touchpoints in the dealer's environment.
8. Create a database for the dealers in the region and formulate an email strategy to communicate with the dealers on a regular basis.
9. Investing in SEO and SEM online to promote the product line and after-sales services.

How is the company financially structured?

You also need to understand how the company is financially structured. The financial structure of the company is about its debt and its equity. The debt-equity ratio evaluates a company's financial leverage. It provides a measure of the relative contribution of the creditors and shareholders, or the owners of the capital employed in the business. The formula for debt-equity ratio is calculated by dividing the company's total liabilities by its shareholder equity. Each business, depending on the nature and breadth of its operations, has a different mix of debt and equity. The debt-equity mix varies depending on whether the company is private or public.

If a company is public, you will also need to understand the performance of the company's stock in the stock markets and the various factors influencing it.

Understanding P&L (Profit & Loss)

If you work for a company where you are building a P&L for your function or unit, the P&L will be constructed based on the nature of your business.

Here is what you need to understand to easily read a P&L Statement or Income Statement:

Net Sales

Net Sales = Net Cash Sales + Net Credit Sales

*Net Cash Sales: The amount of sales made by customers who make immediate settlement of the invoiced amount.

*Net Credit Sales: The amount of sales generated by customers buying on credit and does not include sales in cash. It also includes sales that are made but not paid for immediately.

The next item of your P&L will cover the calculation of Net Sales. These are usually calculated by considering the sum of the Gross Sales less the allowances and discounts.

Net Sales = Gross Sales – Allowances – Discounts
Calculating Gross Profit is basically taking your sales and subtracting the Cost of Goods Sold.

Gross Profit = Net Sales – Cost of Goods Sold
Cost of Goods is the cost incurred in creating the product or service you are marketing or promoting. An Allowance can be a return or a refund.

Total Income
Total Income = Gross Profit + Other Operating Income

Again, I stress that there are many departments that will have those line items empty on their P&L because marketing and communication departments are usually considered a support unit and not a sales-generation unit.

Most expenses will be direct expenses, and these are:

• Staff cost.

- Marketing and promotion.
- Administration and operating.

Next on your P&L statement will be your expenses. As a department, those expenses will usually include the following.

Staff cost

Your staff cost is going to include the costs associated with remuneration and provisions for your team members. In accurately calculating these, consider:

- Basic salary.
- Other allowances such as housing, food, and transportation.
- Travel allowances to cover the travel required throughout the year for business.
- Telecommunication allowances such as phone bills, both locally and internationally.
- Provisions for any salary increases or amendments required.
- Based on the team's structure you will design in the last section of Chapter 8, you will need to make provision for salary increases or additional costs for training and development.
- Cost of legislation matters such as issuance of work contracts and permits.
- Cost of medical and life insurance.

Administrative expenses

Your department's administrative expenses will include items such as:

- Office rentals or expenses of renting a virtual office, which is a nice breed of offices that became common post the pandemic year of 2020. In addition to rental, there is the cost of utilities like electricity, water, courier charges, and internet bills.
- The cost of purchasing hardware and software for the marketing and communication team.
- Annual memberships of image and video libraries such as Shutterstock and Getty Images. Annual memberships for the editing and design software or other systems used to mainstream marketing work, and, similarly, archival systems.
- The cost of machinery required to run the operations of the marketing department, apart from the computers. This includes photography and videography cameras, lighting, printers, craft supplies, whiteboards, podcast equipment, etc.
- Office welfare. This includes activities that are conducted to increase the welfare of the employees in the department, such as training, attending marketing shows, hosting birthday celebrations, and awarding employees. Other office welfare matters would be team building activities, etc.

Direct Margin or Gross Margin

The Direct Margin is calculated by deducting Direct Expenses from Total Income.

Direct Margin or Gross Margin is often expressed as a percentage. When calculating the Direct Margin, the items to look for most of the time will be:

Divisional Margin

The Divisional Margin is calculated by subtracting the operating cost of the division from the profits it generates.

Gross Profit or Gross Income

Gross Profit is the profit a company makes after deducting the costs associated with making and selling its products, or the costs associated with providing its services. Gross Profit will appear on a company's income statement and can be calculated by subtracting the Cost of Goods Sold (COGS) from Net Sales.

Operating Profit

Operating Profit is the profit made from business operations (Gross Profit minus Operating Expenses) before the deduction of interest and taxes.

Here is a simple P&L statement template.

Item	Formula	Year 1	Year 2	Year 3
Net Sales	A			
Cost of Goods Sold (COGS)	B			
Gross Profit	C=A-B			
Other Operating Income	D			
Total Income	E=C+D			
Expenses: Staff Cost Marketing and Promotion Administration and Operating				
Total Direct Expenses	F			
Direct Margin	G=E-F			
Rent Bonus Provision Bad Debts Stock Adjustment Provision Exchange Rate Variance Depreciation				
Total Indirect Expenses	H			
Operating Profit	I=G-H			
Interest	J			
Net Profit	K=I-J			

By this we end The View in Numbers Framework which should be able to help you understand the profitability story of the company, the prospects of your marcomms budget and how best to optimise it.

7

ENVISIONING YOUR DEPARTMENT FRAMEWORK

'It is not in the stars to hold our destiny but in ourselves.'

— WILLIAM SHAKESPEARE

This chapter will assist you in envisioning your marcomms department. Envisioning is not the mere practice of coming up with a vision statement. A vision is a great goal that you aim to achieve in the future; envisioning is the overall canvas of actions that will lead you to this great goal. It is about the means to get to the desired end.

This is the phase where you will bridge the gap between the findings of the discovery phases described in Chapters 3, 4, 5 and 6 and the series of deliverables that are needed from the marcomms function to address the findings in those chapters.

To complete this exercise, you will do the following:

1. Summarise your findings.
2. List and prioritise the types of marcomms services needed.
3. Explain how these services will be offered.
4. Apply a weightage approach to the marcomms service you will deliver.

1. Summarise your findings

Let us start by compiling a holistic list of the challenges and gaps discovered. We will begin with the ones you realised in the **First Impressions Framework** of Chapter 3, which focused on three broad areas.

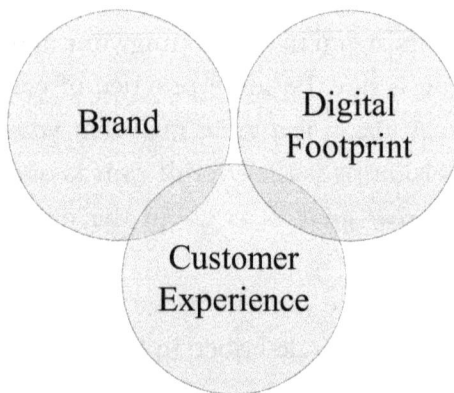

Here is a tabular example:

Category	Examples of Challenges
Brand	• Corporate brand identity is missing or not up-to-date. • Brand story is not compelling or memorable enough. • A catchy brand tagline is missing. • The brand colours are not distinct or are similar to those of a direct competitor.
Digital Footprint	• The company did not establish a strong presence on LinkedIn. • The corporate website is old and requires and a mobile friendly version. • There are missed opportunities of selling online. • Customer data requires updating. • Searchability can be improved through better SEO and deployment of SEM strategies.
Customer Experience	• Sales staff are inconsistent with their product pitches. • Customer complaints on social media are not handled in a timely fashion. • Some promotional advertisements were misleading. • New communication channels such as live chats or chatbots are necessary in this product segment and have not yet been applied.

Next, list the type of marcomms actions required to address those challenges.

Here is an example created for the **Digital Footprint** finding demonstrated in the previous table. To turn your solutions into measurable actions, provide an estimated deadline for the delivery of these solutions.

Item	Suggested Marcomms Solutions	Lead Time
LinkedIn	• Establish a corporate page on LinkedIn portraying the company's image with regular posts and engaging content. • Invest in a followers' campaign on the platform to generate footfall on the page. • Derive a content plan to update the page at least four times a week. • Use the platform's available advertising tools to promote the page.	3-6 months
SEO (Search Engine Optimisation)	• Conduct an SEO audit on the present website and find an explanation for the lack of top ranking in the search. • Present a new SEO keyword strategy. • Revisit the Google Maps listing of the brand outlets and update the imagery and details. • You may need to supplement your SEO with SEM campaigns.	3-6 months
Reviews and Ratings	• Improve the overall star ratings on Google by generating new positive customer reviews. • Design a campaign and training for sales staff to encourage the generation of positive online reviews. • Address negative reviews. • Deploy an instant feedback strategy to online reviews by the company.	1-3 months
Other Social Media Matters	• Derive a social media influencer strategy. • Get existing channels verified.	3-6 months

Next you will be summarising the requirements and observations from **The View From the Top Framework** of Chapter 4.

Demonstrate your understanding of the company's higher purpose according to your earlier discussions with the leaders on **The View From The Top Framework** in Chapter 4.

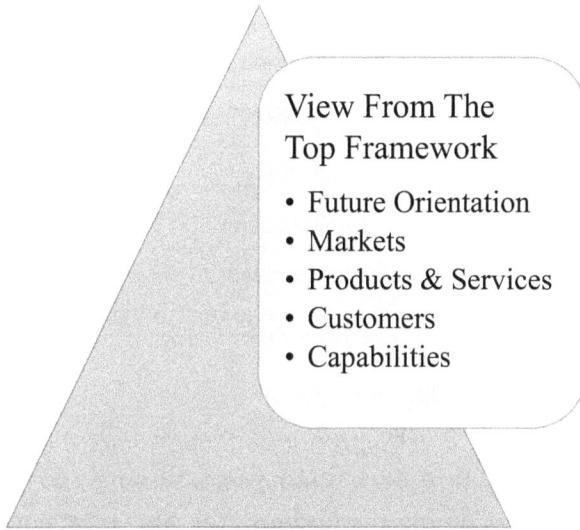

View From The
Top Framework

• Future Orientation
• Markets
• Products & Services
• Customers
• Capabilities

Item	Suggested Marcomms Solutions
Future orientation	• The company is diversifying its products into new geographical territories and needs to strengthen its product offerings. • The company is facing severe competition from cloud-based offerings and needs to transition to an online business. • The company plans to go public in the next 48 months and requires an establishment of a financial PR strategy.

Item	Suggested Marcomms Solutions
Markets	• The company's market share growth is stagnant. • The company requires new lines of businesses to grow its market share. • The company needs a more innovative approach to its product development and services.
Products & Services	• The company requires services to be digitised. • The company requires an omni-channel marketing-based solution.
Customers	• The company needs to widen its customer-targeting. • The company requires a customer journey improvement exercise.
Capabilities	• The company needs to revamp its digital capabilities by employing the right skillset.

The discussions on markets allowed you to fully understand the state of the market, be it in its infancy or declining, the trends in the market, and its upcoming disruptions. You also have a clear understanding of the company's market position and market share. From your review of products and services, you came to understand what products sell best, which are the most profitable, and what marketing strategies are required.

Then you can apply the same to your findings from **The View From The Bottom Framework** in Chapter 5.

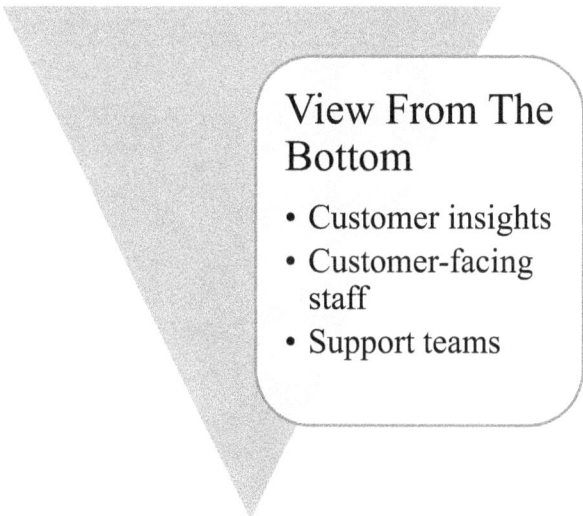

View From The Bottom

- Customer insights
- Customer-facing staff
- Support teams

Item	Suggested Marcomms Solutions
Customer-facing & front-end staff.	• Better access to data that shows the customer's search journey prior to interacting with the customer-facing staff.
Back-end & support functions	• The company requires an ERP solution that can digitize its IT support and Procurement and HR functions.

You can now summarise the most prevailing challenges and list the marcomms solutions that can address them. Here is an example.

Challenge	Details	Marcomms Solutions
Market Share	Company wishes to increase its market share by 3.5% -5% annually.	Introduce new product extensions. Look into regional expansion.

Challenge	Details	Marcomms Solutions
Technology	The company is operating on multiple technology platforms and planning to transform to an omnichannel platform.	Conduct a full branding exercise for the new omnichannel system. By doing so, map a new customer journey and identify new customer touchpoints for the brand.
Quality	Improvement in the quality of services and overall customer experience.	Conduct customer research. Introduce new solutions or service packages that improve the quality of the customer experience.
Customer Success	Increase the present customer satisfaction rating.	Launch a social media customer response strategy. Monitor and report customer feedback. Launch a testimonial campaign. Launch a customer success program.
Profitability	Improve the profitability margins.	Launch a new merchandising strategy. Launch campaigns to increase purchase value and repeat purchases. Revisit the pricing strategy. Plan a new PR strategy that will increase the brand value and improve the brand perception in the market. Introduce cost savings in the marketing execution.

2. Map the marcomms solutions against the prevailing challenges

These can also be split between corporate communications, branding, and marketing. I will offer you the three diagrams to help you list and prioritise your marcomms services. You can also get more details from Chapters 17, 18 and 19.

Your department will be offering either all or some of the below. Additionally, as mentioned earlier, the services may be added with an expected timeline.

Your work may fall under one specialised discipline such as marketing or a combination of marketing, PR, and branding or more. To better understand how much of each you need to cover, use this guide to check the areas that the discovery phase identified as needing to be addressed.

Marketing	Corporate Communication and PR	Branding
• Strategic planning. • Customer marketing disciplines (market research, promotions, partner marketing). • Website development and search marketing. • E-commerce & M-Commerce development. • Advertising and demand generation. • Experiential marketing. • Entertainment marketing. • Event management. • Roadshows and exhibitions. • Pricing and promotions. • Marketing on social media channels. • Programmatic digital advertising. • Gaming. • Mobile app development. • Emails strategy and management.	• Public relations. • Media relations. • Media training for company speakers. • Executive profiling and communication. • Internal communication. • Internal publications. • Investor relations. • Crisis communication. • Corporate philanthropy. • Sponsorships. • Annual reports. • Social media content creation. • Website content creation. • Corporate blogging. • Corporate archives creation and maintenance. • Creating corporate image and video asset libraries. • Tracking of corporate milestones for timeline and history stories.	• Brand identity development. • Conducting brand personality workshops. • Brand architecture and naming strategies. • Rebranding or refining existing brands for divisions and company businesses. • Establishing brand positioning and messaging. • Creating a branding strategy. • Designing of logos and sub-logos. • Formulating brand guidelines for design, style, and tone, including typography and colour palettes. • Branding of company office and commercial environments. • Packaging. • Branded collateral and giveaways.

Here are examples of how you can then describe the services of your department.

Marketing and promotion services

Marketing Channels

Traditional   Digital

| Personal Selling | Cross-Selling | Events/ Roadshows | Advertising | Email Marketing | Social Media | Digital Display |
| Direct Selling | Sales Promotion | Social Selling | SEO/SEM | Mobile | Online & Web Commerce |

- Generate more sales through the formulation and design of marketing campaigns and improved lead generation.
- Oversee promoting the company's products and services in respective markets.
- Design new products or services that will meet the growing and changing customer needs.
- Carry out market research to identify growth opportunities and gather feedback from customers on their experiences and ratings of the company's products and services.
- Gather the valuable data related to customer behaviour and industry trends.
- Provide the direction needed on the company's pricing strategies and accordingly derive the marketing messages that will mirror the perceived value of the company's products and services.
- Oversee marketing budgets necessary to produce desired growth, revenue, and market share.

Corporate communication

| Corporate Communication | | | | | | |
| Internal | | | | | | External |

| Brand Archives | Corporate Reports | Corporate Publications | Crisis Management | Investor Relations | Media Relations | Public Relations |

| Internal Communication | Leadership Communication | Corporate Forums | Sponsorships & Events | News Management |

- Coordinate brand communication from a strategic level with stakeholders and oversee the execution of the brand communication at a tactical level.
- Introduce different types of communication disciplines together in a centralised fashion so that the knowledge and skills are safeguarded, all communication tactics are directed in a coherent strategy, and consistency in messaging and tonality is achieved.
- Assist businesses or company divisions in their task to reach out to prospects, customers, investors, and the community, while creating an overarching image that represents them in a positive light.
- Publish brand messages that will invoke a positive and favourable response to the company and its products and services.
- Have ready a crisis communications plan.
- Plan and execute the company's events and sponsorship agreements.

Branding & design services

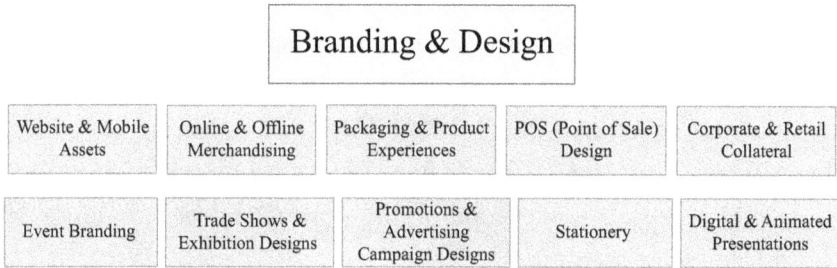

Branding & Design				
Website & Mobile Assets	Online & Offline Merchandising	Packaging & Product Experiences	POS (Point of Sale) Design	Corporate & Retail Collateral
Event Branding	Trade Shows & Exhibition Designs	Promotions & Advertising Campaign Designs	Stationery	Digital & Animated Presentations

There is so much that goes into branding. The above chart shows the assets that need to be created for a company. Here are examples of branding initiatives that your department could be launching:

- Design a brand-new mobile-friendly website for the company that carries a seamless customer journey.
- Supplement the website with a virtual merchandising strategy that enhances the customer experience.
- Upgrade the packaging of the products to address the increasing customer attraction to sustainable packaging.
- Create informative 2D or 3D animated video demos for the company's products and services.
- Conduct a brand refinement exercise and launch updated stationary and visual assets.

3. Explain how these services will be offered

In deciding how the services of your function will be offered, you need to understand the degree of centralisation required for efficient decision making and timely rollout of projects. As companies grow and diversify, the lines of authority may become disabling. It is important to ensure that work flows smoothly by finding the right balance in centralising your operations.

If you're working for a small company with one line of business, it would be taken for granted that you have one central department. If you work for a large conglomerate with multiple brands spread across many cities and countries, you need to have a central function along with satellite offices and you need to follow a de-centralised approach to some of the marcomms services. You may also have separate and highly specialised teams for marketing and communications.

While a centralised structure gives you great control, it may be costly and less efficient. It could slow down the speed of work required to help a company gain a competitive edge. A decentralised approach works well only if a company has well-established systems and processes, and brands have a firm brand identity that guarantees consistency. A matrix or regional approach is a fair balance between the two.

Whatever approach you choose, you need to remain flexible and keep an open mind that you may need to shuffle around priorities as you go. No structure is set in stone. Adaptation and change will come up, and your team structure may require adjustments. Markets, customer sentiment, and even competition change course much too frequently. This requires agility and the openness to change course where and when needed. Most importantly, whatever structure and line of authority you choose, accept the fact that mistakes will happen.

Give yourself and those around you the room to try, fail, and then try again.

In understanding how each of these areas will be addressed, you can decide if they will be centralised within. Here is an example of how a Marcomms department identified which services would be centralised and which would be decentralised. The model below is ideal for a holding company or a portfolio business spanning multiple countries or cities.

Centralised Services	Decentralised Services
• Strategic management and communication advisory. • Branding and brand messaging creation. • Corporate philanthropy and CSR. • Public relations, media relations and reputation management. • Executive profiling and personal branding for senior executives. • Media and public speaking training. • Sponsorship evaluation and validation. • Internal communications. • Corporate publications. • PR agency management. • Corporate website handling. • New and contracted vendor evaluation and assessment. • Issuance of policies and procedures.	• Marketing campaign planning and budgeting. • Marketing campaign management and execution. • Tactical advertising; sales and promotions. • Digital advertising, search engine optimisation, search engine marketing. • Email and SMS marketing. • CRM customer relations management. • Campaign leads generation and conversion tracking. • Corporate events planning and execution. • Product placement and activation. • Social and digital media management. • CRM development. • Mobile app design and management. • Marketing research. • Partnerships and cross-promotions.

4. Apply a weightage approach to the marcomms services you will deliver.

Depending on your diagnosis and discovery results, the role of your department is going to be dispersed across the three disciplines mentioned at the beginning of the chapter: marketing, branding and corporate communications. The areas are truly intertwined and cannot be looked at individually. One leads into the other. I did, however, break them into three diagrams because a visual representation can explain what type of work falls under each discipline.

The first step in identifying the role of your department is to understand the weightage of each of the three disciplines. To best understand how to set up the role of your department, identify to the best of your ability the percentages for the first three to five years.

If you have joined a start-up or a long-standing company that has not upgraded its branding work, then the area of brand may have a higher percentage than others, but that may be the case for the first few years. Similarly, if the company plans to add a lot of new service offerings or is in the process of new innovations, then branding would be a top priority.

When I worked for a manufacturing conglomerate that had aggressive expansion plans with a pressing agenda to go public, my initial discovery phase clearly showed that although the company's marketing practices were rather traditional, there was a lot of room to transition into digital marketing. Yet, the fact that the company had plans to go public meant a lot of communication and PR and communication had to take place. The Group's previous generation of senior management kept a very low profile and did make any public announcements or build much media engagement. This meant it was important to establish a corporate communication strategy and create a positive and favourable reputation for the company.

Here is what the journey looked like:

Year	Marketing	Corporate Communication	Branding
Year 1	30%	30%	40%
Year 2	35%	35%	30%
Year 3	40%	40%	20%
Year 4-5*	40%	50%	10%

As you gain full clarity from the earlier chapters of discovery, you will be able to create a clear path of work for the years ahead on this job with the information in this chapter.

8

THE TEAM THAT WILL GET YOU THERE

*'Great things in business are never done by one person.
They're done by a team of people.'*

— STEVE JOBS

By now, you have a fair and clear understanding of the company's vision, you have identified the gaps and challenges, and listed the marcomms services you will offer. Next, you'll need the right team that will get you there.

In this chapter, we will look at the team structure and skillset required for a marcomms function.

A team structure reflective of business nature

I will intentionally avoid adding any organisational charts in this chapter because these are unique to every company. I will instead explain what job roles exist under the disciplines of marcomms.

If the nature of your department will focus on marketing, then begin by hiring marketing professionals. If the nature of the work requires corporate communication and branding, then make that your priority and then move on to other fields. Your team structure will reflect the nature of your business and types of services your department will be offering.

If you inherited an existing team, asses their capabilities and see if their potential is fully utilised and how else you can add value to the deliverables of the department. Part of your team structure will include outsourced vendors and agencies. Working with agencies is also covered in the second half of this chapter.

Marketing team

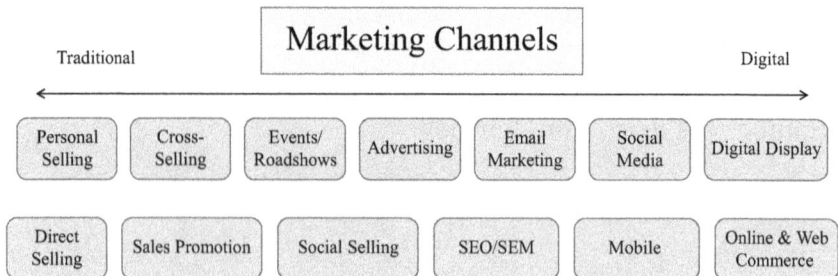

Traditional			Marketing Channels			Digital
Personal Selling	Cross-Selling	Events/ Roadshows	Advertising	Email Marketing	Social Media	Digital Display
Direct Selling	Sales Promotion	Social Selling	SEO/SEM	Mobile		Online & Web Commerce

The marketing spectrum ranges from digital to traditional channels. The disciplines of marketing are many and will vary depending on the nature of your business and the type of products you sell.

Let's look at some of the most commons jobs in the marketing field.

Brand marketing executives

A brand manager or executive will oversee the performance of a brand from a marketing and branding standpoint. They could work on one or multiple brands depending on the breadth of the company's operations. They are responsible for ensuring all marketing campaigns are launched to the best standards and are effective and yielding the expected returns to help the brand grow. They overlook activities that fall under the wide spectrum of marketing and brand design.

These are the executives who do take to heart the STP approach at work. They are capable of effectively segmenting customers. They have the knowledge of how best to target customers with the right pricing and promotions.

Marketing plans take into consideration the implementation and roll out of the 4Ps of Marketing, and these are Price, Product, Promotion and Place. Marketing executives work closely with the sales and operations teams to roll out the campaigns that help the company achieve its targets in sales, profitability, and market share. They are involved in pricing strategies, promotion design, product design, and network expansion for brands.

Marketing executives are also responsible for identifying target audiences. They often create customer personas and work on tailor-made messages and campaigns to reach the different segments of their audiences.

They also take part in the pricing and placement strategies of the products and services the company promotes. They can run marketing campaigns, brand activations, events, sponsorships, roadshows, and exhibitions when needed as well.

They handle the development of annual marketing plans and the design of marketing budgets. They assign budgets to every campaign and every marketing channel. They monitor the budget spend and report on its results.

Finally, marketing professionals also track the performance of the marketing campaigns and the marketing budget. They are tasked with reporting on the performance of the campaigns in terms of leads and conversions.

The rapid decline of the conventional brick-and-mortar businesses had us witness a rise in digital marketers. If you are working for a retail or an e-commerce company, then your marketing team will be heavily focused on digital marketing, social media selling, lead generation, customer acquisition and retention.

Let's first look at the role of a retail marketer.

Retail marketing

Retail marketing is the business area that bridges the relationship between the manufacturing company and the companies distributing the products to markets. Retail marketers are the ones who can deliver marketing plans that allow those products to reach potential customers. Their main performance indicators are linked to sales revenues and to the awareness built around the product. They are usually focused on increasing the popularity of a product, they deploy plans to generate footfall to the retail outlets be it physical or digital and they need to be creative in how best to engage customers.

Retail marketers run campaigns and promotions to encourage first-time and repeat trials. They are responsible for increasing footfall towards a store or traffic to a mobile app or website. They carry out awareness campaigns and retail promotions to help drive product visibility and improved performance.

They conduct market research and competitive analysis to achieve the correct positioning for the products and solutions being sold. They work closely with the manufacturers to help achieve the right brand offering suited to the markets in which they operate. They advise on how best to increase customer satisfaction and provide market data to help customise product design to their regions.

Retail marketers also work on enhancing the retail environment through store designs, merchandising and product displays. They are responsible for upgrading the look and feel and experiences in the retail channels, both online and offline. They also work on packaging and delivery.

Digital marketing

Digital marketers are responsible for the success of digital advertising and digital media campaigns such as display, PPC (Pay-Per-Click), and near-field and mobile advertising. They usually have a very thorough understanding of the digital media and social media channels. With their knowledge they can assign the right budget to the right channels.

In their work, they continuously study how every digital channel is generating leads and how those leads are turning into conversions. The quality of leads and sales conversions fall under their work. They usually work with the internal operations and customer contact centre teams to improve the conversion rates at every step of the customer journey.

They are involved in the design of the digital campaigns and provide feedback on which ad layouts and formats are working best for their audiences. They are also responsible for generating attention grabbing ads with great copy and content that drives interest to the brand.

Digital marketers are also expected to contribute to customer acquisition. They design, manage, and implement campaigns that create awareness and help acquire new customers.

Digital marketers are expected to defend their spend by furnishing reports on the digital performance of their media plans. They regularly provide reports on the performance of campaigns.

In addition to their knowledge in social media, digital marketers grasp the dynamics of SEO (Search Engine Optimisation) strategies, SEM (Search Engine Marketing), retargeting, geographically based targeting, and email marketing strategies.

Roles in digital marketing include digital media buyer, optimisation strategist, website and mobile application developer, lead acquisition specialist, customer acquisition specialist, and campaign analyst.

Online businesses will also hire technical specialists in SEO, content developers and email specialists.

Technical SEO and analytics

Online businesses highly depend on their searchability index. This means, a dedicated resource will be looking after the technical elements that allows optimised crawling of the company's website.

An SEO analyst will be charged with the company's SEO strategy. A company's SEO strategy is focused on using the right keywords to promote the business online. This person will be an expert in creating content that contains the right keywords and terminologies that enable top search ranking. They will look into the website pages and refine the keyword mapping and SEO meta data linked to the pages that are of most importance in the customer discovery.

They also work closely with the digital media agencies that take charge of the paid digital media for the business. They guide website developers on refining the website architecture and online browsing structure according to reported customer behaviours online.

They relay all their SEO knowledge and findings to the social media and content creation teams to help them build the right pipeline of leads to the business. They are also in charge of updating website content such as product descriptions, blog content, and other pages with the needed SEO receptive keywords.

Additionally, they will monitor competition in the market using digital analytics tools to advance their own brands searchability ahead of competition.

They are also in charge of generating monthly reports pertaining the company's online searchability status. They are usually fluent in Google Analytics platforms for evaluating website performance.

Email marketing executives

Email marketing is a prevailing digital marketing tool for both B2C and B2B businesses. An email marketing executive will design your email content strategy. They are often experienced in customer targeting. They know how to tailor-create content that matches the different groups of customer personas. They plan the frequency of the email shot campaigns. They could also be responsible for the SMS campaigns of the brands.

Email specialists dive deep into the customer persons and not only allocate the right concept campaigns and promotions, but draft personalised messages to them. Depending on the importance that your company places on email marketing, you might need talent dedicated to content writing and talent for email design. In some instances, this is an outsourced task. You can find out how to build customer personas in Chapter 18.

Content development executive

A content development executive is responsible for building the online content for the company's website and social media channels. In this role, the executive is working closely with the website developers and SEO analysists and the email marketing and social media team in charge.

A content developer makes sure that the company's website is SEO optimised by drafting short-term and long-term content that carries the desired keyword structure.

This person knows the market trends, customer language, popular search terms and the language adopted by competing brands.

He or she could also be charged with populating the company's blog and social media content calendars with highly engaging topics. They need to have the right copywriting skills and the ability to come up with catchy headlines and newsworthy blog posts.

Content writers can also work under the corporate communications team and assist with press releases and news dissemination. They could be contributing to the company's internal newsletter, corporate magazine and news pieces.

Social media executive

A social media executive will have deep knowledge about the social media platforms that are best suited for the brand messages. The social media team will be responsible for the content strategy of the brand. They identify the best themes and pillars for the content strategy. They also develop community engagement plans and design feedback systems for real time response to the followers and online community of the brand. They put in place tactics to increase the following and engagement on the brand's social media channels.

Social media executives work alongside the digital marketing team. The team develops relationships with social media influencers to run testimonial and product trial campaigns. The team oversees running social media activations like competitions and quizzes. They are experienced in content creation in all its different formats.

The social media team is also responsible for the community management of the social channels. This includes managing responses to social media posts, and other online enquiries.

Finally, social media executives are responsible for reports on social media listening tools, community engagement and competitive reporting.

Corporate communications

	Corporate Communication	
Internal		External

Brand Archives	Corporate Reports	Corporate Publications	Crisis Management	Investor Relations	Media Relations	Public Relations

Internal Communication	Leadership Communication	Corporate Forums	Sponsorships & Events	News Management

Corporate communication is the accumulative set of activities that create a favourable impression about a company or a brand in the mind of its stakeholders. The corporate communication team coordinates brand communication to build brand equity and protect the company's reputation in the market.

The difference between marketing and corporate communication lies in the targeting exercise. Marketing focuses on customers and potential customers. Corporate communication focuses on multiple stakeholders like employees, vendors, media, governments, and the public. Marketing is intended to influence people to purchase a product or a service. Corporate communication is intended to shed a positive light on a business and make it a favourable and trustworthy entity. Corporate communication deals with publicity, investor relations, corporate reporting, corporate publications, sponsorships strategies and corporate events.

Corporate communication also focuses on internal communication to make sure employees are well-informed, well-trained, and motivated. It also tackles leadership communication which includes the messages and appearances of the leaders of the company.

The team also covers the work related to crisis communication. Job roles in this field include PR and media relations, internal communication, event management and sponsorship professionals.

PR and media relations executives

PR and media executives are in charge of the company's news and earned media content. They create news through a suit of publicity tactics such as press releases, interviews, photo captions, news briefs, official media statements, opinion pieces and press stories. They assist in product launches and new store openings by hosting corporate events and press conferences.

They oversee the drafting and distribution of company news both internally and externally. They ensure the news achieve the maximum possible reach by creating favourable relationships with the media outlets and influencers. They oversee the quality and quantity of earned media coverage created for the company. They work against multiple KPIs such as press clipping, coverage value and the brand's SOV (Share of Voice) in the market. They also monitor news of the company's competition in the market. They often work against specific publicity measures that are aimed at raising the profile of the company in the market.

Media relations involves developing and managing relationships with journalists and editors that are beneficial to both parties. These relationships are based on an exchange of information that generates compelling stories. Media relations done right can help you position your company as a leader in the field and your senior executives as industry experts and can get you good reviews. The media relations team responds to media inquiries and pitch media stories to the press. More on this topic is covered in Chapter 13.

Public speaking is fundamental to raising awareness about a business by its people. To be an effective public speaker, one requires certain skills which enable message delivery in a compelling and impactful manner. The PR team facilitates media training workshops for the company's spokespersons. They arrange for their appearances in the media such as radio, TV, podcasts and other types of interviews. Additionally, they secure panel discussions and speaking opportunities for the company spokespersons in industry forums. The PR team also works on earning the company industry accolades and recognitions. The team also handles crisis communication and any reputational issues related to the company.

Internal communication

Chapter 14 is dedicated to internal communication. An internal communications specialist handles the internal announcements and events of the company. They oversee internal corporate publications such as news bulletins and newsletters as well as the company's intranet platforms.

Internal communication teams work on delivering year-long communication plans for the company. You will find plenty of explanations on this discipline in Chapter 14 of the book.

Large companies will also have dedicated roles for brand activations, events, sponsorships, and CSR (Corporate Social Responsibility) executives. These are covered in detail on Chapters 15 and 16.

Branding and design roles

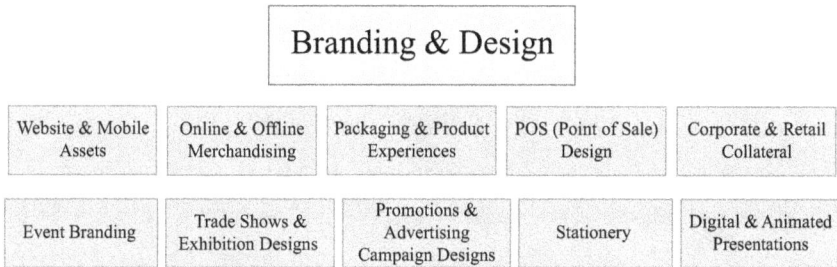

Branding & Design				
Website & Mobile Assets	Online & Offline Merchandising	Packaging & Product Experiences	POS (Point of Sale) Design	Corporate & Retail Collateral
Event Branding	Trade Shows & Exhibition Designs	Promotions & Advertising Campaign Designs	Stationery	Digital & Animated Presentations

The branding team looks after packaging design, new campaign designs, and branding of the retail environments, both physical and digital.

The design team may also have an in-house production team that carries out photography and videography. If the design team oversees most of the campaigns running without the support of an outside agency, the scope of work may necessitate hiring copywriters. Copywriters are talented individuals who can write attractive headlines and content for the advertisements that work on online and offline platforms. They specialise in language that works in harmony with the digital sphere.

Graphic designers are responsible for creating the brand assets. The different types of brand assets are covered in Chapter 12. They include logos, stationery, merchandising, POS (Point of Sale), leaflets, brochures, and promotional material. Large online businesses also employ in-house online merchandising professionals.

Roles under this discipline include creative director, art director, graphic designer, animator, photographer, videographer and editor.

Balancing the skillset in your team

It is important to strike a balance in the skillsets and specialisation areas of your team. For example, if you have hired a team that is proficient with execution, then you'll need to add a powerful strategic thinker. If a team is focused on lead generation and analytics, then that would leave little room for creating experiences and thematic campaigns. In this case, it is important to balance out the skillset with a member from an events-based or branding background or a communication expert who can add an extra dimension to the deliverables.

Identify the skill gaps in your team on an annual basis and bring in the skillset needed. This skillset could be problem-solving, creative thinking, digital strategizing, or content creation. Marcomms professionals who have worked at the agency-side bring in a creative flair while those who have worked solely on the client-side bring in sales optimization plans.

Your structure will be reflective of the percentages of the marketing and comms that your department is designed to do. These were identified in the preceding chapter. The more marketing you do, the more marketers you need. If you are expected to provide communication support with little marketing advisory, then you will be looking for PR executives, media relations executives, content creators, sponsorship specialists, events and social media executives.

High performance teams

In the prevailing market circumstances, there is little absence of talent. Rather, there is a great pool of talent. When faced with not finding the right talent, I suggest you hire a consultant or an agency to help you until more clarity is formed on what are the specific roles you need.

When creating winning teams, make sure you bring on board those who share your values and aspirations. As a person who learned well from experiences, I defined two personal values that I looked for in people joining my team. These are curiosity and creativity.

Carlos Zapeda, VP Transformation and Growth, Moët Hennessy USA, says, 'Leaders and organisations that foster intellectual curiosity are actually able to better identify ideas.'

In turning your team into a high performance one, you need to share with them the vision of your department and define their job roles and KPIs. The team needs to be united under one mission. You will get clarity when you set and clearly communicate your expectations from the team. Establishing clear deliverables allows them to predict their role. Finally, tracking the progress of the team and each individual separately instils ownership and accountability on their part. Providing timely feedback through open and honest conversations allows them to feel looked after. What breaks a team apart is lack of confrontation and misalignment on values. These can be easily resolved when you implement an 'always-on' objective feedback system.

Working with other support functions

It is important to work collaboratively with the support functions of your company. These include HR, procurement, audit and others. I personally focus on finance and technology departments at the beginning. Both functions are important to the success of your marketing and communication work. Finance needs to understand the commercial value of your work. This requires that you present the return on investment to your branding, communication, and marketing work. The IT team is expected to assist you in creating a seamless customer journey by supplementing your work with efficient platforms and systems.

In managing those relationships, it is also important to carve out the responsibility of partner functions and agree on the means of creating the output desired. This is best done through SLAs (Service Level Agreements), which are explained in Chapter 10.

In-house and outsourced functions

The decision of what services to outsource will be based on the breadth of your operations, company size, and the number of brands you handle. It may also depend on your company's appetite for hiring.

In deciding to go in-house or to outsource, investigate the following factors:

- Quality and nature of creative services required for campaigns; are they tactical or thematic?
- Frequency and volume of work required.
- Nature of the brand or brands; a newly established homegrown brand would require a lot more assets than a well-established or a franchised brand.
- The type of technology required for executing your marketing plans and media.
- The types of reports that you need to generate.
- The go-to-market timelines.

Here is an example of a department handling a one-brand company:

Type of Service	Marketing	Communications and PR	Branding
Delivered from mother brand/manufacturer/ franchisor.	Strategic planning. Consumer marketing. Market research. Campaign calendar.	Press releases. Annual reports. Social media content creation. Website content creation.	Packaging. Brand identity and brand architecture. Brand guidelines. Logos. Stationery. Branded collateral and giveaways.
Outsourced to an agency.	Website development. E-commerce development. Advertising and demand generation. Event management. Roadshows and exhibitions. Brand and corporate events. Marketing on social media channels. Programmatic. Mobile app development. SEO and SEM.	Distribution of press releases and media monitoring. Media training for company speakers. Executive profiling and internal communication. Creating corporate image and video asset libraries.	Branding collateral updates.

Type of Service	Marketing	Communications and PR	Branding
Managed in-house	Pricing and promotions. Emails strategy and management. Entertainment marketing, including celebrity and influencer collaborations.	Media relations. Internal communications. Internal publications. Corporate philanthropy. Sponsorships. Corporate blogging.	Stationery adaptation. Newsletters. Internal communication.

Why writing and content creation matters in our field

The latest CMO reports, and industry trends have attested that writing is a prerequisite for a successful marcomms career. Many reports prove that everyone – that is, all corporate professionals – is now in the communications game. Communications stem from creativity and the ability to create the best expression of a brand. And it is in this that the team that you need to have must be malleable, agile, and willing to communicate.

In a study conducted by *The Drum*, where 300 C-level marketing executives were interviewed on the latest trends in the industry, 23% responded that the ability for content creation is one of the top skills in high demand.

In her book *What the new breed of CMOs know that you do not*, MaryLee Sachs outlined the new aspects of a CMO role that are needed, and these were 'Beyond knowing the customer, increasing the interactions with the customer, and beyond knowing the market, creating a system of engagement that maximises value creation at every touchpoint.' This means, imagination and the ability to work on marketing and communication deliverables that permeate every touchpoint. This can only be accomplished by an ability to write and tell stories. All marcomms professionals are storytellers and are in the business of relaying messages. If they do not have that skill, they'll need to work hard at earning it.

The traits of the team

Make a list of the common positive behaviours that you wish to find in your team members. Here is a list I have made:

- Curious.
- Eager to learn.
- Great communication skills.
- Thinks beyond the cookie-cutter approach.
- Demonstrate the ability to get creative.
- Empathetic listener and understands how to sell ideas.
- Admits failure gracefully.
- Receptive to feedback.
- Takes on full ownership of work.
- Is passionate about marketing and communication.
- Invests in his or her career growth and self-development.
- Reads books (this is a personal trait of mine, and I wish to see it in my tribe).
- Sets personal goals, beyond the job, and achieves them.

Structure of the team

The structure of the team will be reflective of the company you are in. Start-ups and commerce businesses will predominantly have a marketing team and as they grow, they will invest in corporate communication. A lot of companies start with a one-person department who delivers work on the full marcomms structure, usually through a predominantly outsourced model. Some companies may have the retail marketers working closely with sales and operations. If your team handles multiple brands, you may need to have brand managers who overlook the entire scope of every brand. You may as well need a dedicated PR, customer-retention, loyalty, social media, and digital teams. It all depends on the size of the company.

As brands grow and expand, their marcomms departments could invest more in an inhouse model where they have full-fledged digital, creative, design and PR teams.

Since structures are pretty much dictated by the breadth of operations. The classic structure will have a CMO sittings on top, followed by leaders of the disciplines of Brand, Marketing and PR. They in turn manage both in-house and outsourced teams. What you need to remember is that the structure of your team will be dynamic and will change as the business grows and changes.

Why and how to choose an agency

Once you have identified your department structure and deliverables, you will most likely look at a hybrid mix of in-house teams and outside agency partners to deliver your campaigns.

Here are the most common types of agencies:

- Research.
- Advertising.
- Social media.
- Digital media buying.
- Web development, app development, and search optimisation.
- Public and media relations.
- Event management.
- Creative and brand activation.
- Branding.
- Mystery shopping.
- Customer experiences and CRM (Customer Relations Management).
- Media monitoring and reporting.

This book will not be complete if we do not touch on the protocols of working with agencies. The right agency partner will provide you with access to specialised fields that are otherwise expensive or too complicated to be handled internally. Creative agencies, for example, have the strategic teams to provide you with great insights about the behaviours of your target audiences and the market trends when it comes to the consumption of products and types of media.

Agencies invest and deploy the latest technologies in the field, and these may be too expensive for a single company to adopt. Agencies employ multi-disciplinary teams that allow your campaigns to be carried out by very experienced people, be it research analysts, campaign strategists, creative directors, writers, graphic designers, or media planners.

Agencies employ and train specialists in key fields, be it analytics, lead generation, SEO and crisis communication, content creation, speech writing, media training, or video productions to name a few. The work environment in agencies fosters creativity, and it is not an environment a company can easily replicate on the business side. By being exposed to other clients and brands in other industries, agencies can add fresh perspectives to your strategies and provide input about the latest and best practices.

Partnering with agencies

The relationship between you and your agency is a partnership. Radim Malinic, award-winning creative director and author of the 'Book of Ideas' series, describes the relationship between agency and client as follows: 'A creative collaboration is a bit like dating: we present only the best versions of ourselves at first, and sometimes, things don't even get past that first date.' While your agency will always come to the rescue, building a productive relationship that is built on trust and more importantly respect is key to your success.

Sometimes landing the right agency partner means that you immerse yourself in writing proper and comprehensive briefs. It also requires building respectful and healthy relationships with the teams that will be working on your briefs. You would also need to get a full comprehension of the creative process and come to terms with the time it takes for a proper campaign or agency deliverable to materialise.

In landing an agency, be it for an annual or a project-based one, be sure to host a series of chemistry meetings with the team that will be taking care of your business. Make sure that your team and the team at the agency are open to working together with an established level of comfort.

When hiring an agency on a long-term basis, try to carry out a trial period for a short time to make sure you are satisfied with their methodologies and output. If the agency is set to hire a team to work on your brand, then feel free to get involved in the recruitment process, especially if this resource is supposed to be working in a 100% capacity on your business.

Agency pitches and briefs

Over the years, I have seen pitfalls and injustice when it comes to inviting agencies to pitch on new business. My experience is limited to the Middle East and North African region, so this is not a global generalisation. Let us address the elephant in the room and talk openly about the appropriate way to approach an agency for a pitch.

Guarantee the confidentiality of the material and promise not to use it yourself

Firstly, let's discuss ideas being stolen from agencies or replicated by clients without the agency's consent. I am not going to sugar-coat the term 'stolen' because it happens, and frequently. We hear of stories of agencies pitching creative ideas that don't land them the Client to then see a very similar interpretation of the idea launched by that Client. Expecting agencies to volunteer their utmost creativity and then getting it passed on to an in-house team or other agency team is utter corporate infidelity. As tempted as you could be to do so, or perhaps pressured by management to do so, I do hope you have it in your heart to understand that this is unethical and unfair.

There's no such thing as a free lunch

Secondly, let us talk about clients expecting agencies to pitch their best assets forward for free. Again, I am specifically referencing the regions in which I have worked in. The times have changed. Not all agencies have sufficient teams today to carry out massive pitching for free. Paying a fee in exchange for the work presented shows that you are serious about engaging with the agency.

Get those briefs written properly

Thirdly, let us talk about briefs. The process of briefing is simple. If you provide an incomplete brief, you get incomplete work. The outcome of your brief is simply a representation of your input. In a nutshell, it's a GIGO situation, and there are two ways to look at it. It's either 'garbage in, garbage out' or 'good in, good out' and we most certainly choose the latter.

Briefs are to be respected and worked on. A brief is not a copy-and-paste from your corporate website or email sent from the sales team. They should provide an accurate representation of current business problems or challenges. They should provide authentic and accurate insights into your customers, full and comprehensive details on your products and customer journey. They should state clear budgets and timelines too. Whatever it is you are going to write a brief for, please take the time to make it complete.

Start with what you don't want

Creative briefs require clarity. They need to include references to the work done before and supplemented with material such as research findings, brand guides, logos and visual assets, and dos and don'ts from past experiences. Be specific on the type of campaign, the messaging, and the audience group you're after. Revisit the STP (Segmentation, Targeting and Positioning) exercise in Chapter 1.

Successful briefs provide realistic and enlightening insights on your customers. Later in the book, I will reference customer person exercises. These must become the foundation to your briefs.

If you don't have a clear idea of what you want in your campaigns, you can always start with what you don't want. For example, a brand owner may know very well that they are not open to anime-style graphics. If you do not wish for agencies to submit work that could be a repetition of previous work, then share that work with them and ask them not to repeat it. By the same token, if you benchmark your campaigns against specific players in the field, direct or indirect competition, then share those ad references in your briefs.

Handpicking the decision makers on creative work

Too many cooks spoil the broth. When selecting creative work, I suggest you don't widen the circle of decision makers. Creative matters are creative. That is, they are not black or white, and you won't get the buy-in of all stakeholders. The best approach is to limit the number of decision makers on marketing and communication campaign approvals.

Selecting agency partners

While pitches have been an industry norm – where a potential client floats a brief and asks agencies to bring their best ideas forward – it has fatigued the industry and, for many, has been deemed unprofitable. A good way to start is to host meetings with the agencies and get to know them well.

A lot of agencies will showcase stunning reels and award-winning work during the business-pitching period. Although they show great references, they may not reflect the actual potential of the teams that will handle your work. Call to meet and get to know the teams of the agency that will be handling your work. You can request references and customer testimonials as well. In those meetings, derive a method in which an agency can showcase its portfolio of work and explain its methodologies in handling briefs. In those discussions, the agency team can also share case studies of similar assignments that were delivered.

Procurement and sourcing of creative business services

Following the formal process of RFPs (Request for Proposals) means paper processing and lots of documentation with minimal human interaction. If you work for a company that has a specific procurement process, you will need to sit down with the procurement team and ensure a process that enables human interaction. Over the years, I came to learn that I do not expect an agency or a production house to submit their creative ideas based on a written brief sent by email only. A Q&A session with meticulous and detailed briefing needs to take place for agencies to submit desirable creative tenders.

During the procurement process, ensure a non-disclosure agreement is signed so both parties can protect their intellectual property. Once an agency is selected and onboarded, make sure the necessary contracts outlining the scope of work and payment terms agreed are in place and signed.

How agencies charge

Agencies either charge on a project or campaign basis or they charge a monthly retainer fee. Retainer fees reflect the salaries of the teams recruited by the agency to deliver work for your company. These are considered an extension of your team and in many instances, some could work from your offices too. The prices charged by agencies are very different from each other depending on their calibre and quality of their work. You can review an agency's rate card and decide how it best fits your budget.

Your key takeaway from this chapter is that a clear vision of your department will be shaped by a methodological thinking process that enables you to predict the scope of work realistically and accordingly identify the team members that will fulfil this scope.

9

BUDGETS AND CALENDARS

'For all of its uncertainty, we cannot flee the future.'

— Barbra Johnson

Sometimes in life, we find ourselves extremely clear and confident about what we need to do. Then, somewhere along the journey, we face twists and turns, bumps and crossroads, and lose sight of our path. We get distracted, and our plans don't get executed on time. What follows is stress, panic, and loss of focus.

Budgets and calendars are essential tools that allow you to remain on track with achieving your goals. Budgets bind you to a specific forecasted future and help you stay within your means.

Calendars offer a very much needed element of predictability and foresight into your year. Once you are aware of what needs to be delivered and by when, you'll be able to plan your time wisely.

It is within this state of mind that one can harness the pleasure of creativity and agility. If you are unable to foresee how your work is going to be done, then you are going to exhaust your brain capacity with worry and stress, which is counterproductive.

With the right budgets and calendars in place, you will enable the flow of good practices in an enjoyable and organised way. Your campaigns will reaffirm your storyline and will be able to deliver messages that are purpose-driven and not price- or promotion-driven.

Any search on Google for marketing calendars is going to return a lot of results and you will get many templates for marketing calendars and budgets that you can use. The key point of this chapter is not to give you yet another one of those templates, but to provide you with a body of work that will help you craft the budgets and calendars that make the most sense for your business.

Marketing calendars

Building a calendar that reflects your planned activities for the entire year will enable you to make wise decisions and help your team work together with clarity towards pre-set goals. By visualising the entire year, you become prepared for high seasons and better equipped for addressing the challenges of the low seasons.

While the calendar must capture the big picture, it also should lay out the short-term goals and tactics required to achieve optimum results. To build this capacity, your calendar needs to carry more than one version.

Apart from the holistic vision, the absolute benefit of a calendar is that you can track the progress of your brands and your team and visualise what lies ahead.

Making your calendars useful

If your calendar is looking like a shopping list of jobs mapped against many weeks with an endless spectrum of colours and pins placed sporadically like darts on a board, you are doomed not to benefit from it.

Here are a few handful tips for building useful work calendars.

- Build your calendar on a dynamic platform that is easily accessible to your team and the entire company.
- If that is not available, build multiple versions of the calendar, a topliner one for the management and a detailed one for the team.
- Add quarters, weeks, and months as time references.
- Include critical work that takes place before and after campaigns or projects.
- Do not create a calendar that is campaign-focused only. Make sure the calendar maps out seasonality and reflects major events that take place while your campaigns are being rolled out.
- Create detailed versions of your calendars for key projects. These need to show what actions are required before and after campaigns are rolled out. For example, if you wish to roll out a new brand in a market by April, then your calendar needs to show the date by which the brand's new legal agreement needs to be signed, the retail outlets delivered, the agencies on the ground hired, and the budgets signed off.
- You may need to produce multiple versions of your calendar – one that is based on quarterly deliverables, and one that is based on campaigns that are key to delivering.
- Try to simplify your calendars by breaking them into ones driven by campaigns and ones that are driven by discipline.

- Build a holistic annual calendar to reflect on the total number of deliverables for your department in a year.
- Share your holistic calendar with key stakeholders of your company.

Calendars are a solid pedestal to your strategy

The more dynamic and accessible your calendar is, the more stakeholders you can communicate with. The main elements are the channels of Marcomms, the projects listed under each channel and the time indicator for the projects to seek completion. Technology has opened a world of ease for management of work, which means you can choose a calendar that is easily changed and readily accessible. Land yourself a calendar template that is interactive and easy to change.

Calendars will also help your team translate their brand objectives and seasonality into campaigns and see how these need to be placed across the year. Create multiple versions, ones that are summarised and ones that are detailed.

When setting smart calendars, start by laying out the department's big plans for the year.

Year	Examples of objectives
Year 1	Refresh corporate brand.
	Launch a digital strategy.
	Open x new outlets.
	Launch x new brands and partnerships.
	Establish a CRM function.
	Generate PR value of x.
	Increase lead generation by 20%.
Year 2	Launch corporate brand in countries x, y, z.
	Launch e-commerce operations.
	Launch x new brands and partnerships.
	Introduce a CSR strategy.
	Complete customer database clean-up.

Each Year can then be broken down into quarters, months or week or a combination of the two. The time element of the Calendar is usually the top right part of the file or what is usually known as the X-axis of the graph. The left-hand side column of the calendar or what is known as the Y-axis can either list the main categories of Marcomms for example marketing campaigns, promotions, sponsorships or events. The Y-axis can be expanded to include the brands that these projects fall under or the KPIs or both. Here is a very simple illustration of a calendar.

	Q1	Q2	Q3	Q4
Campaign(s)		Campaign Launch		Post Campaign Report & ROI Analysis
Event(s) & Roadshows	Event & Roadshow briefing and preparation	Launch of Events A&B		Roadshows A,B&C
PR Campaign(s)	Cover Story A			Interviews D,E,F
Sponsorship(s)	Sponsorship A	Sponsorship B		

Here is another example of a more elaborate Calendar. In this example the timeline is broken into weeks and the main marcomms categories reflect multiple projects.

MARCOM Annual Calendar [Insert Year]

ACTIVITY
BRANDING
Production A
Campaign A
SPONSORSHIP
Sponsorship A
CSR / CHARITY
Charity A
CORPORATE EVENTS
Employee Event A
End of the Year Strategic Retreat
End of the Year Marketing Retreat
INTERNAL COMMUNICATION
Internal Magazine
Internal Newsletter
PRODUCTION
Printing A
Corporate Events & Exhibitions
Exhibition A

154

Categories included a Marcomms calendar

Thematic and tactical campaigns

Design a detailed calendar that shows your campaigns as well as the work that is required to carry them out. Campaigns are either thematic, that is brand-driven, or tactical, that is promotion or price driven. This means, milestones pre and post the campaigns can be added. For example, if you are planning a sell-out campaign by January, you will need the pricing and promotion costs signed off at least three weeks prior to the launch date. You also need to consider by when you need your artwork briefed in, approved, and ready to be published. Finally, you need to set a date for publishing the campaign results and decide accordingly if the calendar will remain as is or whether the upcoming campaigns need to change.

Month	Campaign	Work Required
January	Sell-out campaign.	Pricing sign-off. Promotion sign-off. Campaign plan and budget sign-off. Artwork sign-off. Media plan sign-off. PR plan sign-off. Post-campaign reporting.

PR campaigns and Corporate Social Responsibility (CSR) initiatives

Add the PR and CSR plans to your annual calendars to arrive at a comprehensive marcomms calendar. Many marketers consider PR a subset of the marketing campaigns, but this is far from the truth. Under PR falls media initiatives that on their own can contribute to the brand's equity and impeccable reputation in the market. For a brand to make its way to influential stakeholders, planned out creative messaging is required, and these tactics need to be treated as being as important as marketing campaigns.

Events, conferences, and trade shows

Add your events, trade shows, conferences, and annual gatherings. Whether these are trade shows that your brand participates in or are related to your industry, these are important times for you to acknowledge and mark on your calendar.

Add any marketing-related conferences and festivals that your team can attend and benefit from. There is so much knowledge that can be gained from these events, and it's worth noting them on a work calendar.

Reports and Contracts

Add report submission to your calendars. A major part of what communication professionals deliver is reports. These could vary by discipline. Examples of topics of reports include campaign performance, leads and sales generation, media outreach, brand performance, customer satisfaction, ESG reports, annual reports and budget spends. These could take a back row and get delayed once the workload intensifies; thus, it is important to factor them in on your calendars.

Add contract review and renewal days. The field of marketing and communication is highly dependent on third parties such as advertising, media, and monitoring agencies. This tactic will help your contracts get renewed on time. Renewal of contracts is a time-consuming process, especially if your company's procurement policies indicate a requirement to tender for agencies and vendors every year.

Topical days

Mark the topical days and occasions that carry an element of activation of engagement at your company. Include a list of the days that are celebrated in your region and the industries. Examples would be Black Friday, environmental days such as Earth Day, celebration times such as Christmas, New Year, and national holidays. With brands trying to make their way to the hearts of their audiences, conducting an exercise of identifying topical days that can help your brand and company tell a story has become an integral component of a brand calendar.

Major events

Marketers and communicators build their narrative on the overall sentiment in their communities. Major events taking place during a year can drive some of your creative ideas or activations. They can also help you come up with new ideas for promotions. It would be wise to add these to your calendars.

A smart addition to your calendar would be a list of major world events that are taking place in a specific year, for example, the FIFA World Cup or Olympics. While your company may not be directly involved in them, marketers are often asked to link those in one way or another to their plans, either as brand messages or as events.

Annual meetings, anniversaries, and other celebrations

Make a list of these occasions and celebrations, some of which are common and straightforward, and others that are more related to your brand, the industry you're in or the country. Companies usually host a series of high-level events that include AOP (Annual Operating Plan) meetings, strategy retreats, CEO roadshows and employee recognition ceremonies. These often require a lot more work than one thinks. The process of event management is tedious and requires hunting for new venues, sourcing speakers on new topics and aligning the calendars of many senior stakeholders. Chapter 16 provides details on the work required to hosting corporate events.

Brand activations could be related to the CSR initiatives that your company supports. From Valentines to Read in a Bathtub Day, brands can create intelligent content and activations around these days. These are great windows for further connection with your communities.

Technology upgrades and renewals

Add any technology platform scheduled upgrades and media platform subscriptions that require renewal and review. This could be renewal of website server hosting, software subscription upgrades, and purchases of new technologies that are required for your delivery.

Resource availability

And, finally, add your planned team vacations and training days. This will be helpful in managing the workload and taskforce required to activate.

Calendars enable accurate budgeting

A calendar is also a great foundation starter to your budgeting exercise. By now, you have arrived at a solid understanding of the objectives, the percentage of marketing and comms relative to revenues, what markets need to be tapped into, and who your customers are.

You also analysed the communication channels that need to be utilised to get you to achieve your goals. All these put together the total budget you have for the year.

Marketing and communications budgets

Budgeting is a straightforward task. Simplicity is the best policy. I've fiddled around with many budget templates over the years, and I often found a detailed one a lot better as it allows you to provision for everything that would fall under the remit of a marketing and communication function.

Take your total and make informed decisions on how it will be distributed into two families – a budget for the marketing and communication work and another for the costs associated with your team, office, and administration.

Marcomms Budget	Staff and Office Costs
• Research and development • Promotions • Traditional advertising • Digital advertising • E-commerce platforms and websites • Social media • Printing and production • Roadshows and exhibitions • Events, activations • Sponsorships • Branding • PR and media relations • Internal communication • CSR (Corporate Social Responsibility) • Agency fees	• Staff costs • Rent • Office welfare • Back-end automation

Digital advertising

Digital ads are online, targeted, and data driven. They are easily placed, monitored, and measured throughout the phases of the stages of the buying funnel. A buying funnel would differ from B2B to B2C but would always carry three key stages, which are awareness, consideration, and purchase. The world of digital marketing and advertising is evolving every day. In this space, you can consider mobile apps, mobile phone messaging, emails to targeted lists, lead capturing websites, online blogs and newsletters, email shots, search engine marketing, and search engine optimisation tactics. Chapter 17 offers a comprehensive breakdown on digital advertising.

Social media

The building and maintenance of a digital footprint for the brand online includes website building, blogs, podcasts, search engine optimisation, search engine marketing, programmatic, and any investments in an online marketing channel that enables the brand to amplify its reach. This includes social media as well. Budgeting for digital will cover the expenses of hiring digital teams that will be communicating and monitoring your brand online.

Traditional advertising

Advertising is your bait to capture the attention of your customers, both existing and potential. Some advertising is corporate and created with the intention of creating awareness about your brand. However, most of the time, advertising is created with the intention of generating leads for your business.

While the world of digital is soon to become a main driver for new-age business, many businesses continue to benefit from traditional advertising. The reason why I would split traditional from digital is because you need to monitor how these two categories are being invested in overtime periods and what type of leads are being generated from each.

Traditional advertising would include TV, radio, out of home, print newspapers, magazines, or other publications that offer reach to your target audience.

Research and development

Marketers and communication practitioners use multiple types of research. The way you use research would probably evolve over time. Any type of market research on pricing, product, and brand perception pre and post campaigns would fall here. This category will also account for brand audits, polls, surveys, focus groups, and feasibility studies for your brand and products.

Printing and production

This would cover costs that are paid on the production of creative assets and messages that get published on both your traditional and digital advertising spaces. Here are a few examples: printing of stationery, brochures, flyers, creation of podcast material, video and audio content, photography, and animation of banners.

PR and media relations budgets

This would include costs incurred in generating publicity for your organisation and brands. Fees that go towards generating publicity including the dissemination of press releases that generate news for your brands. Media relations is about building relationships with journalists and media organisations.

PR and media relations are covered in detail in Chapters 13 and 14.

Internal communication

As the name implies, internal communication entails communication with a company's internal stakeholders, from the dormant to the definitive and demanding. Internal communication includes newsletters, reports, memos, and corporate events.

Internal communication is covered in detail in Chapter 14.

Roadshows and exhibitions

This includes the costs of participating in the trade shows. This would range from the cost of renting the space from the exhibitor to the build-up of your stand, permits and registrations, cost of promoting products, hiring entertainment, raffling prizes, and recruiting professional hosts. Here is a brief list of costs associated with roadshows and exhibitions:

- Rental of exhibiting space from the trade fair management.
- Permits and fees.
- Build-up of the stand including the cost of material, transportation, warehousing, and supplementing with the necessary utilities like electricity and lights.
- Setting up screens and display material on the stand.

- Brand activations like using augmented reality displays and VR games. These could include mall displays and pop-up stores as well.
- Production of brand assets such as Podcast series and reels as well as marketing collateral such as promotional material.
- Booking advertising space available in the show vicinity to amplify the presence of your brand.
- Transportation, travel, and accommodation fees.
- Corporate dinners and lunches.
- Hiring of promotors and models.

Events, activations, and sponsorships

In this category, you would account for the costs associated with the events that are usually carried out throughout the year. These may include awards ceremonies, planning sessions, strategy retreats, operating plan meetings, dealers' get-togethers, and employee functions.

Brand activations could also fall under the events category.

Corporate events could be any non-mainstream ways in which a brand is being brought to life through interactive experiences with potential and existing audiences. It is usually a one-time event that allows the brand to get up close and personal with audiences. Brand activations can exist by themselves or be inspired by a mainstream marketing campaign. Buzzwords for brand activations would be 'experiential marketing', 'sampling', and 'in-store activations'. An example of a brand activation would be a pop-up store displaying limited-edition items or an augmented reality game where the products are experienced.

Corporate events are covered in detail in Chapter 16.

Sponsorships are very similar to brand activations and could fall under that umbrella, but they are usually put together by an independent organising committee and brands pay a fee to participate. Sponsorships often allow brands access to key stakeholders or large masses of potential customers. Depending on the scale of the sponsorship, brands can have access to spaces where they can display their products, conduct demonstrations, and interact with fans and followers, whether physically or virtually. Sponsorships often allow a brand to come closer to the communities in which they operate and influence.

Apart from the fees of participation, you'll need to allocate additional funds to make sure their engagement in a sponsorship is effective.

Sponsorships are covered in detail in Chapter 15.

Branding

Lately, the term 'branding' has become overcomplicated and sometimes used with the intention of brand building rather than the actual act of branding. For some, the term brand includes any act that expresses the brand such as activations and even sales promotions. But I am old school, and for the purposes of this chapter, I will stick to the traditional definition of branding.

Branding includes the development of corporate identity, which is a compiled guide explaining the essence of the brand and its application. A brand guide includes a compressed version of the brand story and history, often with a keynote from the brand founder or CEO. It introduces the brand profile, mission, and values. It then demonstrates the symbolism and visuals that are associated with the brand. It introduces the relationship that exists within the brand family between the brands that fall under the mother brand.

The cost of branding goes through highs and lows depending on the state of the brand. If a company is going through an aggressive expansion or a structural change, such as a transformation from a holding company to a public one or a joint venture, costs associated with branding would go up over that time. These costs relate to the brand development. This may contain branding agency fees, research on the brand, brand identity development, brand messaging, and environmental branding.

Branding can be done in-house if your company has a professional design team or outsourced to a specialised branding agency. Branding is discussed in length in Chapter 12 of the book.

Staff and office costs

Staff cost

Staff cost includes the cost of your staff's take-home salaries, the cost of benefits offered to them such as transportation, travel, housing, medical, and life insurance, the costs incurred by training and development, salary adjustment toward inflation and increments, bonuses, and other matters. Under your staff cost, you would also account for paid internships and part-timers.

Office welfare

Every company would have its defined list of what falls under office welfare, and these costs should be accounted for. Included would be an estimation of meals, office cleaning, stationery, furniture, maintenance services, and miscellaneous legal and professional fees.

Rent and utilities

This is the cost of your office rent and utility bills.

Technology and back-end automation

In some companies, back-end automation does fall under office welfare. The reason why I advise keeping it separate from back-end automation is that some of the technology platforms are shared with other departments and businesses in a company.

These costs would include subscriptions to design software, website hosting, cloud services, CRM-related automation, HTML email services, automated press release dissemination, campaigns, and social analytics, etc.

The field of marcomms is malleable and highly dependent on project management skills. I have come to know many marketers who are brilliant at creating ideas but have struggled so hard at manifesting them and often blame timelines and workload.

Efficient budgeting and calendar designs will help plan out your weekly schedules, learn about your monthly deliverables, and anticipate how long projects will take. Use your calendar to help you determine who from the team needs to be working together at certain times, and this will help you plan for team holidays and travel.

10

PROCESSES AND
LEGAL MATTERS

'Thoroughly read all contracts. I really mean thoroughly.'

— BRET MICHAELS

For corporate departments to operate successfully, they need to put in place workflows and processes and adhere to legalities in the field. This chapter will focus on how to create a principled environment that operates on pre-defined processes and policies.

I will briefly introduce you to four areas that are highly critical to the success of your department. You can refer to these as the 'enablers' and they are laws, SLAs (Service Level Agreements), processes and policies.

Enablers			
Laws	SLAs	Processes	Policies

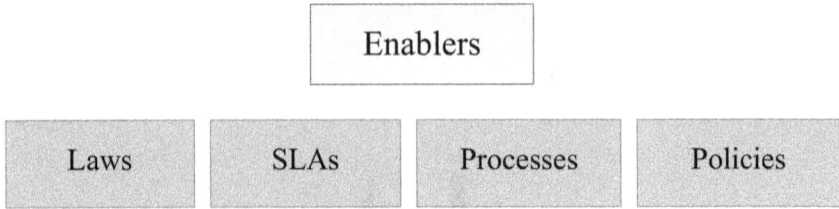

The above enablers will facilitate your operations and will reduce conflict and roadblocks you may face at work while you grow the scope of your department.

Whether you are a beginner starting out in the marketing and communications field or you have accumulated years of experience, working with the right legal framework will help you operate with ease and build harmonious relationships with your stakeholders.

Laws and legal matters

Regulation in the form of laws and codes of conduct ensure that the work carried out is ethical and acceptable in your industry and territory.

Just like in other business fields, there is a legal aspect to everything you do in marketing and communication. If you want to establish and market an e-commerce channel, for example, you need to understand the laws for buying, selling, and advertising online. If you want to establish email campaigns, you need to be clear on how to collect email address information and how to get the consent and permission of your customers to do so. By the same token, you need to apply the country's laws on permission marketing and abide by the rules of customer privacy laws.

Familiarise yourself with the laws that govern pricing and promotions. They outline what permits and guidelines are required to run sampling activities, roadshows, and raffle prizes, hire promoters and models, and more.

You also need to understand what laws govern advertising and publishing of messages in your territory. For example, not all countries allow advertising campaigns that mention or display the name of competing brands or even draw indirect comparisons to them.

The laws on e-commerce and data privacy are constantly evolving. If your company's campaigns conflict with these laws, your company could face hefty charges, and you may suffer reputational damage.

Next are the laws governing the fields of media and public relations. When running PR campaigns, you need to decide if the news and the stories you are broadcasting fall within the appropriate ethical and legal boundaries. There is always a call for the truth in corporate claims. You also need to ensure that the PR and media practices of your company are servicing the best interest of the stakeholders. The claims in your news need to be verified, accurate and up to date so they do not to leave any room for speculation.

An important point of focus would be respecting the privacy of individuals, be it customers or employees or anyone mentioned in your campaigns. For example, employees being photographed at a company event must provide their written consent to having their photos taken and then used in advertisements or social media posts.

This chapter will shed light on the following areas:

- Invasion of privacy.
- Defamation.
- Intellectual property rights (copyrights and trademarks).

- Deceptive advertising.
- Data protection.
- Compliance.

Invasion of privacy

Privacy laws deal with information about employees in corporate content such as newsletters, photo releases, advertisements, publicity, and published media content. They also deal with the privacy of the customers and the data they contribute voluntarily or non-voluntarily when dealing with a company, especially with online transactions, enquiries, and services. They also govern the information about the business entity itself, and what information can be published about the company or not. Marcomms professionals need to look after the privacy of employees and customers by doing the following:

- Make sure the personal and financial data of customers is being protected against identity theft and financial fraud.
- A company's marketing and sales campaigns need to carry the security and data safety features that protect the privacy of a customer's personal information. For example, companies must have the right security systems to safeguard and safely handle the verification of passwords for online and mobile purchases, the encryption and decryption of electronically transmitted data, the verification of digital signatures, and the storage of a customer's biometric and payment data.
- Customer data should always be updated and regulated. This also means employees need to be trained on how to protect customer data and never leak it. The same applies to products and services.

- Customers need to be given the choice to 'Opt Out' of direct SMS and Email marketing campaigns.
- When publishing data about the company's performance, or the company structure, make sure the data is accurate and verified. You also need to seek official permission to share it.
- Ensure that the company's communication and published content does not carry any racial comments or promote stereotypes, whether done intentionally or unintentionally.
- Have employees and customers sign waivers when participating in content shoots or volunteering content that will be published by the company.
- Seek permission to publish photos, opinions, or testimonials of both customers and employees in marketing and PR campaigns.

Defamation

Defamation is the use of negative language about a person or entity that ends up harming their reputation. An accusation of defamation is often backed up by proof of monetary loss or mental anguish and can cost companies hefty amounts. Defamation can occur in your press releases or social media content. It could also happen in advertising campaigns when trying to reference competition or compare your offering to theirs. In addressing matters related to a company's competition, marcomms professionals need to ensure they are not causing any harm or reputational loss for others.

Intellectual property rights

Intellectual property is an intangible property owned by a company in the form of inventions, ideas, names, labels, or literary, artistic and design work. In the marcomms field, you need to be most familiar with copyrights and trademarks laws.

Copyrighting is the legal way to attain protection and ownership of an idea or design work such as product design and even a product's ingredients or production process. It protects the commercial assets of a brand such as recipes, formation, processes, and marketing assets as well. These include tagline and custom type font. It is usually requested for a fixed number of years or an unlimited number of years in a specified territory or worldwide. It also gets segregated by industry. Copyright laws protect the inventions and solutions provided by companies from being copied or stolen by others.

Trademarks are meant to protect the identity of a brand and its logo. Trademarks are used extensively in branding. Trademarks allow your brand a higher recognition and reduce the chances of others copying you. Like copyrights, trademarks are for specific industry categories and geographical locations and is usually valid for a period of ten years before it gets renewed. Not only do you need to trademark your work, but you also need to ensure that your work is original and not copied.

Deceptive advertising

Deceptive advertising laws govern the claims and information being published in advertising campaign material. They call for a company's claims to remain factual and not promise benefits that do get delivered. Deceptive advertising also governs how prices, discounts, and promotions are articulated. It also calls for seeking permission in testimonial campaigns.

Data protection laws

Data protection laws protect consumers from deceptive commercial acts. They call for transparency in dealings, and lawfulness and fairness in trade. They request that companies collecting data protect their data, respect its confidentiality, and not use it to breach the confidentiality of consumers.

Compliance

Compliance is the willingness of companies to act according to the laws and regulations. Companies usually employ a compliance officer or would have a full-fledged compliance department.

The acceleration of digital is pressuring marketers to constantly create new content or engage with content creators. Compliance requirements call for accurate reporting of product specifications, references, ambiguities, and dismissal of misleading claims. Other compliance matters would include disclaimers on websites, product specifications, and packaging information. Compliance also sets rules around the value and types of corporate gifting and giveaways. When dealing with celebrities, vendors and social media influencers, Compliance policies would place a requirement to screen these individuals to ensure they have clear and legitimate official records.

Compliance addresses the infamous code of conduct. An employee code of conduct is a legal charter that defines the acceptable behaviours and attitudes of individuals working for a company. An employee code of conduct entails transparency in communication. It also implies accessibility to types of information employees need to carry out their work properly.

For communication professionals, a code of conduct will call for ethical dealings with the media. This implies that they provide the media with sufficient and accurate information to help them formulate correct and factual stories.

Compliance also addresses bribery and corruption. Bribery and corruption can involve offering, promising, giving, requesting, or agreeing to receive, whether directly or indirectly, any kind of payment or benefits, which could be in the form of gifts or entertainment, to get preferential treatment from the media or your vendors.

Compliance is also all about understanding the risks involved with your communication and marketing activities when rules are not followed. Such risks could fall in areas where a team or employee is not protecting confidential business data or customer data or is even delaying the payments of vendors and freelancers.

SLAs (Service Level Agreements)

SLAs serve as mini contracts between two parties who agree to source services from each other. SLAs occur between corporate departments of the same company. They are very common with vendors and third parties who have been commissioned to carry out projects for a company. SLAs are used with internal and external stakeholders.

SLAs are true enablers to the success of a marcomms department. They become more in demand if you operate in a large multi-brand company with operations across multiple countries or territories. The more diverse the spectrum of services you offer as a department, the more you would need an SLA to regulate the working relationship with other departments and stakeholders.

SLAs reduce any misunderstandings or conflicts that can arise when two teams are delivering work of the same nature. SLAs set out the expectations and correct responsibilities regarding work deliverables and lead times. They define an exhaustive scope of work and reduce ambiguities. SLAs are usually subject to change and need to be revised at least once a year.

What to include in a marketing and corporate communication SLA

A marcomms SLA can begin with an overview of your department and the role it plays in a company. We identified these roles in Chapter 7. For example, the role of the marcomms department is to coordinate brand communication from a strategic level both internally and externally to protect the reputation of the company.

In addition to the types of services offered, the SLA needs to define how the department teams will deliver work together in terms of your timelines, workforce, and business processes. You may want to mention the number of resources and human-hours offered and include all the processes required to carry out the services. If calculating human-hours is not feasible, then agree to a percentage of an employee's time to be dedicated to servicing a brand or a business division within your company.

To increase clarity in your relationship with internal stakeholders, state if the services offered are being delivered through an in-house model or through agencies and outside companies. You can explain how the cost of the services will be incurred and the basis of your charges.

If services are charged on an hourly basis, then a rate card needs to be established. A rate card is a pricing menu listing the cost per hour of the services offered. The costing can also be based on the type of deliverable.

The topic of lead times is important to address in an SLA. I would add a clause on the time window for each level of service and would mention a prime time and a non-prime time as other elements, such as seasonality and availability of resources, change.

In drafting your SLA, make sure it is not one-sided and that both parties have services to deliver. Finally, make sure this is a legitimate document by adding clauses on default and failure to deliver and make sure that services and timelines mentioned are reasonable and attainable within the capacity that exists within your team.

Documenting process workflows

In the marcomms field, you will be dealing with stakeholders who may not have a full understanding of how your processes take place. This leads to a recurring challenge of you defending your timelines and budgets.

Many of you may have experienced late briefs. Your company is about to launch a new service facility and you get briefed only three weeks before the official launch. You are taken by surprise and try to push back on the date set for the grand opening. What, then, would be the best way to do so? A workflow document could be what rescues you.

By creating a workflow process document, you will be able to demonstrate the correct way of getting work done to your stakeholders. Additionally a process mapping exercise can help you automate your work if a future adoption of technology is one of the things you are planning.

What processes and workflows do I need to explain?

It pays to get all your processes mapped out as workflows. Once workflows are in place, they will help you and the other team members working on a task to focus on improving results and quality rather than second-guessing the way to get there.

Within the realm of marketing and communication plans, workflows are important because they bring the capacity for predictability and measurement of outcomes. Workflows help in communication between the teams and in setting realistic expectations.

You can draft a workflow diagram or break down a process of pretty much any type of service you deliver. It could be launching a new brand, running a campaign, drafting a press release, or designing a new business card. The objective here is to not repeat your explanation of a process like a broken record and to be able to stand your ground when demanding a budget or timeline to deliver a job. Every step needs to specify who the owner is and how long it usually takes for execution.

This is a simple, yet a potentially daunting exercise, and it can be built over time. In mapping out a marketing process, indicate the time it needs, and the steps it requires. The process should include the preparation phase of a job as well. For example, a process for designing a lead generation campaign for a product needs to include the initial steps of getting a budget secured, ensuring product is in stock, and making sure a brief has been filled in and signed off. It should also state the stakeholders involved and in the approval of work.

Calculate the time required not only for every step of the process but also for review and feedback in between. Moreover, your process should reflect the time required by other departments; for example, procurement and finance will be part of your process.

Where possible, map out the process in a pictorial or graph form and include names and contact details of persons involved.

Here is a sample workflow for a brand activation or event:

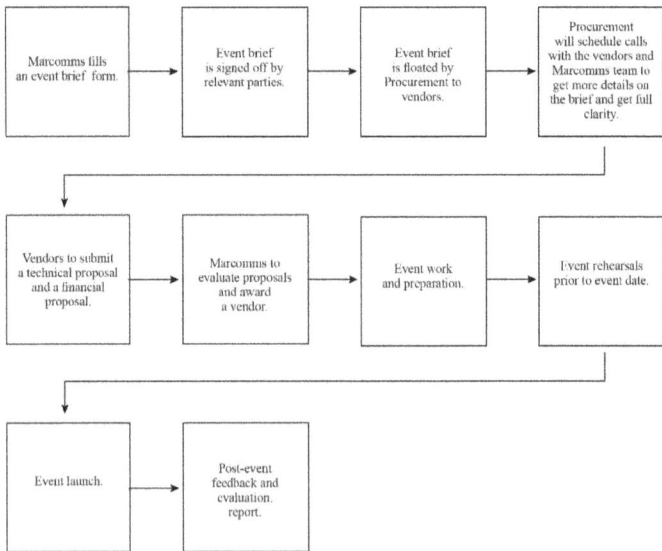

```
┌──────────────────┐    ┌──────────────────┐    ┌──────────────────┐    ┌──────────────────┐
│ Marcomms fills   │    │ Event brief      │    │ Event brief      │    │ Procurement      │
│ an event brief   │───▶│ is signed off by │───▶│ is floated by    │───▶│ will schedule    │
│ form.            │    │ relevant parties.│    │ Procurement to   │    │ calls with the   │
│                  │    │                  │    │ vendors.         │    │ vendors and      │
│                  │    │                  │    │                  │    │ Marcomms team to │
│                  │    │                  │    │                  │    │ get more details │
│                  │    │                  │    │                  │    │ on the brief and │
│                  │    │                  │    │                  │    │ get full clarity.│
└──────────────────┘    └──────────────────┘    └──────────────────┘    └──────────────────┘

┌──────────────────┐    ┌──────────────────┐    ┌──────────────────┐    ┌──────────────────┐
│ Vendors to submit│    │ Marcomms to      │    │ Event work       │    │ Event rehearsals │
│ a technical      │───▶│ evaluate         │───▶│ and preparation. │───▶│ prior to event   │
│ proposal and a   │    │ proposals and    │    │                  │    │ date.            │
│ financial        │    │ award a vendor.  │    │                  │    │                  │
│ proposal.        │    │                  │    │                  │    │                  │
└──────────────────┘    └──────────────────┘    └──────────────────┘    └──────────────────┘

┌──────────────────┐    ┌──────────────────┐
│ Event launch.    │───▶│ Post-event       │
│                  │    │ feedback and     │
│                  │    │ evaluation.      │
│                  │    │ report.          │
└──────────────────┘    └──────────────────┘
```

Marketing and communication policies

Start-ups and newly founded companies may not have formal policies that cover the area of marketing and communications. It will happen at least once in your work life that you will be asked to put in place a marketing and communication policy, or to review and expand existing ones. Even long-standing businesses could be carrying policies that have become outdated.

Communication and marketing policies identify the types of behaviours that will reflect negatively on a company's operations and reputation. They will help you respond and not react when a violation takes place.

We live in a digital world where information on a product or major organisational change can easily leak to the public. Communication policies help protect the company's reputation. They integrate efforts between departments, ensuring consistency and quality of work delivery. They reduce cases of wrong news, rumours, and miscommunication and come in handy in the times of crisis.

Do I need to write a policy from scratch?

The answer is yes and no. It all depends on the company you are working for. Some companies may not have policies at all while others may have policies that are worth a review and a refresh. Once you understand the essence of every policy and what it needs to cover, you can correctly judge what needs to be done. Some companies may have well-established compliance and legal functions that create those policies, and some may not. If your company has a legal officer, then they can help you in drafting and reviewing your policies.

A marketing and communication policy will tackle the dos and don'ts of a company's external and internal communications. It also addresses the desired behaviour of the company's employees on social media and other external forums. The policies also address protocols to external news and media engagements.

What would a typical communication policy include?

Communication policies also tackle matters related to respecting and protecting the privacy of a company's stakeholders; these include employees, customers, partners and even competition. Marcomms policies honour the privacy rights of both past and present customers. Additionally, they address behaviours and set expectations on how employees are expected to communicate both internally and externally. They lay out the dos and don'ts of communication in dealings and specify desired protocols of written and verbal communication.

External communications policy

An external communications policy will also govern how public relations practices are conducted. It addresses what information can be included in a press release, announcement, Q&A document, print, audio or video interview, and how information is communicated and distributed, as well as who is permitted to speak to the media and what type of media training they need to have completed.

The policy will list the protocols for media interviews and round-tables, what subjects can be discussed, and what would be considered sensitive information that should not be shared with the media. If an employee is contacted by a media representative or has received a complaint, how are they supposed to respond? An external policy emphasises that news and announcements are made in a timely manner where all stakeholders, internal and external, are informed at the same time.

Internal communication policy

In an internal communication policy, employees are guided to speak respectfully about their employers and communities. They are cautioned against engaging in behaviour that will reflect negatively on the company's image and reputation.

Internal communication policies also touch on the use of copyrighted materials and encourage employees to write in a knowledgeable, accurate, and professional manner. The policy honours the privacy rights of all employees and brands, past and present, by explaining how to seek their permission before writing about any topic that might breach their privacy. If an employee is developing a website or writing a blog that will mention the company and its potential products, employees, partners, customers, and competitors, the company would guide the employee to clearly emphasise that all views expressed are his or hers alone.

Social media policy

As the Gen Zs enter the workplace, they bring with them a parallel life of social media activity and side hustling. Companies must embrace the change and yet regulate it. Social media policies can create a happy a medium between the employee's activity online and their own brands reputation. For example, a lot of companies encourage their employees to become social media influencers. Social media policies can address how employees need to represent themselves and the brands they work for.

However, the success of a company's social media strategy is contingent on the collaboration of employees in the process, so a policy needs to be clear and inviting rather than prohibitive and restrictive. Communication managers need to find creative and organised ways to turn employees into online brand custodians. Social media policies will lay out the dos and don'ts of social media usage for the employees. They also outline what is considered acceptable and what is not for the employees.

Other policies you may need as well can be related to the sourcing of services, confidentiality, procurement, and technology adoption.

This concludes the part of the book that is related to the blueprint for establishing a marcomms department from scratch. The second part of the book include chapters on communication disciplines such as PR, Sponsorships and Events. These were written with the intension to help you get a quick and full understanding of the key areas in branding and corporate communication. The last few chapters are guides on how to put together a comprehensive marcomms strategy deck as well as skills that will help you excel in your career.

11

THE BRAND PERSONA FRAMEWORK

'The brands that will thrive in the coming years are the ones that have a purpose beyond profit.'

— RICHARD BRANSON

Marcomms professionals working for portfolio businesses or start-up owners might find their companies in a dire need of personality with panache. Defining a personality for a company allows it to define its true purpose. A brand purpose, in turn, gives birth to a vision and a set of values to live by. These permeate the spirit of the business and generate a performance-driven culture that generates high levels of affinity with customers.

This chapter offers you a **Brand Personality Framework.** The framework is composed of a set of questions that, when answered, will help you arrive at the best personality articulation for your company. At the end of the chapter, you will be offered tactics for mastering the artistry of brainstorming with your company's key decision makers to help you achieve this framework successfully.

What is a brand personality?

A brand personality is the representation of a brand as a real person. Let me caution you here – a brand personality is not a checklist of adjectives. It is more like a biography of a person. It talks about their upbringing, their motives, what they dream of, and what they plan to do in the future. It explains what inspires them and what drives them forward.

Arriving at a brand persona helps a brand build meaningful and enduring relationships with its stakeholders. It is an engaging process that connects the brand with a myriad of audiences on an emotional rather than a transaction level.

What is a brand persona framework?

The brand persona framework is a simple exercise that when applied, provides marcomms professionals with clear personality for the brands they are looking after. It is one of reflection and intro-spection. It requires research and brutal honesty. It is a shared exer-cise amongst multiple stakeholders that know the brand and interact with it.

Often carried out as a guided brainstorming session or series of sessions, the brand persona exercise can either be outsourced to a professional branding agency or attempted in-house following the framework presented here. Those sessions should not be restricted to the owners or senior executives of a company. They need to be held with participants who represent every target group of the company. I usually encourage actual customers to be present in those sessions.

Associating a human characteristic with a company has been attempted by marcomms practitioners for decades. The conversation is traced back to the early 70s which was further refined in the late 80s by different scholars. The earlier interpretations of a brand personality were driven by product attributes more than human attributes. A brand was not described as a human but as an inventory of the practical benefits a product owns.

In 1997, the famous Aaker's study relaunched the brand personality exercise and, instead of product attributes, outlined five human personality dimensions for a brand. The framework was a great revelation at the time but has, since then, served its purpose.

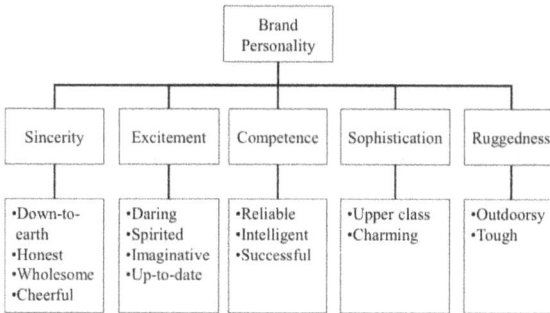

Brand Personality				
Sincerity	Excitement	Competence	Sophistication	Ruggedness
•Down-to-earth •Honest •Wholesome •Cheerful	•Daring •Spirited •Imaginative •Up-to-date	•Reliable •Intelligent •Successful	•Upper class •Charming	•Outdoorsy •Tough

Today, marcomms practitioners use more free-flowing approaches when putting together a brand personality.

But why do I need a brand personality?

Humans are the species that rule the Earth! Baaam! Isn't that silly of me to say? Perhaps. Asking why you need a brand personality is like asking why humans rule the Earth.

We are truth-seeking creatures. We live our lives searching for deeper meaning in the simple events we encounter. Thousands of books have been written on the hidden meaning of child's play. Our brains constitute the powerhouse behind all this mishmash. Our brains respond to matters that stir emotions. Hence, our love for soap-opera shows.

This universal truth did not only give birth to doctrines, but it also gave birth to brand persona and customer persona exercises for marketers to be able to attach emotions to their brands.

On a pragmatic level, a brand personality exercise paves the way to a brand story and a corporate vision and brings the right brand values to life. A solid personality reference facilitates connected story-telling for marcomms professionals.

Anything else?

Let's quickly talk about brand perception, intimacy, and value.

Apart from the fact that a brand personality helps in the articulation of a brand vision, it also creates a dramatic shift in shareholder value as well. By repeatedly telling your story, you will create a positive brand perception, which, in turn, creates brand intimacy, which is then measured as brand value.

Let me break this down for you:

Brand perception is how your customers perceive your company. For example, a brand may be perceived as luxurious and expensive when, in fact, it is price competitive. Take, for example, brands that monopolise an industry such as utilities and telecoms in some countries, they could be very customer-driven but the fact that they are operated by exclusivity might give out an impression to some that they are not.

Brand intimacy is what your customer feels towards your company. It could be neutral, positive, or negative. Brand intimacy is not always related to your social engagement levels, star ratings, sales, or even profits. It could be circumstantial or seasonal. Take, for example, hand-sanitiser brands during the COVID-19 pandemic. Customers built greater levels of intimacy with sanitizer brands during the outbreak than they would otherwise. This level of engagement wouldn't occur in a non-pandemic year. Brands who suffer seasonal shortages of stock or an unfortunate rumour could experience a temporary drop in intimacy until they resolve their issues.

A positive brand perception will help create harmony between you and your customers. If you would like to dig deeper into understanding how brand intimacy is measured, I advise you to read the book *Brand Intimacy* by Mario Natarelli and Rina Plapler.

Brand Value is the intangible value a brand adds from the practice of consistency and integrity in its behaviour. A company's brand value is usually larger than the company's actual book value. Global agencies such as WPP perform brand valuation studies, which are complicated assessments that take into consideration multiple factors. As a result, shareholders get higher returns from brands, and it all starts with a coherent personality.

What is the Brand Personal Framework in this book?

Having conducted rounds of tested and tried frameworks to identify a personality for a company or a brand, I will present you with a simple framework that I developed to help you arrive at an honest-to-goodness personality exercise for your company. The framework is a collection of open-ended questions. The questions are presented in the order in which they are to be discussed.

Q1: If your brand were a person, what gender would they be?

Many brands may start off being gender-specific. For example, Coco Chanel was certainly a female gender brand catering to females seeking style and a unique high end fashion flair. Over the years, the brand started catering to both genders. Tommy Hilfiger was a male brand catering to males only, and with time, catered to both males and females of different age groups. The gender of your brand may not necessarily reflect the owner's gender or the customers' gender. Annie Lennox famously said, 'I love to be individual, to step beyond gender.' A lot of new-age brands, especially technology ones, choose to fall in a gender-neutral category, and your brand can do so if that is appropriate.

Q2: If your brand were a person, how old would they be?

Simple as it sounds, answering this question can be tricky. A lot of people might associate the age of a brand with the age of its founders. Take for example, a young entrepreneur in his early 20s, who invented a mobile app that can scan and screen the health of elderly people whose age range begins at 50. In this instance, the age of his app brand should not be 20 years old, nor should it be 50 either. His app should come across as a mature healthcare professional who is in the early stages of middle age, 35 to 40 years old. This way, the brand can convey the element of maturity and trustworthiness.

When I was holding a brand persona session for a long-standing family business and this question came up, the majority of the participants in the session described the company as an old mature male whose age ranged between 60 and 70 years old. The company was about to celebrate its 50th anniversary, and its former chairman, who was one of the founders, had recently passed away at an age crossing 70. The son of the founder was present during the session. He stood up and objected to suggested age for the brand. He reminded the room that the founders of the company were very young at the time it was established; they were vibrant youthful men in their twenties when they began their journey of trade. He also explained that the company needs to be perceived as young in order to continue innovating and attracting young talent.

Q3: If your brand were a person, where would they live?

In answering this question, it would be very interesting to tell a tale of many journeys. The brand could have been a person who was born in a country and emigrated to another and became a multi-cultured person. With this migration, the brand blended two cultures. We see this type of blend in modern restaurants that launch fusion cuisine experiences. The person would have probably travelled to cities and parts of the world that inspired his or her business ideas or innovations. My company recently adopted a solar technology that was German-engineered, developed in France and sold in the UAE. They may have seen moments of truth during their travels and decided to open a business to make an impact on people's lives. While travelling to Argentina, American entrepreneur and founder of TOMS Shoes, Blake Mycoskie, witnessed the hardships children not able to afford shoes faced. That inspired the birth of his brand. A lot of brands are born with a local or regional outlook and over the years transition to global ones.

Q4: If your brand was a person, what field would they have studied?

Boasting about a degree is of least importance by far in this exercise. The world knows very well that a formal degree is not a guaranteed path to success. In answering this question, you are trying to get a glimpse into the ways in which this person learned the secrets of the trade. Was he an apprentice turned CEO, a son of a well-heeled businessman who learned from his dad, or perhaps, she was a Harvard graduate turned music composer? Where and how the brand learned the secrets of the trade makes up one of the most compelling parts of the story. Comparably, learning about their failures or downturns and how they turned them into breakthroughs makes up a big chunk of the brand narrative, which, in turn, affects an entire company's culture as well as its outlook on growth.

Q5: If your brand were a person, what would their dreams be?

In understanding a brand purpose, it is important to understand its dreams and aspirations and how they evolved over time. Was the dream to build a small trading house that turned into an economy accelerator? Was it building a school that is inclusive to make education accessible to minorities, and with the grace of things, turned into the largest learning platform in the world? Was it a small business that turned into a grand portfolio business?

Q6: If your brand were a person, who would they look up to?

Who are the people that your brand admires and emulates? These do not necessarily need to be famous figures; they need to be those who influenced the way your brand does things. Many Emirati brands look up to the UAE's founder, the late Sheikh Zayd Bin Sultan Al Nahyan. Many brands in the technology sector look up to the tycoons of industries such as Henry Ford, JP Morgan and Steve Jobs.

Q7: If your brand were a person, what would their values be?

I love this quote by Elvis Presley: 'Values are like fingerprints. Nobody's the same, but you leave them all over everything you do.' The conversation on value is one of depth and connectedness.

Values are unique to every person, and there is no specific number of values to stick to. In these sessions, participants often begin with a long list of values and then make them shorter. There are over 300 different words that relate to values. What is important is to choose those that are best in sync with the brand. Here is a list of values that are often used in the business world: *Adaptability, Sustainability, Creativity, Family, Performance, Boldness, Mastery, Happiness, Awareness, Balance, Diversity, Passion, Teamwork, Excellence, Performance, Mastery, Inclusion, Care, Integrity, Principled, Accountable, Leadership, and Ambition.*

The corporate values for Amazon, for example, are customer obsession, long-term thinking, eagerness to invent, and taking pride in operational excellence.

Q8: If your brand were a person, what would their beliefs be?

Just like people, beliefs pave the way for your success or block it completely. As you embark on unveiling the deeper layers of your brands, it is important to bring to light the beliefs they uphold. This exercise is a great starter for any taglines you would need to come up with as part of your branding exercise. In a session I held once, adding value was a very prominent belief that soon turned into a tagline: 'Adding value all the way.'

Like values, beliefs drive a company's quests and operations. Many organisations have beliefs that can be articulated as this: *There is always a better tomorrow. No hard work goes to waste. Planet Earth needs looking after. Everyone deserves a good life. Do your part and help create jobs for the youth.*

Here is another example from Amazon. The brand's vision statement reflects its beliefs "to be Earth's most customer-centric company, where customers can find and discover anything they might want to buy online, and endeavours".

Q9: What do people say about this person, i.e., what is their reputation?

Understanding your brand reputation is simply understanding how it is perceived by people. If the brand does not exist yet, it still is important to make a list of how you wish the brand to be perceived.

Research and surveys are very important at this stage of this exercise. Customers' expectations for a brand get higher year on year and getting in the game of customer satisfaction is now everyone's business. The internet and the element of anonymity when it comes to rating and providing feedback on brands has heated up the love-hate relationship with them.

To arrive at answering this question sincerely, marketers need to bring home new metrics that go beyond views, likes, leads, and conversions. Try to unravel the emotional relationship your customers and employees have with your brand through satisfaction and performance surveys. Identify its awareness level and how your stakeholders emotionally respond to your brand. I touched upon metrics and analytics in Chapter19.

Q10: What does your competition say about you?

While you can estimate what competition says, using researched results will help you understand how your target audience are benchmarking you against competition. This is a moment of truth in this framework where you exercise outspoken honesty. The SWOT Analysis conducted in the earlier chapters of the book should be able to assist you with this.

Q11: If your brand was a person, what brands would they admire?

Brands power brands. Explore the brands your company admires. Is it Apple for disrupting industries? Or is it Amazon for making shopping easy and convenient? Or is it Virgin for boldness and creativity? Or is it Disney for making dreams and celebrating imagination? It could be Marvel for their ability to turn imagination and playfulness into products for people of all ages.

If you are operating a holding company or a portfolio business, you would most likely admire the brands you franchise as well. The brands you admire do not need to be in the same industry you operate in. For example, you can admire brands that are innovators and dreamers. Or brands that have re-invented themselves, or brands that have outgrown their markets and portfolio beyond their core business.

A CEO of the bank I worked for was always inspired by Apple. 'I want to be the Apple of the banking industry,' he would often say in meetings. His statement was so powerful, it allowed the bank to launch a series of first-of-their-kind innovations, and the bank was awarded the 'Most Innovative Islamic Bank in the Arabian Gulf' a few years into its operations. The entire organisation was in sync with its innovation agenda.

Q12: What is the outlook of your brand?

As digitisation and artificial intelligence are taking over our lives, answering this question requires a straight look at the facts and hard truths. It could be a new frontier in the metaverse, decarbonisation, zero emissions, e-commerce, intelligent manufacturing, robotics, expansion, or consolidation.

Q13: What is your brand's tone of voice?

Just like humans, levelling up your persuasion and influence requires you to own a unique compelling tonality. Your tone of voice reflects your confidence, authenticity, and great intentions. The world is now connected more than ever, and customers are in touch with brands on a lot more touchpoints than one can keep up with. This is pressuring brands to own their unique tone of voice.

John Grisham once said: 'In life, each of you is an original. Each of you has a distinctive voice. When you find it, your story will be told.'

As brands embark on publishing their own unique content, resembling an authentic tone of voice will help them connect better and faster with their audience. But who decides what is the best tonality for a brand? You sure don't want to leave this in the hands of an intern or a distant brand manager at some agency. This is an inside job, and one that the marcomms team must address.

A good place to start is to document the tonality of the founders and the owners who started the business or other competing brands in the market that you aspire to be like. One way to do so is to recall and collect early conversations that took place at the time of the brand formation and strategy sessions by the seniors of the company. These could be the accumulation of the discovery meetings you had, as described in Chapter 5.

Make a list of the compelling and famous phrases that come up and describe them as a style of speech for the brand. Document and archive interviews and written content related to the founders and CEOs of the company, including announcements and messages from them to the organisation. Listen to the way key executives of the brand speak, reference statements from the founders and leaders, and take note of quotes they repeat and quotes they are famous for. Role-play how the founders would interact with a customer, handle a complaint, elevator-pitch their business, or tell stories at the beginning of a speech.

As you put together a manifesto for your brand's tonality, try as much as you can to use descriptive sentences:

- Friendly yet informative.
- Conversational and down-to-earth.
- Transparent and factual.
- Truthful and honest.
- Playful and comical.
- Witty and helpful.
- Motivational and inspiring.
- Passionate and authentic.
- Avoids short and snappy responses such as 'no'.
- Speaks with confidence; says 'certainly' instead of 'yes'.

During my tenure at one of the region's pioneering portfolio businesses, I put myself on a quest to speak to everyone who interacted closely with its founders. What I found out is that they put great emphasis on customer service and the importance of keeping customers happy and confident in their service centres. This paved the way to a tone that was customer-driven and sought nothing but the customer's ultimate satisfaction with the brand.

Q14: What emotions does your brand evoke?

Today, the interest in the relationship between emotions and memory is not restricted to fields of science. It is a space for brands to thrive in. Emotions create memories, and brands fight their way through to a piece of a person's mind.

In understanding the brand personality of your company, explore what emotions the company and its experiences evoke in a customer. The best reference I found for this exercise is the nine families of feelings introduced by Dr Lucia Capacchione in her book *Living with Feeling*. Here are a few of her families:

- Happy: delighted, blissful, excited, enthusiastic, gleeful, joyful, grateful.
- Sad: down, gloomy, grieving, disappointed.
- Angry: enraged, irritated, furious.
- Afraid: anxious, fearful, nervous, scared, panicked.
- Playful: childlike, adventurous, creative, light-hearted, free, lively, spontaneous, whimsical.

Once you identify the emotions, trace them to the services, attitudes, and behaviours you want your brand to be associated with.

By answering these 14 questions, you will then be able to create the framework for a brand personality.

The Brand Personality Framework

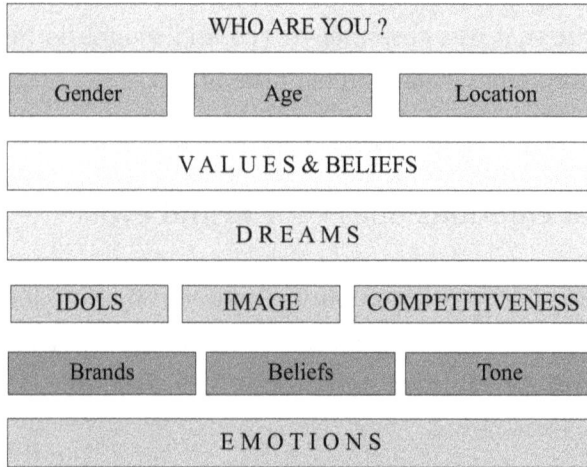

WHO ARE YOU ?		
Gender	Age	Location

VALUES & BELIEFS

DREAMS

IDOLS	IMAGE	COMPETITIVENESS

Brands	Beliefs	Tone

EMOTIONS

All right. I get it. How can I achieve a productive brainstorming session for completing the Brand Persona Framework?

A lot of us have attended a brainstorming session before but may have felt it was not as productive as it should have been. Asking people to be open and collaborative is not easy.

Here are a few tips for running fruitful ideations sessions:

- Affirm that the session is a safe space for all, despite their rank and position in the company. If the session is attended by the business leader, ask them to provide an opening remark acknowledging that feedback in its different forms and colours is welcome.

- Break down any judgments or limitations. You will need to moderate the session and be quick to park on the side any criticism coming through. Do so by making the attendees aware that the meeting is not to set limits on what's said.
- Listen and observe. Note down the details being shared, especially stories untold or expressions and advice provided by the business leaders.
- Deliberate with respect, giving every participant their chance and right to defend their idea and their feedback.
- Open up to possibilities by encouraging the crowd not to shy away from ideas. The intention of the session is to generate and shape new avenues that are good for the brand.
- Stop and block when needed. There will be participants who are overpowering by nature. This could be due to a personality trait or a sense of entitlement they carry within themselves. They may unconsciously cut others off or talk a bit more than they should. Stop them by politely pointing out that time is precious or that you need to hear from others as well.
- When it comes to the number of participants, choose quality over quantity. As mentioned before, in addition to the senior management team, include members from the sales and customer-facing staff. Choose team members from the sales, after-sales, and service teams who can speak about the customer needs.
- Host the session out of the office environment. A relaxed and informal setting dissolves the inherent hierarchal dynamics of the office structure. Taking the participants away from the office and placing them in a neutral spot will ease them into generating creative ideas and providing thoughtful opinions.
- Include icebreaker exercises in your session. An icebreaker is an informal game or team activity that dissolves the tension between

the participants. It could be as simple as starting the session with a personal story and asking others to do so as well.

- Invite sketch artists to visualise and illustrate ideas and expressions discussed by the groups.
- If you have commissioned agencies, then invite them and their creative teams.
- Use tools like paper, boards, colours, images, glue, and cut-outs of photos and words that can be put together to form boards that contain the answers to the questions in the framework.

It may be many years into your career before you come across the opportunity to build a brand persona exercise. For some, this could be the very first thing they do, but we all know that the career path of communicators is never linear. If you do come across this branding exercise, trust me, you have hit the jackpot. It is fun! This is one of the most exciting practices in the field.

12

BRANDING, STORYTELLING, AND CORPORATE IDENTITY

'The most powerful form of brand storytelling is when customers don't recognise that they are being marketed to.'

— WALTER & GIOGLIO

The process of branding is not a loosey-goosey list of things that can be whipped in a sitting or two. The process of building a brand is a chain of discoveries. Much like the development of a business strategy, building a brand will call for the inclusion of multiple stakeholders and the setting of clear objectives.

The completion of your **Brand Persona Framework** in the previous chapter will help you work on what comes next, a brand story, a catchy tagline, and a brand identity guide.

The predicament with branding is that marketers sometimes fall into the trap of creating brand literature that talks more about what the brand does than what it should do for its customers. In building your brand narrative, be wary not to turn it into a story of the company's mighty existence. I call this the 'sales trap'. As a communicator, your biggest mission is to keep your customers at the core of your branding delivery.

In *Building a Story Brand*, best-selling author Donald Miller explains that his book does not describe how to tell your company's story. 'A book like that would be a waste of time,' he says. He continues to explain, 'Customers don't generally care about your story; they care about their own.' Branding, therefore, is the process of understanding yourself as a brand, your customers and, of course, your employees for the sake of serving them better.

You will arrive at the right branding with a whole life ahead of it by keeping your customers at the heart of your work. Chapter 18 will explain and give examples of customer personas. The trick to those persona exercises is not to take them lightly and to complete them as a prerequisite to your branding work. Rather than offering this as lip service, it is time to dig deep enough into the desires, dreams, needs, and wants of your customers. You need to honour their problems, insecurities, and the limitations they perceive in their lives.

In the next section, I will offer you an easy-to-follow technique to arrive at your brand's unique positioning statement. It is simply the summation of multiple practices I've encountered over the years.

Brand positioning

Simply put, brand positioning is how marketers shape the perception of the brand in the eyes of their customers. American marketing author Philip Kotler defined brand positioning as 'the act of designing the company's offering and image to occupy a distinctive place in the mind of the target market'.

A successful brand positioning exercise is the second phase after creating a brand persona. It uncovers what makes a company or brand different from its competitors. The brand journal offered three aspects that should be considered to help you arrive at a positing statement. These are:

1. Understand what your customers want. Chapter 5 covered that.
2. Understand what the capabilities of the company are. Chapters 3 & 4 covered those.
3. Understand how each competitor is positioning their brand. Chapter 19 helps you identify your competition.

In addition to understanding your capabilities, customers, and competition, you need to understand the differentiating value that you provide. This is often referred to as USP.

What is a USP (Unique Selling Proposition)?

A USP answers the question: 'Why would customers choose you over others?' Donald Miller offers three questions that, when answered, can help you arrive at a USP.

1. What does the hero want?
2. Who or what is stopping the hero from getting what they want?
3. What will the hero's life look like after they get what they want?

In case you're wondering who, the hero is, it is your customer.

Allow me to throw in an example to help demonstrate this point. I will try to answer the three-above questions in the context of an automotive dealership that is trying to differentiate itself by offering a special sales and after-sales service programme that includes a host of benefits that go beyond the traditional offering of a typical dealership.

There are a lot of offerings in the market, but our hero wants to find a credible multi-brand one-stop-shop to help them buy a car conveniently and smartly. Our car dealership offers a wide selection of automotive brands at very competitive prices that can be bought online with full price transparency and with the option of trading in your old car. The customer journey extends beyond the sales experience as we provide you with a service contract that can be paid in monthly instalments supplemented with an employment protection payment plan. This means, if for any reason, you lose your job, we help you restructure your payments. Customers can get up to seven years of warranty and free road-side assistance. Not only that, our programme offers you a chance to exchange your new car for a different model of your choice if you are not satisfied with your initial purchase. We have the right team that will understand your needs for today and tomorrow.

The USP for this product will be somewhere along the lines of 'Your entire automotive needs will be taken care of by our professional sales and aftersales team and well-trained technicians who will look after your car for the next seven years at the best market prices'.

A discussion on USP can take up a whole chapter. Once you have answered the questions above, you can move on to putting together your USP Statement. The statement needs to briefly describe who you are, what your values are, and what you offer in the context of what your customer needs.

Your USP statement needs to be compelling but realistic, based on facts and not claims. The statement needs to focus on customer needs identified and, finally, be delivered in a very punchy, brief, straight-to-the-point manner.

Brand storytelling

Brand storytelling is the act of manifesting the company's USP in a series of messages that stir emotions and create purposeful connections. These messages are intertwined in the many forms of corporate messaging of the company. Unlike other types of stories, brand stories are continuous and ongoing. In other words, they are constantly changing and do not have one ending or one version. Brand storytelling is the subtle art of telling your tale in different forms and on different occasions.

In case you are still not sold on why a brand needs a story, just take yourself back to the time when you were a child. There must have been many stories that resonated with you because you felt they carried a message and inflicted an emotion.

The art of storytelling today emulates an entire industry of its own. Stories manifest in movies, novels, TV series, and content that lives all around us. The reason why Marvel is a top brand is because it mastered the art of storytelling to people of all ages and walks of life. Parents love Marvel stories as much as their children, from toddlers to teenagers.

When Harry Potter turned 20, *Vogue* magazine published an article to explain how it became the best story that there will ever be by delving into why parents, children, and grandparents love it. The article spells out that at the core of Harry Potter is a story that every person relates to. *Vogue* magazine describes it best by saying: 'The book instils knuckles down to intrinsically human qualities. There's bravery on multiple scales, from facing bogarts to killing Voldemort. There's loyalty – Snape's actions are the very definition of the word – and the plot focuses closely on the importance of trusting both your own instincts and those in your inner circle.' It is the connection with those values that make the brand surely a most memorable one.

Humans relate to stories with emotions. In other words, our brains enjoy and resonate with a flow of events when told in a story format. Brands that connect with customers emotionally live longer in the lives of their customers. While one would argue that business stories cannot be as dramatic and sensory, marketers know better that this can be done.

How to draft a brand story

You do not need to be Apple or charitable TOMS to own a brand story. Every brand deserves a story, and every marcomms professional needs to know how to create one. SMEs and start-ups have wonderful stories too, and when told right, they help them earn their shares. The connected world of today now makes your story accessible and allows it to live online forever.

Conversations on brand storytelling have been making headlines for years, but I never truly understood it myself until I read a handful of books and blogs about it. Before we delve into creating a brand story, let's agree that a brand story is not the first paragraph on your corporate website nor is it the first slide of your Google slide deck. Beyond any doubt, it should live on as many customer touch points as possible.

A brand story is a series of stories woven into your corporate messaging. In these narrations, communicators, and marketers seed in reminders about the company's USPs and how they benefit customers.

In their book *The Laws of Brand Storytelling*, Ekaterina Walter and Jessica Gioglio define brand storytelling as the art of shaping a company's identity using narratives and techniques that facilitate an emotional response and establish meaningful connection between the company and its customers. They reference macro stories and micro stories. Macro stories are ones that many marketers have mastered, and they live in corporate profiles, marketing campaigns and press releases. These are the evident stories of visions, profits, business innovations, and industry achievements. Micro stories are referred to by the authors as the 'always-on approach' to continue building on the macro story. These live in your corporate feed, corporate content, social community engagements, blog posts, CEO speeches, and other narratives such as customer testimonials and employee endorsements.

In their training deck on corporate storytelling, Select Training and Management Consultancy bring our attention to the importance of stirring emotions in your narrative. Emotions are sometimes more important than logic, and your brand story will become memorable when it activates parts in the brain that allow the receiver to relate to their own experiences when learning about your brand.

The best way to understand a brand story is to shift your mindset from a 'story' to a 'storytelling' approach. Allow me to list down the ingredients needed for cooking up your own delicious brand story (and please keep it handy):

• Your brand persona.
• Your customer persona(s).

- How you are different to others when serving customers. Your USP.
- What have you failed at when offering customers?
- How are you fixing those gaps?
- How does your customer feel about it?
- How all of this is inherent to your brand's purpose.

Donald Miller offers the following simple framework for telling a brand story. He describes a character who wants something but encounters a problem before they can get it. At the peak of their despair, a guide steps into their lives, gives them a plan, and calls them to action. That action helps them avoid failure and ultimately succeed. The character is your customer or target audience, the problem is their needs and wants, the guide is your brand, and the end is the outcome generated because your brand is in their life.

Humanising your brand

The human element is most crucial in your brand story. In fact, a corporate story needs its heroes to be humans or as close as possible to what humans relate to. In the book *The Laws of Corporate Storytelling*, the authors list the following groups as potential heroes of your stories:

- Customers and their families.
- Employees.
- Partners.
- Franchisees/licensees.
- Industry peers.
- Influencers.

- Volunteers.
- Mascots.
- Causes.
- Change movements.
- Hashtags.
- Social media trends such as TikTok challenges and Snapchat filters.

Where do businesses tell their stories?

As briefly explained earlier in this chapter and as discussed in Chapter 3, your brand story lives on every touchpoint in your customer journey. Your employees are a living and breathing embodiment of your brand story and need to be part of it too. Brand storytelling lives on all channels of communication: corporate websites, landing pages, annual reports, sustainability reports, social media posts, blog posts, press releases, corporate newsletter, and even in the live conversations of your employees. Brands have recently expanded their narratives to TikTok reels, induction kits, LinkedIn life tabs and Wikipedia pages.

Your brand story then makes its way into the messaging of your leadership and your corporate roadshows. It takes on different versions in your online content and, most importantly, it makes its way to your employees and earns their belief until they are turned into brand ambassadors.

If your brand story keeps your customer as the hero, it can take on any length and form. You know you are doing well when you can ask and receive a straightforward answer. Try asking Google this: 'What's the brand story of Apple?' And enjoy the results you get back so easily. Clear and crisp, here is an exemplary brand story. Founded by two college dropouts, its pioneering expansion into various industries and new services such as Apple Pay, and iTunes helped to propel Apple into becoming America's first $700 billion company.

As the world turned upside down in 2020 with the COVID-19 pandemic, countries and pharmaceutical giants entered the vaccine war. The world was in a dire need of that shot. While, within 48 months, the world had more than a handful of vaccine options, many related to the Pfizer offering. The vaccine carried a new mRNA innovation that was created in a laboratory to teach human cells to make a partial piece of a protein. The shot promised protection but was never tested before, which in many cases would have caused the public to grow sceptical. But the new brand for Pfizer and BioNTech won the public's attention because of the human story that lied behind it. The vaccine breakthrough was the brainchild of a husband-and-wife team of researchers: Ugur Sahin, 55, and Ozlem Tureci, 53, who were based in the German city of Mainz and were immigrants of Turkish origin. People saw a story of immigration, dreams, love, and a higher purpose to help humanity in the story of the vaccine.

What not to do in corporate storytelling

Here are things to keep in mind during your corporate storytelling:

Your brand storytelling is not a historical listing of events. That is called a timeline and could be a micro story. In your storytelling, touch on historic events but let them fall into the backdrop of what drove your brand to serve people better. Then move on to what influence you have on the lives of your customers and communities.

The proof is in the pudding. Show proof of your brand's achievements by clearly stating the intentions that lie beneath them. In stating your intentions, keep a friendly dialogue, and provide a reason for others to believe in you. People love intentions, and more so, reasons to believe.

Do not go on blasting out claims, state facts instead. If you are bigger, better, the best and all, please have others say that about you. Do not fall into the boastfulness trap, and do not resort to corporate bluff using acronyms, industry jargon, and business buzz words that could alienate your brand from your audiences.

Bigger buzzwords are not a reflection of your attempt to solve problems for your customers. Richard Branson was a ruthless, ambitious workaholic who, instead of claiming to be one of the most successful businessmen on the face of the planet, said he wanted to rebel against the autocracy of the corporate world and make business accessible to the masses. He changed the PR narrative for conglomerates and how CEOs and business tycoons are portrayed. The media quickly picked up his brand story. He is often described as a young man who started out as a school dropout and now has wealth estimated at USD 2.7 billion while owning close to 200 companies. He is seen as the provider of thousands of jobs, and a passionate man who introduced life-changing benefits to his communities.

Elevator pitch. As a marketer or communicator, you understand people's attention spans are getting shorter. According to a study run by Microsoft in 2015, the human attention span has dropped from 12 seconds to 8 seconds in the year 2000. This means, you need to balance the length to the frequency of the corporate storytelling narrative. You will need to use higher frequency and shorter formats and add variety and creativity to your chronicle. When doing so, apply the logic of elevator pitches to your brand story – make sure you can grab attention, establish a connection, and leave an impression quickly.

Use enough dialogue. Marcomms professionals of the past era were taught to communicate in one-way streams. The world of corporate communications has changed so much that one has no choice but to host a dialogue with your audiences to get them to listen to you. What made the story of Adam and Eve so famous? Was it the nudity? The apple? Or the dialogue? 'Eat anything you want, except the fruit of that tree.' Adam and Eve had a conversation with God. In your storytelling, keep the dialogue open, ask questions and wait for answers. Welcome suggestions and prompt your audiences for feedback.

Finally, please keep your narrative simple and memorable.

The use of taglines

Professor Joep Cornelissen provides a simple and clear definition of a tagline: 'A tagline is a short and memorable phrase at the end of an advert or other corporate message that aims to either sum up a company's claim or to reinforce and strengthen the recall of those claims.' Taglines can be easily created once the USP exercise is complete.

Here is a checklist that will help you arrive at a good tagline:

- Taglines reflect a universal truth.
- Taglines are unique to the psyche of your audience. Nike's famous line 'Just do it' does not speak of their products at all; it speaks of the spirit the world's greatest athletes.
- Taglines use everyday language.

- Good taglines are not a repetition of what is out there nor are they a copy from competition.
- Taglines are best kept to five words or less. The shorter the tagline, the better.
- Compelling taglines are free of time-bound promises; like a stunning National Geographic photograph, they are timeless.
- A tagline is not a sales pitch, and, thus, should not sound like a statement coming out of a salesperson's mouth.
- Taglines are positive. Positivity can come in many forms. It could be uplifting, dreamy, witty, motivational, cheery, or simply down-to-earth.

Here are examples of popular taglines:

- The happiest place on Earth – Disney.
- Let's go places – Toyota.
- Think Different – Apple.
- Open happiness – Coca Cola.
- The best or nothing – Mercedes- Benz.
- I'm lovin it – McDonalds.

Taglines are a great anchor to your brand aesthetics, accompanying logos, and headlines.

Design a brand identity guide

Once you are clear on your brand persona, stories, unique selling proposition, and tagline, you are now in a great place to start putting together your brand identity guide. Creating a brand identity requires painstaking planning. A brand guide, as the name implies, needs to hold your hand as you journey into bringing brand communication to life. A brand guide cannot be abruptly outwitted with shortcuts. Companies that rush into the creation of their brand guides find themselves in a position where they need to re-work them within a few years.

I have seen many in the field jumping on the re-branding bandwagon once they take over a brand. Let's face it – visually speaking, changing identities is the easiest way to say, 'Hey, I've made an immediate and visible change in no time.' Be warned, this is dangerous. I almost cringe every time I hear of a new Head of Marketing or Comms who just recently joined a company and has jumped into a logo facelift exercise.

Branding is the DNA of a brand. It doesn't change with time. It changes with years – gradually and slowly. Even when a logo or a brand identity is over 10 years old, please take the time to understand the brand well before opting to change it.

Before jumping on a brand identity change or a logo fix, consider these matters. First, the logo has been around for over five years, and the design needs retrofitting to new emerging media platforms. In this case, it is critical to understand if a new logo or a facelift is required. Second, the company has experienced a significant change in its formation. They could have gone through an ownership change, a change in leadership, a merger or acquisition, are planning to go public, or have undergone a major transformation in their market offering. The company could be expanding into new territories or market segments.

Brand guide

A brand guide includes an introduction to the brand and all the visual and sensory assets that bring it to life including images, graphics, type font, videos, and sensory elements such as sound (sonic branding), and even smell (scent branding). In the case of a brand guide, we can comfortably claim that 'the more, the merrier' philosophy applies.

Here is a simple list of the elements of a brand guide:

- Introduction to the brand.
- Logo(s).
- Brand architecture.
- Fonts & typefaces.
- Colour palette.
- Iconography.
- Imagery.
- Applications.

In addition to the brand's purpose, vision, mission, and values, a guide will showcase the brand persona. It elaborates on brand tonality in depth. Then it explains how the brand will manifest visually through narratives, logos, imagery, and how it will live in brand touchpoints such as stationery, signage, any static or moving visual, audio, or sonic branding, and in any possible interaction with a customer, be it a greeting, a communication, even a social community response. This also includes the environmental branding which is the design of physical spaces representing the brand, these are usually retail spaces and offices.

You can put together this section of the brand guide from the results of Chapter 4, The View From The Top Framework, and Chapter 11, The Brand Persona Framework.

Logos

Logos are the most powerful visual representation of your brand's promise. Within its small colourful world, the company provides the seal of trust and tells its story.

There is no formula to creating a logo. Logos are an artist's interpretation of what your brand persona and brand promise are. The artists are often briefed on the company's purpose, brand persona and brand USP prior to working on the logo designs.

If you are working for a company that plans to either launch its logo for the first time, or refresh its logo, you need to study the market and make a mood board of the logos that the company founders find attractive. Try to get an understanding of what they like about those logos. Is it the formation, like the typography, or is it the colours and styles of graphic elements? Secondly, it would be good to study what logos look like in your industry, but please do not opt for a copycat approach. Your logo is unique to you and only you.

A brand guide would not only present your brand assets but also tell its story. There must be a meaning to the patterns, shapes, strokes, blocks, and the graphic elements created.

In portfolio businesses, the brand guide would also offer logo lockups, composite logos, and bi-lingual logos where necessary. Your brand guide will also demonstrate how the logo is used on packaging, stationery, virtual and physical displays, uniforms, name tags, and other spaces it is supposed to be placed in. The brand guide would also consider how the logo is interpreted in 2D and 3D formats.

A brand guide will explain how the logo can take on certain forms when presented on challenging spaces such as mobile banners or signages, which are usually horizontal and narrow. The guide will specify what the smallest size the logo can be. How it can be turned into a badge or a pin. How it will look in a black and white version too.

Research your industry or product category and understand where you stand in terms of font styles, colours, and patterns. It is the reoccurrences of displaying the logo that makes it recognisable. A contemporary type of font is not for every brand. A typeface for a tech company may not work for a manufacturing or an industrial one. The same would apply to the colour palettes and the primary and secondary colours you choose to represent you. The more business or products you have in your portfolio, the more colours, and patterns you would need on your colour palettes.

A logo lock-up would include the design of your logo alongside your tagline and is best if designed with different layouts in mind and not left to chance. A brand guide would specify how the tagline is displayed with the logo, and if it can be displayed on its own or not.

Brand architecture

The term brand architecture refers to the nature of the connection between the company's main brand and the different brands it operates. The term architecture intercepts the type of relationship that exists between the parent brand and the rest of the brands in terms of design and the overall look and feel. There are three types of brand architectures: monolithic, polythetic, and hybrid. A monolithic brand architecture stipulates that the logo and artworks of all brands look the same with a slight variation from the design of the parent brand. There is an element of consistency between the brand names and logos, reflected either in the wordmark, font types or colour scheme.

Classic examples of a monolithic architecture would be the Virgin brands, Marriott Hotels, and FedEx brands.

In 2015, Google revealed its rebranding exercise, and the new brand architecture is a great demonstration of a monolithic type of architecture. The main sub-brands that fall under the Google umbrella, Gmail, Google Meets, Google Drive and Google Maps, follow the same colour scheme and design elements. The monolithic architecture was inspired by the vision of the company to offer a seamless customer journey driven by technological innovation.

A monolithic architecture is often more suited for B2B portfolio businesses that are branched out into multiple industries or serve a large array of stakeholders. They are often used by government and semi-government entities as well.

A polythetic brand architecture is one where the designs of the parent brand and product brands are not related to one another. The world diehard B2C brands that operate a wide range of products and services adopt this style. The nature of the business requires the freedom to create varying brands with unique USPs to address different needs of different customers. The classic example is the Unilever brand family. The logo design of the world-encompassing conglomerate that aims to become a sustainable commonplace for customers does not share any commonalities with the brands its sells such as Ben & Jerry's, Dove, Knorr, Vaseline, and many others.

The hybrid brand architecture type is a mix of both and is often an evolution of one of the previous forms. It happens when a portfolio business ventures into homegrown brands, B2C, or B2B fields. Microsoft, Coca-Cola, Volkswagen, and Amazon brand families are hybrid.

Fonts and Typefaces

It is important to give your brand typography its fair share of study-ing too. A brand's typography is one of its greatest assets and lives on most of its communication. When selecting typefaces, take into consideration the population of people using it and decide if you wish to go for a custom-made one or a system-ready one. The bigger the brand, the better it would be for it to invest in designing its own type-face. The best example I can think of is the font of Emirates Airline. You need at least two typefaces – one for headlines and one for body copy. Headlines can be bold and wild, and body copy can be sub-tle and use something like a Calibri or Arial font depending on the nature of the brand. For an airline or a telecom brand, you might opt for a grand, custom-made font. Otherwise, you will be choosing from a default system font.

Colour palette

A brand guide will also cover the colour pallet for the brand. Colours can be inspired by the industry but not necessarily, especially if the company is instigation a sector disruption.

When I was part of the branding team giving birth to a new and progressive Islamic banking brand in Abu Dhabi, the founding committee had the desire to make this brand very appealing to the young generations. In discussing the colour scheme of the brand, the CEO pointed out that most of the Islamic banks used the traditional dark tones of blue and green. He then said: 'We could be green or blue, but we chose orange.' Orange is a colour that communicates vibrancy, newness, and renewal. From that day onwards, not only did the branding carry the vibrant orange colour, the marcomms team was inspired to adopt a fresh tone in the bank's communication. We used informal and friendly language and encouraged the employee to remain friendly in their interactions with customers. In the design of the communication and brand assets, we took cues from colloquial language and lingos adopted by the Emirati culture. We struck a balance that was casual yet confident, new yet trustworthy.

Iconography

Iconography could be unique graphics that represent the brand's sub-offering. They could represent a company's services, field of business, or category of solutions. While you can find plenty online from websites like Shutterstock, you can design your own and make them unique to your brand's look and feel. In leading the communications for Al Masaood, Abu Dhabi's largest family business, pitching the business presented a challenge as the company was investing in multiple industries. The company had major stakes in the city's automotive, industrial, and construction sectors. Using iconography was a great way to describe the conglomerate's business lines in a smart and visual way.

Imagery

The visual and imagery section of the guide is what brings the brand to life. They say a picture is worth 1000 words. It is a very important part of the branding suite, and the more you are invested in it, the more value you add to your brand.

In this section, you can include the type of imagery that represents the brand. This is the imagery that will be used on the brand's digital assets such as websites, social media, emails, apps, and on traditional assets such as vehicles and print advertisements. A brand's imagery can be unique to the brand by using a certain type of photography, lighting, effects, and colour grades.

Brands can carry more than one class of imagery: for example, text only, lifestyle, and illustrations.

Applications

The final section of the brand guide shows examples of all the brand elements put together and how those manifests into applications. Applications can be a brand's mobile app designs, website design, adverts, office design, packaging, and any other form of messaging design.

Branding is the connectivity of all the above

In his book, *Building a Story Brand*, the *New York Times* bestselling author Donald Miller described a brand story as 'the secret weapon that will grow your business'. The branding elements discussed in this chapter, like logos, typefaces, imagery, and taglines, glue together a brand essence. The elements collectively make a brand a distinct entity. Keep your brand alive and thriving by creating each of the elements discussed in this chapter. The process is very enriching for your career.

I hope that this chapter has assisted you in building your brand foundations. The next chapter will delve into the PR and media relations aspect of marcomms.

13

PUBLIC RELATIONS AND MEDIA RELATIONS

'Publicity is absolutely critical. A good PR story is infinitely more effective than a front-page ad.'

— RICHARD BRANSON

I am a graduate of marketing and business administration. The first 12 years of my career were spent enjoying creative campaign development and budgeting for multimillion-dollar media plans. My first job on the client-side required that I oversee public relations. My initial understanding of PR was limited to drafting and circulating press releases as a by-product of marketing campaigns. A decade later, I know that PR is telling a grander and more noble story that generates a more authentic and credible image for a company.

The Public Relations Society of America defines PR as a "strategic communication process that build mutually beneficial relationships between organisations and their publics."

If you are on your way to handling public and media relations, I am here to tell you that it is not just amazingly interesting but very uplifting to your career. PR is the side of the story that an advertising campaign is unable to tell. It is fluid, insightful, and stirs emotions that help in connecting the brand to the wider audiences. Most importantly, it generates great reputational equity for companies. Ted Rubin rightly said it in his famous quote: 'A brand is what a business does; reputation is what people remember.'

If you studied journalism and PR or have spent most of your career in this field, you may not find this chapter very beneficial. But if you are making your way from sales, marketing, commerce, or advertising to corporate communication, I promise you this chapter will help you out.

What is public and media relations?

Public and media relations are the communication tasks that contribute to a positive and appealing image of your brand. If a marketing campaign brings in the leads and sales enquiries, publicity campaigns bring in the curiosity and admiration for the brand, and the word-of-mouth awareness that creates affinity. Public relations practices such as the publishing of press releases and pitching interviews for company officials or hosting press conferences position the brand in a positive light. It allows an insider's view into the company and the type of culture it fosters. PR gives a company a noble voice and a unique position in the outside world. It builds a company's reputation and helps it establish trust with an entire ecosystem of stakeholders.

Broadly speaking, the discipline of public relations incorporates news dissemination, media relations, reputation management, crisis communication, PR strategies, events management, sponsorships, and executive profiling, or what is more commonly referred to as leadership communication.

We spoke about the three types of media in Chapter 3 and those were owned, paid and earned. PR falls in the earned category. It could also fall in the paid category if you have paid for a speaking opportunity, publishing of an opinion piece, an advertorial or an interview with the press.

Similar to advertising, PR is measured. There are specific formulas for measuring the value of PR. While they differ from one industry to another, it is usually a multiplier of two or three to the actual cost of advertising. PR can be measured by press clippings and campaigns. PR campaigns are a series of five to six press releases or interviews on the same topic. PR reports calculate the value of coverage generated on a monthly, quarterly, and annual basis. PR managers often benchmark their PR value against previous time periods, and against their direct competition. With social media prevailing, a lot of the online content is now considered an earned media value. Today, there are social listening tools that can help you be accurate in reporting your publicity value.

PR is the longer format of the corporate narrative. PR stories are not restricted to the products or the services a company offers. One could argue that PR is more credible than marketing because it is generated by third-party sources such as news agencies and media influencers. Just like marketing, successful PR and media relations rely on two factors for success:

- **Creativity**. Creativity doesn't only stand true for marketing and advertising. Creativity takes your publicity ahead in leaps and bounds. Some people think that you are either born with it or not. The truth is creativity is earned through practice. By simply observing all the great ideas that are out there, you can broaden your horizons and become creative. Being creative in PR means you are not only sending out news about everything you do, instead you are weaving engaging stories about how your company is positively influencing lives.
- **Personalisation**. Corporate messaging gets traction and attention once it is tailored to its recipients. New software and publishing platforms allow you to segment your PR audience to gain more attention through relevant messaging. PR publishing software, for example, can help you target your news by type of magazine, social media influencer, vlogger, etc. With this, you can get different news drafted with different propositions to attract the attention of recipients.

Today's content revolution on the internet has made messaging accessible to anyone who holds a smartphone in their hands. This means PR is now a lot more engaging and visually appealing. PR is an ongoing narrative and should not be bound to business seasonality.

What if I do not like or know how to write?

If you don't enjoy writing, I am sorry to break it you, but you won't succeed in PR and communications. I have seen our industry welcoming a lot of new communication practitioners that lack not just the ability to write but the willingness to learn the skill. No one is born good at writing, the good news is, it is a muscle you can grow. It takes the discipline of reading, devouring content and writing to get it right. All you must do is practise. Start by reading the daily news, journaling, and re-drafting your day's emails. Practise by blogging or writing compelling social media content until you feel confident to review and comment on press releases and other communication assets. I often ask junior PR members on my team to read the headlines of the day and re-write them in their own words for 20 minutes for a couple of months consecutively. If you experience writer's block, which we all do, remember that writing is all about re-writing. Do not think that your first few drafts are the final versions – just edit, review, and repeat.

I touched upon writing as a skill for a marketing and comms professionals in Chapter 12. The truth is the entire field of marcomms is one of expression and influence and writing is a tool that one must possess to be able to make it through in the field.

From my experience, I would advise that you do not fully rely on a corporate writer or the services of a PR agency in writing the content for your company. This is the narrative of your brand. Train your team to be as fluent in written communication as they can. Defining the tonality of your brand through the Brand Persona Framework in Chapter 11 will tremendously help. Communicators are the owners of the brand's tone and sentiment. They are the ones who can create connectedness in the brand story and, thus, need to oversee its press content.

What is media relations?

Apart from your ability to read the news and write compelling stories, you need to build a relationship with the media community. Media relations involves developing and managing relationships with journalists and editors that are beneficial to both parties. These relationships are based on an exchange of information that generates compelling stories. Media relations done right can help you position your company as a leader in the field and your senior executives as industry experts and can get you good reviews and news coverage.

What if I am starting PR late in my career and I've never had relationships with the media?

Your relationship with the media is never based on your age or the number of years knowing each other. It is a beautiful connection built on mutual respect. It is all about engaging beyond the norm of press release and the façade of the PR agency to enrich each other's knowledge. You will need to reach out to them with the right approach and the right content, and you will get the rapport you are looking for. Building a solid relationship with the media requires continuity more than longevity. It needs a quality connection over one based on quantity. In the next section, I've included tips on this subject.

The best way to successful PR is having a good story

Make sure you have a good PR story. A good PR story should meet the interest of the journalist or editor, not the brand owner. Alex Singleton, an outstanding PR consultant in the UK, explained this by quoting 'What journalists actually need from you are story ideas that interest their readers.' Journalists are more in touch with the sentiment of the market. After all, they are in the business of news. Corporate PR is challenging because what companies think of as big news is not necessarily big news in the eyes of the public or the press.

In creating your story and making it newsworthy, ask yourself some questions, such as: 'Am I talking to my CEO and board in this piece of news?' A PR message filled with claims doesn't draw anyone in. A good story delivers news. The definition of news is extracted from the word 'new', meaning it either hasn't happened before or hasn't happened before in a specific context. It should be genuine and focused on the element of newness and what benefit it holds for the reader or the viewer.

Building your relationship with the media

Interacting with the media might be intimidating at first. At the beginning of your relationship, they will hold the upper hand and their control of the dynamics will remain for a long time until you gain their trust, and they buy into your corporate story. In building this relationship, take to heart the following tips:

- Focus on the publishers that cover stories related to your industry. This is not a funnel approach; this is a megaphone one. Start small with niche publications and then insert your news into the broader realm of media titles like business magazines and newspapers.
- Serve your news fresh and hot off the plate to the media you are most interested in. As you work your ties with the community of editors and journalists, offer them exclusive pieces of news that support their work.
- Provide the journalists you are most interested in connecting with extra information that can add value to their content. Give them the access they need to the spokespersons of your company. If you promise them a meeting with the CEO, please make it happen. You can also work with them on exclusive pieces on big projects and launches.
- Respect the media and value their time. If they ask for a meeting, snippets of reports, evidence of claimed success, facility visits, or something else, please entertain it and organise it in a timely fashion.
- Maintain the relationship beyond the times you need to get your news published. For example, if your company produces an industry report or have assigned a research company on a study that yielded interesting results which can be made public, share those findings with the media that regularly publishes for you.
- Be present and reply to their calls and requests whenever they reach out.

Manage your media list actively

In earlier times, media lists were enormous. I would scroll and scroll through the contact details and names of publications on a list, and this was for the Middle East region only. I know that in the US and Europe, media lists could contain over a million contacts. With the advancements in database management and digital dissemination platforms, one can easily segment their media lists. It is also disheartening to note that the industry has shrunk, and there are not as many media contacts as before. Yes, your lists may contain more titles, but these today are online platforms and not real publishing houses.

In creating and managing your media lists, have a personal list that you built based on your close and important media contacts. These contacts would be journalists, influencers, and editors who you have come across at media functions, PR society meetings, and press conferences. Review the list of your media as frequently as needed and keep it up-to-date. If your business operates in multiple industries, you will have to create an industry-specific list for each of the businesses you are looking after.

As you work on your list, understand the circulation power of these publications. It was easy in the old days as the circulation was merely the number of copies printed. With the digital world taking over, you can delve deeper and understand the online analytics as well – website visits, email shots, open rates, and click-through rates.

Space out the frequency of your news

Study the frequency of the news in your industry and try your best not to spam the media. This gets harder when you are handling multiple brands or when you have strict KPIs to meet related to the number of clippings and SOV (Share of Voice). One way you can avoid spamming is not to write one version of your press release only. You can write multiple versions of the press release addressed it to a segmented media list. You can also create a PR campaign with five or six press releases covering segments of the same story over a pre-defined period. Getting into the practice of building your monthly and quarterly PR calendars can help you prepare in advance for news and find a way to introduce variety to your content.

Get creative with your news

The success of your PR and media relations is based on creativity and delivering fresh ideas to the press. A monotonous PR plan that only publishes announcements or soft news is unexciting to the press and will eventually lose its momentum.

Creative executions in PR not only help big brands but they are also extremely helpful for start-ups and SMEs. These can be achieved by telling interesting stories in the form of customer testimonials, employee stories, industry innovations, market trends, sponsorships, infographics, results of polls and surveys, and a company's positive contributions to the community.

Build personal relationships

Reach out to journalists in person and through emails and on social media. Make sure that you have been reading their latest articles and tweets and that you understand their viewpoints and interests. Note down any coverage they have given your company recently and thank them for it. In writing or reaching out personally to the journalists, do make sure that you do not spam their inboxes with messages. Most importantly, do not leave you're your relationship with the media in the hands of your agency or junior members of your team.

Allow the relationship with the media to go beyond the traditional 'Here is my news, would you publish it?' dynamic. Seek out opinions and engage the journalists with your company wherever possible. When hosting strategy retreats for your company, invite journalists to contribute with opinion pieces and information that is relevant to the topic. If you are holding key events, you can invite them and make them feel as part of your corporate family.

As a communicator, try to write to them on your own opinion about their latest articles and work and provide them with your very own articles and opinion pieces as well.

Pitch your news

Pitching takes up a large chunk of your media relations efforts. Try to regularly pitch for interviews, speaking opportunities, articles, and opinion pieces. In doing so, make sure you are giving the media access to information that they could not otherwise get. Train the spokesperson from the company to provide the answers needed for the journalists.

Build new-age PR tactics into your calendars. This includes using mediums such as recording podcasts and vlogs or hosting webinars. The post-pandemic world affirmed to us that a lot of the news that you need to send out can be done without asking the journalists to travel to you physically.

Additionally, build relationships with credible social media influencers that operate in the capacity of media influencers and produce quality content. Offer them access to your stories, facilities, and management.

Podcasts as a medium have been growing and building traction. Launch your own podcasts or look for a popular industry podcast that you can place your executives on as speakers. In launching your own podcasts, leverage the relationships with your key customers and influencers.

You can also build a series of informative videos on your industries and market segments and share these as nuggets of knowledge for the crowd.

During your exhibitions and road shows, you can add a layer of publicity by broadcasting a series of interviews live on your social media channels.

Create a corporate blog and draw attention to it

I have stressed a lot in this book on corporate blogs. These were mentioned in The First Impressions Framework in Chapter 3 and in other chapters. Corporate blogs concentrate not just on the products being sold but also on the culture and thought leadership aspects of an organisation.

Blogs generated by a company can help the leaders reflect on their experiences in the industry. Blogs are powered by SEO techniques. By creating a corporate blog, you add keywords, titles, and meta descriptions that create visibility and searchability to your brands. In addition, every new blog you post adds new content and links to your website. That helps with SEO immensely because it gives Google and other search engines a reason to re-crawl your website. A blog is a great way to turn attention to the culture of a company.

I have touched upon micro stories and macro stories in Chapter 12 when I discussed brand stories. The same applies to PR practices. PR is not always big bang news, sometimes it is the contrary. Corporate blogs allow companies to share their micro stories. They can capture the attention of the media when researching topics of interest. Take, for example, an automotive journalist wanting to research the status of electric vehicle adoption in his or her city. If the journalist comes across an opinion piece written by a CEO of a car dealership on this matter, he is most likely to reach out to this company for a testimony for his upcoming article.

To enrich the content of your blog and diversify it, you can find a community of social media influencers who are media savvy and are practising ethical and up-to-the-mark media online and collaborate with them on joint articles and add these to your blog.

Blogs can also carry results of surveys and polls. They can draw the attention of the outside world to your company and help you promote your company as an attractive place to work.

Diversify your PR content

Strike a fair balance between soft news and hard news. Soft news is mostly announcements, which could be about executives joining, donations made, community involvement, events, or other promotional activities. These are good to have but don't necessarily add value to people's lives. Hard news, on the other hand, speak about innovations, profitability coming through major developments and strategic alliances, the launch of new technologies, results of business ventures, or published infographics on the performance within an economy.

Your PR content can be product news, innovation and trends, opinion pieces on the future of the industries you're in, offering pieces on the future of the industry and products, publish survey and research results, and write engaging opinion pieces.

Show a human side to your company

We will also discuss sponsorships in Chapter 15 and see how such partnerships are a great amplifier to a brand's PR initiatives. Great brands sponsoring community initiatives can be a very effective form of promotion. In my present job, my company, Al Masaood, one of the leading family businesses in Abu Dhabi, decided to be one of the key sponsors to the Special Olympics World Games that took place in Abu Dhabi in 2019. This is the world's largest humanitarian sporting event for people of determination. The sponsorship consisted of supplying a fleet of 310 Nissan vehicles to transport more than 5000 international athletes and delegates. The PR coverage was great, and it delivered the type of content that journalists enjoy covering.

We got creative with our PR stories; we held safari trips for athletes with special needs alongside social media influencers with similar special needs. We held meet- and- greet opportunities for our customers in the showrooms with the athletes participating in the games. We gave our customers complimentary tickets to the opening ceremony. On Mother's Day, we conducted a series of interviews with the mothers of the athletes and encouraged them to speak openly about their personal struggles in raising children of determination. They shared inspirational stories on how embracing sports contributed to the healing and integration of their children in society. Finally, our senior leaders and board of directors signed up to volunteer in the event and the company gave its employees days off to volunteer and take part in this iconic humanitarian event.

Topical days supplement your PR content

Work on creative PR campaigns that go beyond the classic business theme. In Chapter 17, I touch upon topical days and how building these into an annual calendar can pave the way for rich content. These are must-haves on your PR calendar because they enable your brand to create social conversations that are more focused on human stories than mainstream product ones. Imagine how many technology providers could benefit from content generated on 'Safer Internet Day', or how a water brand could benefit from content on providing clean drinking water to communities in need on 'Clean Water Day'.

Similarly, hosting competitions and awards for certain causes builds up affinity with the media. The famous Japanese brand UD Trucks runs an annual Extra Mile Challenge, a global competition for truck drivers. In the competition, truck drivers are asked to put their heavy-duty driving skills to the test. They are expected to drive, reverse, and park their trucks in challenging and limited spaces. The engagement is high and attracts truck drivers from all over the world. Winners of the competition are offered an all-paid trip to Japan where they are given a tour to the factory of the brand and are recognised by the senior leader in the head office. The brand is celebrating the hard-working drivers, addressing their safety and welfare, and rewarding them for their hard work and long hours on the roads.

Use PR monitoring platforms

Deploy the right software to help you in your media monitoring. Depending on your budgets, you can get very sophisticated with your media database management. I have used Meltwater for years, and they provide an integrated all-in-one platform for social listening and journalists' databases and outreach. These platforms will show you what's working and what's not. The data generated can help you shape and refine your PR content.

What makes a good press release?

So, what makes a good press release? When I first started reviewing drafts for press releases, I was amazed by the rigidity of the language and how formal it was. For someone coming from the advertising world, and who was very fascinated by the art of creative copywriting, the language of a press release felt a lot like the acquired taste of anchovies to me.

Along the way, I started using simple straightforward language that is, factual and reflective of the actual events that took place. Reading through the media narratives over the years, one can see that times have changed. A storytelling approach that is warm and grabbing has now overtaken the corporate and business narrative.

Today, with the internet democratising media, press releases have 'soften up' and a lot of corporate news are using much simpler language.

Apart from language, a good press release will answer the 5Ws: What, When, Who, Where, and Why. It also carries a catchy headline that grabs the attention of the reader. A press release is not a document written just to relay news to the media and editors without making a meaningful contribution to their publishing. It should answer the 'Why' very well. Why has a company taken such a decision, launched such a product or hired a certain person? Once you have hooked the journalist in the story, you need to provide enough details to pave the way for genuine interest in the story.

In her book *A Modern Guide to Public Relations,* author Amy Rosenberg offers the following list of topics that the media will actually cover:

- Executive appointments.
- New location openings.
- New services or new products, whether extensions, add-ons, or completely new.
- Bringing on board high profile and notable professionals.
- Construction, revamp, or expansion of new business premises, physical or virtual.
- Results of new studies and market reports.
- Community involvement or volunteering.
- Events, photo opportunities, and press conferences.
- Recaps on what a company has delivered.
- Performance details of a company in terms of growth and market share.

Your press release speaks about the company's unique selling proposition, which we introduced in Chapter 12. A USP helps the company differentiates itself from its rivals to the readers. It also carries the sentiment of the market. It includes news hooks that speak the language of the press at the time it was written; for example, it could relate to the emergence of a new technology in the field, the near death of an industry, the scarcity of a substance, or the lack of a certain skillset.

To make a press release exciting, consider adding customer testimonials or third-party endorsements. This is one of the oldest tricks in the books, and it still works wonders and brands thrive on it. Fortify your news with insights from research, surveys, and opinion polls. In addition to the photos that are usually attached, use new-age media such as videos that cover events, time-lapses for projects, etc.

The inverted pyramid

To relieve the fear that the important information in your press release may be missed, make sure that it is mentioned at the beginning of the news piece. This is often known as the 'inverted pyramid approach'. The press release needs to explain who the brand is, not just in the boilerplate but also in the body of the communication – unless you are Apple and Microsoft, do not send out your press releases thinking that the journalists know who you are. Explain who you are and what you do. If the news is about an event that took place, add when and where and who took part, and, finally, explain why the event took place.

In terms of format, opt for straight-to-the-point sentences and avoid the run-on ones. Take it easy on the adjectives and big buzzwords unless necessary. Use compelling photos, infographics, and publish white papers in collaboration with educational institutions. Add a boilerplate and sign it off with a reachable name and correct contact details.

Some may advice that a press release must be short in length. In my experience, the length of the press release needs to reflect the substance of the news and the information attached to it. Do not sacrifice relevant information for the sake of brevity.

Additionally, the publishing scene today is full of online portals that publish entire press releases, and the added text can supplement your search engine optimisation plans.

The mass publish syndrome

As a marketer turned comms professional, I have given into the temptation of spamming the world with press releases. Driven by aggressive KPIs, a lot of communication practitioners continue to use a mass publishing approach. In a way, you could be a contributor to the phenomenon of all soft news and corporate announcements. It took a few years to realise that it was getting boring and monotonous. I also had to gather the courage to stop the spamming and, where necessary, reduce the frequency of publishing press releases. You need to strike a balance in your publishing approach by simply asking, 'Is this really news to the press?'

When working with multi-brand businesses or even start-ups that are experiencing accelerated growth, falling into the trap of over-communicating is inevitable. In your PR strategy, you will have to challenge yourself to include creative campaigns and media engagements that are valuable and fruitful and go beyond announcements and self-flattery.

What happens when you don't believe a news piece can be a press piece?

- Suggest an internal announcement instead.
- Turn it into a corporate blog piece or a social media post.
- Create an internal news broadcast video on the same.
- Suggest that this gets sent to one industry publication where it would be pitched as a story.

Know who you're talking to

Understand the public mind. We are students in the ever-changing world of content. In publishing for your customers, study the type of content they consume and are attracted to. This is a very similar approach to creating customer personas. Get an understanding of what content repels them or may not meet their interest at all. By understanding this, you can inject attention-grabbing hooks that will attract them to your messaging.

Keep your email alerts on and do not get into the habit of not reading them. As you go up the chain into a CMO role and the many other priorities get in your way, keep a daily habit of reading your news and monitoring alerts.

Bill Gates famously and rightly said, 'If I was down to my last dollar, I would spend it on public relations.' Public and media relations are main drivers in your department's strategy. With the world of content advancing, there is so much to the marriage between PR and marketing, and practitioners of the field need to work closely and effectively to compound their brands. The bottom line is increased publicity and authenticity.

If you need your news to run and want to guarantee good coverage, make sure you reach out to the media outlets and pitch your news. You could do so through short email pitches, phone calls, requesting a meeting with the editor, blog posts, social media campaigns, and sending supporting photo and video content.

Media training and public speaking

Part of your job remit in PR is to seek the media training that will help executives in your company improve their public appearances and engagements. Media training is a comprehensive way to learn how to deal with large audiences, video-based interviews, podcasts, speeches, opening remarks, and panel discussions. Executive media training will guide your spokespersons how to present themselves professionally, with a healthy degree of confidence and comfort.

A media training course will bust the myth that one can go on camera without being prepared. In fact, one of the very interesting things I learnt about public speaking is that one needs an hour of preparation for every minute of delivery. While, of course, corporate executives do not have that luxury of time, training in this field is required and will help them build their confidence as they engage with the media more frequently.

If you are new to public speaking, then do offer yourself a media training course as well. Nothing is more disheartening than a comms professional stuttering on stage or on camera, or worse, leaking confidential new unintentionally.

A media training course will help you and your seniors prepare for public appearances and improve public speaking and speech delivery. It gets you organised and teaches you celebrity-style tricks such as how to stand at a podium and answer questions from the audience or how to answer tough questions by the media. It trains you to use the right body language gestures and postures, and how to get better voice characteristics, such as pitch and tone. There are specialised courses to help you get the right articulation and pronunciation.

Other benefits of media training include:

- Develop mechanisms on how to cope with stage fright.
- Learn how to deliver messages on camera.
- Learn how to deliver messages using the right body language during offline and online engagements.
- Learn how to host a podcast or record yourself on a phone camera.
- Learn how to dress for camera and lighting – although the world is becoming a lot more informal with the lockdown and the rise of webinars, making sure one is carrying a fresh and sharp look is key to making a lasting impression.
- Learn the right make-up tricks to your skin and face to look healthy on camera.
- Learn how to deliver a speech.
- Learn how to use expressions wisely.

Part of your publicity planning will include the assessment of the public speaking skills of the spokespeople in your organisation and then the arrangement of the media training they need.

The world of corporate communication as we know it today has transformed, and the lines between marketing and PR have completely blurred. Artificial intelligence and communication technologies have transformed the world of communication and PR has become integral to the success of your marketing and promotional campaigns. Marcomms professionals need to make publicity part and parcel of their plans to achieve optimum results.

Like peas in a pod, media relations and the dissemination of press releases go together. And like the chicken and the egg, they feed into each other, and neither takes precedence over the other. Mastering both areas of PR and media relations will surely get you launched into the world of PR successfully.

14

INTERNAL COMMUNICATION

'At the end of the day, we are not selling. We are serving.'

— Dave Ramsey

Businesses start out as passionate quests by entrepreneurs and then turn into communities buzzing with life and relationships that go beyond trade. As businesses grow, so does their vision. Employees are at the heart of this change and drive it forward. Internal communication is the internal compass that guides everyone towards the direction of a company's next destination.

Empowering and energising teams

Simply put, internal communication is the combination of initiatives that empower and energise employees to carry out their jobs to the very best of their ability. Motivated teams are excited about their work and serve customers better. They bounce around with ideas and new ways to do business better.

What is fun about internal communication is that it is extremely fluid and takes on many forms of delivery. It is, as well, a two-way dialogue. What's even more fun is that you are an employee yourself and this means you are a target customer, and you know well what needs to be done to get it right.

Singular and continual

Internal communication initiatives take on multiple forms. Some of the work is carried out as one-off campaigns, others take on the form of an ongoing narrative. One-off campaigns can be an extension of external marketing campaigns and promotions. The latter has the objective of keeping the community of employees well-informed and aware of the company's performance.

Whether you are opting for the first form, the second or both, internal communication, much like other disciplines, becomes effective when it is backed up by a strategy and an execution plan. It also needs to be measured on regular basis.

A playfield for everyone

Internal communication is not restricted to large companies only. We often hear great stories about internal communication strategies adopted in global companies, with case studies shining the spotlight on Fortune 500 brands like Walmart, Amazon and Apple. This doesn't mean that a start-up cannot formulate an internal communication plan. Internal communication remains a necessity for companies of all sizes. In addition to the benefits mentioned above, it is much needed to prepare your company for times of crisis.

Problem solving and innovation

Albert Einstein said, 'We cannot solve our problems with the same level of thinking that created them.' Internal communication tackles training and developing employees. This enables them to get better at problem-solving and thinking out of the box.

Shared ownership

Textbook theories place internal communication under public relations because employees are considered powerful influencers of a company's reputation. Part of your PR plans is distribution of news to your internal audiences. Nevertheless, the overall effectiveness of this discipline cannot be pared down to keeping employees well-informed only. As the pillars stated above show, achieving organisational coherence requires, in large part, the support of key leaders and other teams to unify teams under one overarching vision.

Internal communication, therefore, is a shared function between multiple teams, which includes management, HR, learning and development, QHSE (Quality, Health, Safety, Environment), compliance, and teams that are customer-facing such as service centres and call centres as well as the marcomms team. Think of internal communication as an inclusive discipline that requires cross-functional collaboration.

Fair and reasonable

Despite all the success that internal communication delivers, it is often the underdog when it comes to budgets and planning. The reason comes down to the corporate trait of prioritisation for profits. Since it is a shared responsibility of multiple departments, no one function or team can get the exclusive credit for its success and, thus, interest is lost in executing it. Additionally, unlike campaigns, you cannot always argue that internal communication is bringing in new business or extra savings. Sales and operations take precedence when it comes to budgets. However, we all know that happy employees mean happy customers.

Carrying out successful internal communication initiatives may not require big budgets. The smallest of initiatives, such as a direct message from the CEO thanking employees, goes a long way. Internal communication, therefore, is a fair and reasonable investment for companies to make.

Turning human

Internal communication not only makes your brand relatable, but it also brings your brand's vision to life. As a marcomms professional, you will need to work extra hard at promoting your brand story to the employees, starting from the seniors, and trickling down to the rest of the population. This is done through a series of communication techniques including the preservation of your company's tone of voice.

Dr Susan Drake, author, and professor of business management, made an interesting commentary on internal communication. She said, 'People relate to people and not to stuffed corporate shirts.' In

Chapter 11, I wrote on the power of humanising brands through The Brand Persona Framework. The best way to begin your internal communications work is to complete the brand persona exercise for your company.

People stay for culture

As the saying goes, people work for money, but they stay for culture. In the book *Light their Fire*, the authors showcase the results of several studies that show how employee retention is based on their feeling of clarity and is usually not affected by their pay. 'Not being paid fairly was the least important of the factors that contributed to employees being dissatisfied and wanting to leave.' The book goes on to explain the cost of employee turnover is a lot higher than the cost of internal communication. The point is employees knowing where the company is heading and where they stand in the process can keep them loyal.

Keeping your employees is a lot cheaper than hiring and training new ones. The longevity and loyalty of your team depend highly on their feelings of belonging and worthiness. The feeling of belonging is addressed through the transparency of your communication, and their worth is addressed through the training and engagements offered.

So, what is a company's culture?

Peter Drucker's 'Culture eats strategy for breakfast' is a testament to the fact that culture is the lifeline of a company. Organisational cultures are taught. How? By demonstrating behaviours in a consistent, repetitive, and constructive manner. Culture is the combination of all the factors required to keep the attitude of the company intact and would include its values, beliefs, philosophies, and the overall purpose.

Displaying a company's vision statement in the face of employees is not going to result in the culture you are aspiring to. First, start with a company's purpose. Explain why the purpose is the leading point of all the actions being taken. Reiterate your purpose through the actions taken and communicated. Then foster a culture that is born out of that company's purpose. All of this can be achieved through mastering the art of brand storytelling which Chapter 12 tackled.

So how do you go about strategising for successful internal communication plans?

Strategising for success

An internal communication strategy gets your employees to love your brand only when they understand the brand purpose, positioning, story, vision, and mission values. This strategy will embody the company's understanding on how employees feel about their job safety, their future at the company, and how they are being treated by the company.

Gap analysis

A prerequisite to building and running an internal communication plan is to have a clear understanding of the overall sentiment in the company. Some call this a culture check, this book will refer to it as gap analysis.

Find a way to run a culture check that looks at how well your employees are aware of the company's vision, mission, values, and future orientation. Another check is finding out how happy and motivated employees are and what new skills they need to move with the times and embrace changing market conditions.

In your gap analysis, you will need to identify how well your employees know the following:

- Company purpose and vision.
- The corporate values and if they believe in them or can recommend others.
- The history of your company.
- The articulation of the brand personality and its identity.
- The company's strategy and business objectives.
- The company's target audience, and direct and indirect competition.
- The changing market trends.
- The company's product mix, and best-selling brands.
- The company's unique selling proposition and taglines.
- The future direction of the company.
- The importance of the role they play in the company's journey.

What are the essentials of an internal communication strategy?

Let us now approach internal communication in a structured manner and break it down into deliverables. Here is a five-step process to building an effective internal communication plan.

- Define your objectives.
- Identify your internal customers and their needs.
- Create your internal messaging house.

- Decide on the platforms of delivery, the frequency of communication, and the owners of the messages.
- Launch and continuously review and assess.

Defining your internal communication objectives

Here is a list of possible objectives of internal communication. Defining these objectives needs to happen collectively with key stakeholders in the organisation.

- Launch an annual theme for the fiscal year, taking into consideration where the company stands against its strategic path.
- Create a culture of respect by promoting empathetic listening. Develop tactics that enable the leaders of the organisation to listen to their people.
- Improve excellence in execution through a stream of year-round communication on the company strategy, its materialisation, and how it is broken down.
- Create awareness of the year's strategic initiatives such as the need to improve customer satisfaction, new product launches, or new market opportunities.
- Understand the level of employee satisfaction with their jobs through internal surveys and polls.
- Use employee knowledge and insights to assist the business. Create open channels of upward communication for the company to benefit from the insights employees hold.
- Deliver an updated succession plan for employees to envision their future in the company.

- Increase awareness around corporate policies.
- Improve the equity of the employer brand and be able to attract better talents through existing employees and referral programs.
- Innovate new ideas that benefit the business through interactive sessions.
- Launch and communicate an annual training calendar.
- Spread motivation and inspiration through a series of messages from key stakeholders.
- Have a detailed plan for crises, such as lay-offs, or product recalls.

Defining your audience and their needs

After stating your objectives, it is time to understand your internal audiences. Start by listing down your internal audiences. Here is an example of such a list:

- Board of directors.
- Executive committees.
- Support services departments.
- Customer-facing employees.
- Middle management.
- Business partners such as franchisors or principal brand executives.
- Workers on the production lines.

We spoke about the brand persona and customer persona in Chapters 11 and 12. Comparably, you will need to conduct an internal audience persona exercise for each of your groups. Identify their needs, aspirations, and career plans. Sometimes organisations hold varying brand personas for their internal audiences, and by conducting a brand persona exercise, you will be able to understand the type of messaging themes that suit them and what mediums are best for broadcasting.

Take a long and hard look at the population of your employees. You need to understand the slices of the pie in terms of audiences and choose your communication channels accordingly. Take, for example, a cloud kitchen company; 20% of the employees are white-collar workers who are constantly connected to the internet and can easily log in through their phones and watch a video. The 80% of the population that are blue-collar workers do not have access to their emails while working on sites. This may not mean that 80% of your communication should be targeted towards them, but it certainly means you cannot reach them through a web-based or an email campaign. You may need to allocate a budget to traditional broadcasting such as bulletin-board posters or direct SMS or WhatsApp group broadcasting.

Create your internal messaging house

Internal communication is based on information sharing and creating a two-way stream of dialogue between the corporate leadership and the employees. These conversations are expected to bring clarity and enable your staff to execute your communication in an efficient and timely manner. The best of ideas often come from the bottom of your corporate pyramid. Similarly, utilising the knowledge from this area can be the best avoidant of crisis. When you create systems in which employees can report the red flags and insights, you foster a safer environment. What I am trying to say is that your internal messaging house is a two-way stream.

Here is an example of internal messages:

- Regular communication on how the company is performing by the leaders. These could be done on a bi-annual, quarterly, or monthly basis depending on the length of the company's sales cycles and the breadth of the business.
- Occasional messaging that brings the company's culture alive. This would include reminders of the leaders' philosophies and aspirations, the progress made thus far on certain projects, and strategic initiatives.
- Regular and constant reminders of the company's vision, mission, and values. The messaging could also include open feedback channels from the employees on how well a company is upholding its values.
- Motivational messages in the form of rewards and recognition to employees who are performing in an efficient and professional manner, as well as those who have over-achieved their targets and over-delivered.
- Organisational news on new developments, new hires, financial achievements, market forecasts, marketing campaigns, and any upcoming change to the company necessitated by external or internal forces.
- Topical day activations in the form of engagements that send out a message of encouragement and inclusion to the internal audiences.
- Memos on organisational decisions, policies, and other directives.
- Introductions to new joiners and new employees or partner organisations and information about other HR-related matters.
- Updates on the company's annual calendar of events and major milestones.
- Employee-focused motivational campaigns based on testimonials, sharing of experiences and recognition of good performance.
- Learning and development training calendars.

More than just email

The very first thing that comes to mind in internal communication is email communication. In fact, email continues to exhaust a lot of the ways businesses communicate when, in fact, it should not. Email is an invention of the 70s, and so much has come up that could relegate email to the backseat. The world of communication has become wide and instant, and there is no limit to how a company can communicate. Here is a possible list of forms and mediums that can be considered:

Format	Mediums	Examples
Video	TikTok channels, Snapchat channels, intranets, WhatsApp groups, YouTube channels, display screens in offices and at corporate events.	A video message from the chairman, CEO or founder to all employees recapping the performance of the year. An induction video to new joiners about the company's values and strategy, history, and heritage.
Audio	Podcasts and audio corporate publications (a great companion to employees commuting to the job). Conference calls.	Podcast sessions with company leaders on their experiences and achievements. Audio articles on corporate publications or articles on thought leadership.

Format	Mediums	Examples
In-person or virtual events	Corporate events of differing sizes, such as team meetings, fishbowl-style meetings, seminars, and roadshows.	Awards and recognition ceremonies. Annual operating plan meetings. Focus groups and brainstorming sessions. Virtual seminars. Coaching and team building activities. Q&A sessions and periodic ideation sessions.
Messaging Platforms	Electronic messaging, intranets, websites, printed messaging on bulletin boards, brochures, leaflets, and dynamic induction kits.	Welcome messages both electronic and in-person. Corporate newsletters and magazines. Memos, announcements, and minutes of meetings. Annual reports and periodic reports on business performance. Executive messaging to employees on performance and achievement of goals. Corporate policies. Online polls and surveys.

Decide on the platforms of delivery, the frequency of the communication, and the owners of the messages

As a marketer and communicator, you are going to plan and organise the internal messaging house, making sure the output is timely, correct, honest, clear, and consistent. Keeping employees informed requires a predictable frequency. For example, a company's CEO is expected to communicate with the employees at the end of every quarter, end of year, and beginning of a new fiscal year. Executives are also expected to inform employees of upcoming major structural and policy changes.

Like the concept of corporate storytelling, internal communication is an ongoing conversation. It can be broken down into different types of messages delivered by different mediums. You will need to balance the messages by introducing a variety that is not exhausting to the crowds.

Some of your messages need to target specific audiences such as leadership announcements on recent milestones or changes to an organisational structure. Other messages could be recognition stories about employees and how they are contributing to the company's success. Longer messages could be something like training sessions on customer service.

Once your messages are identified, you will need to decide on the owner and frequency of the message. Here is a simple tabular example of how you can achieve this:

Message	Owner	Platform	Frequency
Regular communication on how the company is performing.	CEO Office.	Video message.	Quarterly.
Occasional messaging that brings the company's culture alive.	HODs (Head of Departments). HR. Marcomms.	Intranet. Weekly newsletter. Events. Roadshows.	Weekly. Monthly.
Regular and constant reminders of the company's vision, mission, and values.	Marcomms.	Snippets in multiple platforms: announcements, induction programmes, memos, intranet, website, corporate presentations, social media content.	Ongoing.
Training Calendars and programs.	Learning & development.	Intranet. Email. Virtual meetings. In-person events.	Bi-monthly.

Channels of delivery

What makes internal communication attractive is the cost efficiencies of the discipline. You would rarely hear of a company that spends more money marketing internally than externally. A lot of what you do is with channels that you own and with audiences who are not interested in you but are committed to you. Here is a list of possible platforms.

• Intranets or internal portals.	• Town halls.
• Weekly corporate newsletters.	• Conferences.
• Memos and announcements.	• Quiz nights.
• Surveys.	• Corporate sporting events.
• Polls.	• TikTok challenges.
• Rewards and recognition ceremonies.	• Corporate blogs.
• Brainstorming sessions.	• Social media platforms for employees.
• Quizzes and competitions.	• Topical day celebrations.
• Podcasts.	• Scheduled management directives.
• Induction programs.	• Shared calendars of events.
• CEO roadshows.	• Corporate publications.
• Training workshops.	
• Strategy retreats.	

Modern companies have moved to delivery channels that are more in line with the times.

Up close and personal. There is nothing greater than face-to-face interaction. It remains the richest form of communication and companies need to use it as much as possible. Your internal communication plan could include creative workshops to update a brand persona, a vision statement, or a revision of corporate values. This can be done with your internal stakeholders as proof that the company believes in how well they understand the business. We spoke about taglines in Chapter 12. A simple communication involving employees in the voting for a tagline, or the launch of a new tagline would be a great boost to employees.

New-age content. Modern companies have moved to new-age digital channels that deliver great content. Podcasts are a favourite of mine and have become an enjoyable platform that people can listen to on their commute or while they are working out or at their desks.

Creating cross-functional teams. Assigning cross-functional teams on certain projects binds employees together through having one common objective.

Offsite meetings and strategy retreats. Strategy retreats are a great way for teams to collaborate, get on the same page, and unite over a future goal for the company.

A creative way of blurring organisational barriers between employees is by creating knowledge teams. These could be employees who have knowledge of certain matters and can provide advice. Their knowledge could be out of a previous or current experience, a hobby, or literature. Another one is creating D&I (Diversity & Inclusion) teams or champions.

News exclusivity. A simple yet effective technique in motivating employees is allowing them exclusivity to the news of the company and its latest products and services. This means sharing corporate announcements and product news with them before the public. You can always allow them a sneak preview into upcoming product launches, a retail outlet, or a test version of a new app.

Internal networking. Networking platforms that allow employees from different functions, territories, and ranks to meet and get to know each other. These could come in the form of shared projects, learning and development quests, research studies, etc.

Ideation platforms. Suggestion schemes that allow employees to contribute new ideas that could benefit the business such as new product extensions, systems, cost reductions, etc.

Employee events and activations. I referenced topical days in Chapter 9. These are a great way to earn the heart and attention of your employees. This could include celebrating World Heritage Day, Happiness Day, Christmas, and other events.

Annual planning and kick-off meetings. Hosting these helps set clear objectives. They explain the scope of work, reiterate where the company is strategically, can source feedback from all corners of the company. It generates alignment on the company's strategic orientation and the company's ambitions.

Annual training calendars. Part of the internal communication calendar will be the learning and development schemes that have been prepared. Training is a great avenue not only to upgrade the skills and knowledge of employees but also to make them feel empowered to learn more on the job and achieve more.

Collaborate with HR and compliance teams. Work with HR and compliance teams on creating a safe avenue for expressing grief or any wrongdoing, such as whistleblowing schemes.

Positive feedback funnels. Feedback avenues and reports allow employees to express their opinions freely and disagree with matters that they find inappropriate. Open and safe channels of feedback are highly effective in gaining trust, which is the essence of a great company culture.

Rich company archives. We touched upon the importance of company archives earlier in Chapter 3. Access to records and historic data, means by which employees can fulfil their tasks efficiently and easily reference historic achievements as a foundation to build ambitious future, can be a great motivator to the community of employees.

Launch, continuously assess and review

The inclusivity factor is what you are after in your internal communication, and it is what keeps your employees informed of which direction their ship is steering. The type of content you generate online would most certainly affect the productivity of your internal audience. It also can be generated by them, as we will see later in this book.

While the norm considers internal marketing a subset of PR, communicators should not reflect the outside news internally but should create internal narratives that create transparency, aligns teams on common goals, unifies their attitudes and languages, and helps them become brand custodians.

Purpose for a North Star

The best compass for a successful internal communication plan is based on articulating a company's purpose. The quote on money cannot buy you happiness stands true not just in life but also in corporate life. Nilofer Merchant explains, 'Money motivates neither the best people nor the best in people. Purpose does.' Once employees are listening to the corporate narrative and understanding the purpose of the company, they stay happy and loyal.

Having a solid internal communication plan results in transparency, inclusion, accountability, and harmony in business relationships. Training and development results in advancement, improvement, and innovation. Internal communication is the nucleus of a performance-drive culture. It brings about powerful results and desired changes.

15

SPONSORSHIPS AND CORPORATE SOCIAL RESPONSIBILITY (CSR)

"We firmly believe that a sponsor should add value to the
fans and make their experience better.
Doing this means understanding your role,
one that goes beyond 'official partner of...and actually give
fans a reason to pay attention to you"

— GED COLLEYPRIEST,
FOUNDER OF UNDERDOG SPORTS MARKETING

When done right, sponsorships provide a speedy and meaningful connection with your audiences. Sponsoring community, business, and sporting platforms spike up the favourability of your brand and helps draw in new and potential customers. They also amplify the love for your brand or company.

Historically proven to be a powerful marketing and communication tool, sponsorships benefit companies of all sizes, whether start-ups or conglomerates. Sponsorships supplement both the marketing and PR efforts of brands and can also be a platform for generating leads and additional sales. Yes, these vary greatly in sizes and forms and need to be done right as they may not always establish the most accurate of returns.

In his latest book on sponsorship strategy, Ken Ungar, C-level sponsorship consultant and famous author on the topic, explains that the sponsorship industry has grown from USD 13 billion to USD 62 billion in just under 20 years. He goes on to explain that, unsurprisingly, 70% of sponsorships fall in the field of sports. Whether you are here to understand sponsorships of sports or other areas such as arts, music, entertainment, education, charity, or even community initiatives, this chapter will help you put together a way to build a sponsorship strategy and execution plan for your company.

The chapter will explain why sponsorships are the propulsion engines to your brand and a creative vehicle that drives home brand love, credibility, and authentic publicity. The chapter will end with an explanation of CSR and sustainability and what are the differences and points of connection with sponsorships.

A quick definition of sponsorships

A sponsorship is a contractual agreement between a brand and a platform, most often referred to as a property. Properties organise and manage teams and initiatives in different fields such as sports and entertainment. In this contractual agreement, the brand receives access to the property's products, services, and audiences in exchange for a fee that is either paid in cash or as VIK (value-in-kind). In-kind payments are done as an exchange of products or services provided by the sponsor to the property running the sponsorship as an alternative to cash. Sometimes, the payment is done as a mix of cash and value-in-kind.

Many of the automotive sponsorships I have run consisted of a VIK arrangement where the company supplements an event with a fleet of cars and transportation logistics and in return is given exclusive rights as automotive partner.

Types of sponsorships

Kim J. Harrison, an award-winning practitioner of sponsorships and PR, identified three types of sponsorships.

- Corporate sponsorships.
- Marketing sponsorships.
- Cause-related sponsorships.

Corporate sponsorships are used to communicate key corporate messages about a company for the purpose of elevating its brand equity and presence. Marketing sponsorships are often used to promote a sponsor's products and services that help in sales and profitability. Cause-related sponsorships are related to humanitarian, environmental and societal causes. Companies enter as sponsors by paying a fee to support certain causes or to donate a percentage of their sales to a not-for-profit organisation.

Are sponsorships essential to your marcomms strategy?

When you study the field, you'll find that sponsorships are very empowering to brands and are integral to the marketing mix. Yet, there is no formula set in stone as to what extent sponsorships should occupy your marketing mix and budgets.

Several elements come into play when deciding how and when to pursue sponsorships:

- The availability of platforms in your region that can help you optimise your marketing plans.
- The existing platforms guarantee the presence of your brand's potential and existing target audience.
- The extent to which the platform can provide accurate reports and calculate the return on investment for your brand.
- The type of market your brand exists in. Is it an emerging market with a powerful economy destined for growth, where traditional marketing methods may not cut it, or is it a mature market that requires differentiation and closer interaction with customers?
- The pricing strategy of the brand. We see that brands with very high price points benefit greatly from exclusive sponsorship platforms. This is very true in the luxury segment. Whereas mass brands that do not hold much differentiation might not benefit from sponsorships as much as they do from other marketing strategies such as sampling and promotions. Yet, there is no formula cast in stone, and decisions are made based on many elements.

Bridging brands and crowds

Airline companies are famous for their multimillion-dollar sponsorship deals. Emirates Airline, the world's fourth largest airline and a flagship carrier of the UAE, has built a monumental portfolio of sponsorships. Over the years, Emirates acquired the rights of leading football teams such as AC Milan, Arsenal FC, the Asian Football Confederation, Real Madrid, and others. They also own other property rights in the fields of tennis, rugby, and horse racing.

Whether you are a start-up or an SME, you can still reach your core audiences through sponsorships. Let's assume you are a start-up app that facilitates online sessions of therapy at competitive rates. Therapists from around the world can now offer online counselling on a platform in a safe and private manner. You could decide to sponsor a community 5K walk for an institution that aims to raise awareness on the issue of mental health. You would expect that people showing up for the walk might be those in need of counselling and advocates of counselling.

Now imagine that you brought an activation element to your sponsorship by bringing in your therapists to provide talks and awareness sessions before or after the community walk. The sponsorship may well be within your means from a budget consideration and has allowed you to promote your app amongst the right audience.

CSR is a much broader realm, and I will touch upon it later in the chapter. Sponsorships provide brands with CSR avenues that match their values and their good-willed intentions towards their communities. Sponsorships help companies build a CSR story, which in turn can allow differentiation and a means to earn further publicity.

Sponsorships allow you to reach influential audiences without going through the hassle of building a platform yourself. By reaching potential influencers of your brand, your brand can experience compounded and unprecedented growth.

The Rolex philosophy on sponsorship is a great illustration of this point. The founder of Rolex watches, Hans Wilsdorf, promoted his watches by inviting world-class athletes to wear them during their sporting quests and expeditions. Heroic athletes from all walks of life wore the Rolex timepieces and conquered their pursuits in mountaineering, swimming, equestrian, yachting, tennis, golf, and more. The brand then made its way to the world of arts and supported elite musicians and singers. Recently, the brand made its debut sponsorships with the movie industry when it became the sponsor of the Oscars. When you study the Rolex brand, you will find that through its sponsorship strategy, it has grown to become one of the leading luxury brands in the world.

Every brand's delight

Sponsorships are versatile. They come in stretchable sizes that work well for brands of any industry. They are an effective marketing channel or branding in the B2B and the B2G sectors.

In addition to enriching your reputation and compounding your PR results, sponsorships allow for product and service trails.

Sponsorships allow your brand to build a niche association with certain experiences. Automotive brands are closely associated with racing and motorsports. If we look at Nissan, the leading Japanese carmaker, chose a rich selection of sports properties such as the UAEFA Champions League and the Formula E, F1 for electric cars. The brand also sponsors regional and local sports that appeal to its target audience, and these range from desert off-roading to cricket.

In strengthening its commitment to the sporting scene of Abu Dhabi, Al Masaood Automobiles, collaborated with Nissan and sponsored Al Jazira Club, one of the most prominent football clubs in the country and in Abu Dhabi. Nissan Abu Dhabi was also an active supporter and sponsor of the Fatima Bint Mubarak Ladies Open, the first-ever exclusively ladies-only professional golf event to take place in the UAE in 2019. Al Masaood also collaborated with Nissan and sponsored the Abu Dhabi HSBC Championship presented by EGA in 2019.

Sponsorships are great means for brands to research new products, gather insights, conduct surveys, and gather more customer data.

When done right, sponsorships are effective lead-generation tools and provide grounds for promotions and product launches and reveals.

Manifesting brand experiences

Sponsorships provide an uncluttered space for brands to bundle their products with experiences. A case in point is the Red Bull popular involvement with extreme sports competitions. The brand is now closely associated with adrenaline-pumping sports through the sponsorship of highly focused events such as the Red Bull Air Race, the Red Box Soapbox Race, and the other events in cliff-diving and snowboarding as well as motocross.

Sponsorships allow brands to also improve their stakes not just with customers and wider communities but with their own employees, investors, and shareholders. Unquestionably, sponsorships allow brands to stand out from their competition.

What are the elements of a sponsorship strategy?

1. Start with the STP segmentation, targeting, and positioning exercise.
2. Identify sponsorship areas that align with your brand objectives.
3. Create a sponsorship policy.
4. Outline the process of evaluating sponsorships.
5. Call for a sponsorship committee.
6. Allocate a budget.
7. Activate your sponsorship.
8. Evaluate the performance.

STP and sponsorships

Remember my STP story from Chapter 1? This method helps you evaluate the sponsorship options on hand. Once you are clear on your segments, find out the level of commonality between the attendees of a sponsorship and your target segments.

Take, for example, a 4x4 accessories brand, for example, ARB. ARB is a leading 4X4 accessories brand worldwide and is a top one in Australia. Personas of ARB customers in the UAE love dune bashing in the dessert, while in Australia, they are into wood bashing and driving in the forest areas. In Australia, the brand would go after wilderness lovers and campers. In the UAE, the brand would go after desert dune bashers and safari lovers.

Siemens Energy, for example, is positioning itself as a leader in digitalising energy solutions and transitioning to renewable energy.

The brand partnered with Expo 2020 Dubai and became a sponsor for this world-class event. Siemens integrated its technologies at the Expo 2020 site across its 137 buildings, turning the expo into the most digitalised, sustainable, and secure edition in the history of expos.

In the positioning section, consider how the sponsorship helps in better positioning your brand. Does it give customers more reasons to believe in you? Does it differentiate you from your competition? Shell, a leading global player in energy and petrochemicals, has become partners with Nissan in the electrical Formula E sport. The alliance between Shell and Nissan in Formula E brought together two leading brands in the development of new mobility solutions.

Identify sponsorship areas that align with your brand objectives

These could well be extracted from the areas of interest identified by your customer personas as well as your brand persona for your company. The lion's share in sponsorships is sports, followed by entertainment. When studying the sponsorship journey of brands, you will find a lot of interest in sports that then expands into art, which then expands to music and cultural events. Sports is an avenue that is loved and watched by millions. People get excited and united at the same time, making this platform one of the most popular for brands to partner with.

Having said that, brands can have avenues of their own apart from these. At Al Masaood, where I work, the company, a legacy family holding company, found great receptivity in cultural sporting events and cultural events that celebrate the heritage of the UAE. The company sponsors the traditional Dhow sailing race, 'Delma Race', in the capital Abu Dhabi, a 125-km race for 60-foot traditional dhows, traditional sailing vessels used in the Arabian Gulf. The company also sponsors the annual camel race, one of the richest races in the world that serves as a revival to old traditions, and the Liwa Date Festival that celebrates local harvesting of the national fruit.

Al Masaood had a privilege to become one of the elite sponsors of the prestigious Sheikh Zayed Bin Sultan Al Nahyan Jewel Crown, the world's richest horse race for purebred Arabians. Al Masood Automobiles, the automotive arm of the Group, participates annually in the Moreeb Dune International Festival, a dune bashing sport festival in the Al Dhafra region in the UAE. The festival hosts a variety of races including cars, bikes, falcons, camels, and horses. The festivities comprise an array of activities that promote the UAE's culture. Racing enthusiasts participate in several challenges like car drag races, bike races, motocross track challenges, camel races, horse races, classic cars competition and the famous Moreeb freestyle drifting track race.

Outline the process of evaluating sponsorships

The best way to evaluate sponsorships is to create a sponsorship policy. A sponsorship policy will guide you to:

1. Identify the opportunity in your markets most suited for your brands with their possible limitations.
2. Specify the areas of eligibility for the brand in sponsorships. In the process, you can identify what areas are a no-go for sponsorship as well. For example, when I worked for an Islamic bank, it was a given that sponsorships with licensed platforms that serve

alcohol were a no-go, as were any properties that promoted non-halal products or weapons or featured any forms of entertainment not in line with Sharia standards.

3. Determine what checks and balances will be carried out on the organisations hosting the sponsorships.

4. Decide on the areas and geographical territories for your sponsorships unless they are virtual.

5. Call for a sponsorship committee. A sponsorship committee does not always constitute the members of the marketing team. Depending on the type of organisation, this may include members from other teams such as Diversity & Inclusion, Government Relations, CSR, and Compliance and Legal and could also include members of the Finance team.

6. Break down the sponsorship evaluation process including the criteria and lead times associated with it.

7. Include other considerations such as required branding, contractual terms of time, delivery, financial commitment, what type of internal communication would be associated with carrying out the sponsorship and frequency, and on what basis the sponsorship will be re-evaluated.

Decide on a budget

Many factors are at play when determining how much of your marcomms budget to allocate to sponsorships. I once found out that 65% of the budget of a company I consulted for was dedicated to sponsorships. Industry norms set the cap at 11% to 20%, but this is not definite and varies by sector, industry, and what key events are taking place during the year. Some brands might witness an increase in their sponsorship budget because their region might be hosting a unique event only once.

How to evaluate a sponsorship

Even if you are establishing a department from scratch, you may be surprised that you have inherited some sponsorship commitments. The arrangement could have been made directly through the CEO or it could have been offered as part of a sales deal. Consider the following points and questions:

Start by validating the sponsorship proposals. First, make sure these do not fall in no-go areas. The no-go areas can be based on a company's ethical stance; for example, weapons, child labour, street fighting, smoking or anything that poses extreme danger to communities could be areas a brand chooses not to get associated with. A proposed platform could be sponsored by a competitor and this, for some brands, means it is a space not to tap into. Perhaps a main competitor has become synonymous with a specific sport, and you may not wish to sponsor that sport if you do not have sufficient funds and the creativity to overpower your competition.

In your sponsorship strategy, you may have identified certain sports and educational avenues. Let's say your company has the following as pillars to your sponsorship strategy: 1. Combat sports 2. Female sports 3. Nutrition 4. Enabling people of determination through the creation of jobs. You are approached by a property that is into water sports, which does not align with any of your pillars or your audience. Here are a few questions to ask:

- Does the audience of the sponsorship represent your target audience or potential new customers? Perhaps a customer segment with a high barrier to entry that your brand is unable to penetrate? Cross-check that there are shared values, aspirations, and interests between the platform and your company.
- What is the potential impact of the platform on your target audience? Will they love you more or prefer you to other brands because of this sponsorship?
- Is there an additional commercial advantage between the platform and your company? Do you produce any products that go into this platform?
- Understand the exclusivity rights of your brand in the sponsorship. Are you exclusive to an industry category or the tier you are in, and how does that play out for you?
- If you are taking on a sponsorship that was previously handled by a competing brand, and this is common, try to investigate and understand why the competing brand decided to discontinue and not renew the partnership. Not researching what your competition has done in previous years means you are at risk of repeating what was done instead of raising the bar higher.
- What data and reports will the platform offer during and post the sponsorship, and will this information be useful for you? Post sponsorship reports would include attendance customer satisfaction and engagement surveys, media reach, and third-party rating reports.
- If the platform is membership-based, what is the renewal rate? If there are tickets sold, what is the growth rate of ticket sales?
- Is there room for creative brand activations? Would you be able to get up close and personal with the audiences?

- How is the sponsorship handled? Is there an in-house dedicated team? Or is it sub-contracted to a specialised event company? How experienced is the property in running the sponsorship?

Understand the media mix of this partnership platform and if that provides the target messages of your brand. You will need to study and review the marketing plans of the property itself and make sure they get executed. What type of media is offered? Let's say you are offered the opportunity to sponsor a golf tournament that is broadcast on TV stations, yet not the ones of your region. You may be paying for media that doesn't reach your local audiences.

Assess the social media presence of the platform. Will they be livestreaming their events? What is the quality of their content like? What are their engagement rates? Have they allocated a budget for social media ads? How is the social media community of the platform being handled?

Activating your sponsorships

When taking on a sponsorship, you need to start with a comprehensive communication plan, then move on to activating. The essential starting point is to trace the journey of the platform and think of messages and activation around the points of contact.

Create a messaging house

Identify your messages, and where they will be diffused along the journey. Think of tailor-made messages, products, offers, and promotions, from one-themed messages to a series of branded content around the theme. Some sponsorships are better activated when brands create a theme around them.

Design your PR and marketing plans

Create a list and timeline for publishing the necessary announcements both internally and externally. Create compelling content about your involvement and explain the reasons why you chose this platform and what the shared values and ambitions are. Create the suite of PR and social messaging accordingly. Expand your PR plan and consider a press conference, a signing ceremony, lining-up of interviews onsite and offsite, pitching speaking opportunities and commentary, and arrange for trophy and award ceremonies.

Design your branded spaces

Upon studying the sponsorship journey and identifying the touchpoints beneficial for your brand, design and produce your branded messages and spaces. Plan your advertising and social media content as well.

Supplement your presence with onsite activations or promotions

Sponsorships are good opportunities for the display of new products or showcase of services in an up close and personal method. Special edition branded collateral, freebies, and raffle draws are other ways to bring your brand to life.

Plan your activations and displays accordingly

These could be giveaways at your stalls, branded collateral, or experiential marketing stunts, raffle tickets, meet the team opportunities, for example, in sports, roadshows with promotions around the theme of the sponsorship, player and celebrity endorsements. Leverage your databases and invite your customers, create an area for VIPs, and engage the media that you closely work with.

Involve your employees

Sponsorships are also a great vehicle for employee marketing and strengthening your employer brand. You can do so by offering employees special privileges like discounted tickets to the sponsorships and, in the process, turn them into custodians as well.

What could go wrong in your sponsorship strategy?

Just like campaigns, sponsorships can turn out to be ineffective. Here are a few scenarios to consider.

- Succumbing to the temptation of sponsoring a platform that is too overwhelming for your company, your budget or your team to undertake. Having gone through it myself, I can tell you it is a sad state of affairs. There are plenty of opportunities out there, and sponsorships are not to be rushed. It is a foolish game to underestimate the work that goes into sponsorships.
- The audiences of the sponsorship are not your present, future, or potential audiences. If STP does not yield any commonality between the property and your audiences and the products, territory, market or values, then this is a friendship without benefits.
- You are utilising your sponsorship by slapping a logo on a board only or your logo is lost amongst many on a very small and cluttered space. Many companies get tempted into sponsorship in exchange for a value-in-kind exchange. You view the sponsorship as an exchange of advertising space only. You don't get accurate measures on viewership, or any awareness created.
- You are not using the sponsorship as part of your PR and CSR plans. Sponsorships are means to tell a story to the media and to get your name out there, and you did not take the opportunity to build on your connected storytelling and enrich or tell your brand story.
- The sales team or an internal member in the company are influencing the decision-making process of the sponsorship. How often do you get a sponsorship because a sales leader is just about to close a major contract with an influential party that is offering a sponsorship in exchange for a sales deal or a discount? Take, for example, a well-known celebrity who is about to place a large order for your latest stock and is bargaining by asking for a major discount in exchange for sponsorship rights on a roadshow they

are hosting. While the deal is promising, the sponsorship may be far-removed from your audience and brand strategy.

- You are measuring your sponsorship by media exposure value only – other means could be additional leads, improved brand image and reputation, and improved customer sentiment. While some sponsorships provide display spaces, they should not be confused with advertising.
- You did not spend enough time negotiating the partnership and ended up buying the rights for a tier in the sponsorship that offers your brand privileges more than it requires.

The COVID-19 pandemic had imposed lockdowns and restrictions on human gatherings in large numbers and hindered the sponsorship and events industry tremendously in 2020 and 2021. This specialty field in marketing made headlines as one of the industries hit hard by the lockdown. In March 2020, CNBC declared that it was predicted that sports leagues would lose more than USD 300 million in sponsorship funding in 2021.

Be that as it may, this channel is one that allows times of togetherness between people and brands. It will bounce back with time. They are among the most creative of ways for brands to connect and resonate with people by creating excitement, entertainment, and soul-fulfilling experiences.

CSR (Corporate Social Responsibility)

'Sustainable development is the pathway to the future we want for all. It offers a framework to generate economic

> *growth, achieve social justice, exercise environmental stew-*
> *ardship, and strengthen governance.'*

— BAN KI-MOON

The topic of sponsorships is rarely discussed without referencing CSR in the context of marcomms. Some may refer to both disciplines interchangeably, but the two are different.

It might be of help to briefly explain CSR now that many sponsorships claim to embrace it or be it. CSR is a much broader discipline than sponsorships. Perhaps it is better described as an overarching approach of a company towards running its business.

Wikipedia defines CSR ad follows:

> *CSR is a type of international private business self-regulation.*
> *While once it was possible to describe CSR as an internal*
> *organisational policy or a corporate ethics strategy, that time*
> *has passed as various international laws have been developed*
> *and various organisations have used their authority to push it*
> *beyond individual or even industry-wide initiatives.*

Large organisations, especially the ones that are into mining and manufacturing or any type of business that is greatly associated with greenhouse emissions or whose operations have a direct impact on the environment, usually employ a dedicated team or regulating body for their CSR implementation. Medium to smaller businesses may employ a CSR officer or delegate the CSR strategy and implementation to either the CEO office or the communication department. In fact, CSR is an organisation-wide responsibility and is not limited to one or two functions within an organisation.

CSR tackles matters such as:

1. How is a company sourcing its raw materials and resources? Does it adopt ethical and fair trade? Is the raw material being bought from sustainable sources?

2. How sustainable are the products and the production methods of the company? For example, are the raw materials of a product recyclable and biodegradable? Are the factories or production facilities producing less carbon emissions with the passing of time or have they signed up to a net zero production? If a company is into the service industry, is it conducting its services with less carbon emissions or in a way that doesn't harm the resources of the environment? Does it treat its employees and vendors fairly and implement an inclusive management policy? Is the company an equal opportunity employer?

3. Is the company earning its market share through ethical and fair means? For example, is a company burning prices and margins to gain market share while killing chances for smaller businesses?

4. What policies does the company have in place to self-regulate? This includes compliance and legal policies such as whistleblowing, ethical procurement, inclusion, etc.

5. Does the company hold itself as being responsible towards the environment? How is it addressing the deteriorating environmental conditions on Earth? Is the company contributing to global warming, water scarcity, and pollution? What is the company putting in place to combat such effects? Did the company pledge to a net-zero operation in a specific timeframe?

6. How transparent is the company about its means of earning profits? What types of reports does it produce and make available to the public?

One of the easiest ways to understand CSR is to realise that it deals with how a company generates revenue instead of what it does with its revenues after being earned. This means, what ethical and environmentally conscious methods are being adopted across the entire operations of the company as it makes profits. This would cover the entire production cycle from the very start of the sourcing of material, to the methods of operations, to how people are recruited, paid, and treated, and finally it trickles down to what service is given to the communities in which the company operates.

In summary, CSR affects three aspects of business and life, and this is often referred to as the 'Triple Bottom Line' effect:

1. Economic.
2. Social – that is, the people.
3. Environmental – matters related to planet Earth.

In this regard, CSR is not:

- **Publicity**. While CSR-driven efforts help companies produce favourable publicity, PR efforts do not constitute the entirety of a CSR strategy. CSR is not PR, the lack of adherence to CSR principles in a company will cost a company a lot of money due to negative publicity and damage to its reputation. Some companies have had to invest millions of dollars in their PR to rectify the ramifications of not following through with their CSR strategies. This is often seen when companies are faced with boycotts, reputational problems such as child labour, resistance to provide transparent reporting on their emissions, and possibly even the inability to attract good calibre employees due to corruption and bad management practices.

- **Philanthropy**. A company's philanthropic quests or charitable contributions cannot constitute or represent its entire CSR efforts. These are only part of it. I caution communication executives to deliver stories on their brand's CSR strategy by limiting it to an act of charity of philanthropy only. What's the use of donating to a 'plant a tree' cause when your products destroy forest lands to get produced.
- **Compliance.** Businesses are expected to have their rules and regulations, and checks and balances in place. The book touched upon Compliance in Chapter 10. Having a code of conduct and an equal pay structure is only part of a company's CSR not all of it.
- **Sponsorships**. While these could be the means by which a company engages and pays back its community, sponsorships cannot represent a company's entire CSR. Sponsorships could be one way in which a company gives back to its community, and their activation could be fulfilling one aspect of the CSR strategy of the company. Sponsorships, therefore, do not represent an entire CSR strategy for an organisation and should not do so.

In recent years, more attention has been paid to how community-driven and environmentally responsible companies are. The pressure on companies to respond to these concerns has been driven by major stakeholder groups including governments, legislation, consumers, vendors in the supply chain, and the public, especially the younger generations.

To better understand a company's stand on CSR, you may ask the following questions:

- How is the company making its revenues and profits?
- How is the company spending its earnings?

- How fair is the company as an employer? Is it an inclusive, equal-opportunity employer?
- How is the company's existence affecting the environment or contributing to its damage?
- How is the company regulating its operations? What policies does it employ?
- How transparent is a company in its reporting? Does it declare its profits and distribution of revenues? Does it measure and monitor its resource consumption and carbon emissions? Does it report on these through ESG reports or others?

Green marketing and greenwashing

Now that we're talking about CSR, let's also bring up the topic of greenwashing. There is a lot of green marketing but limited understanding and commitment from the CEOs and other executives about it.

Green marketing is the promotion of products that are environmentally conscious. These could be products made of recyclable material. They could be biodegradable and not harmful to the environment. They could be better options than other products that do cause harm to the environment. And, finally, they could be products that adopt environmentally friendly packaging such as paper instead of plastic, or renewable energy for their sources of power, such as solar or wind.

Green washing is when you market a product as environmentally friendly when in reality it is not. The term 'greenwashing' was first used as slang and was then added to the *Oxford English Dictionary* in 1999. Greenwashing is the act of deluding consumers regarding the environmentally friendly practices of a company or the environmental benefits of a 'green' product or service.

Greenwashing occurs when marketers overly advertise the green claims of a product when in fact it is not. This puts the brand at risk of criticism or accusations that the company has engaged in misleading behaviour. Which is true. Take, for example, a shampoo product that claims to be environmentally friendly because the packaging is recyclable, yet the inside product is full of toxic chemicals that are very harmful to consumers health or contribute to the deterioration of the climate.

To avoid green washing and embrace green marketing, you need to engage in transparent and ethical communication. Here are some tips:

- Check for the Codes of Responsible Marketing in your industry or sector.
- Evaluate whether promotional activities meet your company's CSR criteria.
- Communicate the results of the CSR activities in your company regularly and openly.
- Make your product claims as specific and factual as possible to avoid misrepresentation and public confusion.
- Evaluate the ROI in areas such as reputation management, employee morale, and community engagement and communicate your results to the public.

Sustainability

Whether marcomms professionals acknowledge it or not, the topic of sustainability is going to play a key role in their work in the years to come. This is true for the simple reason that following the pandemic year, the world can no longer deny the environmental and economic disasters that have come to light. For some, the terms 'CSR' and 'sustainability' are used interchangeably. Sustainability is focused on the environment and is part of a company's CSR direction. In the corporate world, sustainability is undertaking processes and business acts that safeguard the environment – the production of goods and business conduct in the fields of sourcing ingredients, procuring environmentally friendly raw material, and the level of carbon emissions manufacturing products.

Sustainability is most associated with environmental impact but is not only limited to that. It also includes diversity, inclusion for minority groups, and poverty. Think of sustainability as the plan to keep a company afloat, including the safety and thriving of the world around it. Never in the history of communication has the topic of climate change and global warming been more pressing. Climate change is tremendously affecting the prices of raw materials and the working conditions for labour. Sustainability is truly intertwined with communication and can always be supported through sponsorships. Sustainability, however, is a much broader term to both CSR strategies and sponsorships of a company.

Peter Bakker, President and CEO of the World Business Council for Sustainable Development (WBCSD), stated, 'The rules of the game are changing. The world is facing three pressing global challenges: the climate emergency, the loss of nature, and mounting inequality.'

Marcomms professionals, in my opinion, need to get up to speed with sustainability matters. Employees want climate-positive action from companies. This is now demanded by customers and employees, spurring a higher demand for products and services that are environmentally friendly.

Research suggests that 54% of Gen Z think a company's environmental and social efforts are very or extremely important when considering whether to purchase a service or a product.

As these younger audiences become more influential consumers, they are leaning more and more towards eco-friendly products and services, and are paying more attention to climate-related practices by organisations.

The public is growing more aware of the risks of climate change, and both employees and consumers are becoming less accepting of businesses that don't work to reduce their environmental impact. Sustainability, therefore, has become a business imperative.

In ending this chapter, I'd say sponsorships are a highly effective marketing avenue only when carefully studied and planned. Sponsorships do not represent the complete CSR story of a brand, nor how sustainable a company is. They do, however, facilitate means for brands to contribute to communities and become more environmentally conscious.

Sponsorships are integral to a corporate communications plan; it provides memorable moments of truth for brands in an up close setting with their customers. They can help uplift a company's image and increase the awareness with a product or service.

16

CORPORATE EVENTS

'Good fortune happens when opportunity meets with planning.'

— THOMAS EDISON

Events are a wonderful and colourful world of experiences, sensory and exciting by design, memorable and enjoyable in nature. Events are meant to leave their guests with a memorable connection with brands.

Corporate events hold the same goals as general events – to create brand experiences that generate a positive association with your brand in the minds of your customers and employees. Corporate events offer a much needed up-close-and-personal interaction for the brand with its audiences. They enrich a brand experience and are a primary marketing and publicity tool.

Corporate events do not have the advantage of 'frequency' that advertising and PR campaigns have. Campaigns can repetitively drum their customers with the very same message in many shapes and forms. Corporate events lack the repetitiveness factor, and this means they need the instant impact factor. You only have one chance to get it right. Events are considered a one-time encounter and may be forgotten with time. Since corporate events are an interactive extension to a brand and its owners, they are costly if they go wrong. You need time and careful planning to accomplish the goals of your corporate event.

If you are experienced in corporate events, then this chapter will be a good refresher for you. It could serve as a practical induction for a member on your team who is expected to run events as well. If you are new to this, I promise you this chapter is going to come in as handy as a pocket map in a foreign land.

I was introduced to the world of corporate events many years into my career. I found them both incredibly thrilling and stressful. So much planning goes into an affair that is consumed within a few hours or a few days at most. As I learnt my way around them, I discovered that each time you run an event, you add to your learning, and that sometimes, a previous experience in events may not be sufficient to guarantee success in a present one.

Once you set yourself a framework for running events, you will feel much more confident with the task. Throughout the years, I worked on corporate events that hosted a range of 10 to 20,000 attendees a day. Some of these events were private in nature and others were public with an element of live entertainment and broadcasting. The formula is the same for all types of events. What differs is the scale of detail, the operational planning, and most certainly, the time required to prepare. I learnt that you need to be utterly organised and leave no detail to luck.

This is a field where there is always something new and different to try. You would rarely find yourself thinking that you've exhausted all options. Each time you run an event, you will get a lot more inspired to do it again with a bigger or better version.

What are corporate events?

The spectrum of events in general is as stretchable as an elastic band. Here are a few examples of what is considered a corporate event:

- AOP (Annual Operating Planning) meetings.
- New product launches.
- New store openings.
- Press conferences.
- Strategy retreats.
- Training sessions and seminars.
- Ideation and brainstorming sessions.
- Staff gatherings for team building, training, or celebration of a topical day.
- Recognition and awards ceremonies.
- VIP visits.
- Corporate shareholder and board meetings.
- Signing ceremonies for contracts and MOUs (Memorandums of Understanding).
- Ribbon-cutting ceremonies for store openings.
- Trade shows and exhibitions.
- Press briefings.
- Media roundtables.
- CEO roadshows.
- Corporate lunches and dinners.
- Networking events.

- Charity and fundraising.
- Corporate tournaments or sporting events.

Large events like concerts, fashion shows, marathons and the like can also be counted as corporate events, but these require specialised and professional teams to execute them on a large, sometimes enormous, scale. It would be wiser to opt for sponsoring such events and using your time and expertise in promoting your brand on these platforms rather than organising them yourself.

The importance of planning and time management in running events

Successful events don't happen with a blink of an eye, even when being run by someone with extensive experience under their belt, they require time. A date set for an event must be a realistic one. Take a long, deep look into the requirements of the event and do so as early as you can before you commit to a date.

Be clear on the objective of your event

As you begin researching and brainstorming ideas to come up with a theme, clarify and align with all stakeholders involved on the objective of the event. Having a clear goal for your event is like having a frame to the canvas of your picture; it helps you map out the sequence of actions required.

Teams may occasionally swerve when planning an event and end up complicating matters. The initial plan for an event could be a visit from a key influential executive, and the next thing you know, your boss suggests an awards ceremony for high performers and an announcement of a new business venture. The best way to start planning your event is to lock in a clear and a specific objective with your management. Write the objective down in a statement and share it for sign-off with all stakeholders if you need to. If asked to add segments to your event that don't align with the overall objective, explain the complications and risks that may arise from such additions.

Map your event journey

Create a journey for the visitors and write down how you wish to shape their experience. Having a memorable experience is what matters the most in your event. In mapping the guest journey, begin by describing what you wish for them to take from this event and then work backwards. The event journey will identify the key stages and touch points that require attention and branding.

Identify how you wish to bring their attention to the event and get them to decide to attend it. How would you wish for them to engage with your brand during the event and what information do you want them to leave with? In this identification process, consider what behaviours your event visitors are likely to exhibit and what reciprocal interactions you need in place to gain their attention.

Decide on the size and scale of the event

Understanding the size and scale of an event depends on acknowledging the size of the audience. Event experts ask you to allow for a period of 12 to 18 months for planning any event that is expected to host a thousand guests or more. While this could be over-ambitious in the corporate world, it is worth contemplating. It is important that you have an accurate estimate of the numbers of your audiences. You'll also need to group them into types of audiences and then list them in terms of importance. Each group will carry a similarity of some sort; it could be their arrival time, consuming habits, social status, and so on.

It would help to draw a persona for the groups of people representing your event attendees. At the very least, draw these for the key influential attendees. In drawing their personas, you'll be able to arrive at many possible options and ideas that will help you custom-build an event that they will thoroughly enjoy.

Imagine you are about to run a sporting competition for your company. If most of your employees are females aged 35 to 50, would it make sense to run a football competition? What if the owner of your company or your CEO is an avid player of golf? Would you opt for a swimming competition as part of an annual staff meeting?

Setting a date

Regardless of the amount of support and structure you may have, time is essential when it comes to running successful events. Once you agree to a theme, you then need to set a date and a time for your event. It is quite imperative to agree on a date or a few tentative dates for your event and then work your way backwards. A good event needs time for the planning and good execution.

Breaking each task down

The game plan for events involves breaking down each task into smaller tasks and then addressing the time it takes to achieve these.

Sending out the invites ahead of time

You may need to send out a 'Save the Date' invite while you work out the remaining details of the event, including where it will take place. Corporate events do sometimes require that attendees get some work done, like preparing presentations or making a product demo.

Elements of a corporate event invitation

In your invitations, make sure you include the following:

- Date or tentative dates.
- Time in preferably 24-hour format. Be specific with time and mention time segments if they exist. Use Outlook or the corporate mail calendars to lock these in.
- Address and location. If this is a virtual meeting, then make sure a link is shared or ensure the name of the platform on which the event will be hosted is mentioned.
- Dress code and what is optional and what is mandatory. If a dress code is expected to follow a theme, then do mention the theme.
- Mention the itinerary or add a summary of it.
- The names of important guest speakers or VIPs attending.
- Whether attendance is mandatory or optional.

- If admission is paid, draw attention to that and specify the cost.
- Any equipment required to be brought by the guests, like laptops, specific gear, or other sets of clothing.
- Directions and a link to a Google map.
- RSVP details including a reachable mobile number and a responsive email address.
- Last date to RSVP by.
- A link to a website or microsite, if required, with more details about the event.
- A registration link if required.

Write that brief and specify the budget available

If your event is going to be handled by an events company, write a succinct brief to your vendors. I often encounter corporate event briefings that do not specify a budget or a budget cap. Some argue that specifying budgets may restrict the formation of creative ideas, especially when it comes to entertainment and activities. While there is an element of truth to that, it would be unfair to your events team not because a budget will help suggest what really works within your budget.

Choosing a venue

Once you've identified what type of event you are hosting and who your audience is, you'll need to decide on a suitable venue. Here are a few things to consider when deciding on a venue:

- The venue is large enough to host the event comfortably.
- The venue is easy to reach for the attendees.
- Fits within your budget.
- Meets your requirements for sound, light, and entertainment.
- Easily accessible and has enough entries and exits to meet the event capacity.
- Ambience and overall mood of the venue compliments the event theme.
- Internet and cable connectivity meet the event requirements for any broadcasting, live streaming, sound, and light.
- Has the required amount of parking space for those travelling with their own vehicles.
- Has valet parking services if that is required.
- Offers the required amenities such as bathrooms, changing rooms, storage, warehousing, terraces, and outdoor seating if needed.
- If you require food and service from the venue, then you will need to check if their F&B services meet your standards.

The larger your audience, the more important accessibility of your venue becomes. Accessibility investigates what possible hurdles may exist when audiences try reaching the event. These could be traffic, road detours and temporary closures, or weather conditions.

Sometimes events are intended to be far away or remote. Take, for example, a corporate strategy retreat. Some companies select island resorts or out-of-country venues. If this is the case, you will need to understand the flight schedules and other modes of transportation that are available. Suppose there is only a limited number of charter or sea flights to your chosen location – like twice a week only – then you'll need to plan for alternative scenarios in case an attendee missed their flight. You could be holding an event on an island that is only reachable by ferry. You will need to study how transporting your group can work with the existing capacity of the ferries. You also need to find out what other modes of transport, like a helicopter for emergencies, are there as well.

Things to consider when hosting an event in a foreign country

First, you will need to ensure the majority, if not all, of your group can be granted entry to that country. You will need to gain a full understanding of the visa and entry permit regulations. Living in the Middle East, we recognise that not all nationalities have access to all countries and cities, and this could hinder any plans related to hosting in a specific country. Researching who requires an entry permit and how long it takes to apply is on your list of things to do. With events hosted in a country that others need to fly to, you'll need to communicate way ahead of time, research visa requirements, papers required for the visa applications, and the time required for the process of issuing the permit.

Your event date needs to be announced in advance to allow the attendees adequate time to get their papers and travel arrangements in order.

Choose a theme early on

Choosing a theme for your event is often a matter of creativity and it does not necessarily subscribe to a set of prerequisites. The theme of your event could be based on a certain seasonality, or it could be inspired by nature occurrences. It could be inspired by the heritage of the country where the event is taking place. Whatever the case may be, a theme helps you in the branding of the event and it will positively influence the choice of venue, entertainment, menus, and other matters.

Build an itinerary

Event itineraries serve two purposes: to help you plan your event every step of the way and to inform the attendees of how the event will pan out. The itinerary of a corporate event is usually presented in a tabular format and provides a chronological listing of events and the times they are expected to take place. Items that are usually found on itineraries include: expected time of arrival, time of door opening or curtain opening, who is delivering speeches and opening remarks, any tea and coffee breaks, lunch breaks, activities taking place at the venue or on stage, and when the event is expected to end.

Entertainment and team building activities

Corporate events are much more memorable with creative entertainment and team-building activities. Your corporate event could turn into a mundane and tiring excursion if it is not supplemented with some fun.

Experiences and entertainment dissolve the walls people put up around themselves in the corporate world and encourages them to warm up and get to know each other better. When brainstorming entertainment ideas for your event, make sure they are ones the crowd would enjoy, and that they fit within your budget, culture, space, and time parameters.

The choices of entertainment and team building activities are plentiful. You can find agencies that will plan, organise, and run these for you. The agency will have enough knowledge to suggest entertainment ideas that will work well with your audience.

Here are a few ideas for team building and entertainment options that you may consider:

- Live debates: splitting attendees into teams to debate different topics that are not necessarily work-related.
- Trivia style quizzes to test teams on their general knowledge or business knowledge.
- Strategic board games: playing games such as Monopoly.
- Classic team building activities that include an element of speed, following instruction or a kind of sports like pedal tennis or football.
- Drumming: it creates team coherence by having the attendees perform together and in sequences, it releases tensions and grows harmony between the groups.
- Dragon boat race: whenever hosting at a location close to water, dragon boat races are fun to put together.
- Cooking competitions: creating teams that are to cook different types of meals together allows team members to show off their time management and performance under pressure.
- Create your own commercial or short movie: a chance for team members to plot scenes, publish content, and add their humour and creative flair to a production; this is a lovely exercise and leaves the attendees with a piece of content that they can take back home.

- Masterpiece building: teams build artistic masterpieces such as paintings or sculptures. You may experiment with different materials and craft objects.
- Rock my vehicle: teams create moving objects such as boats or cars and test if they work or not.
- Create your chocolate masterpiece: who would say no to an indulgent and aromatic experience working with chocolate and creating a masterpiece from it? This activity will demonstrate the business process from planning to designing, producing, and presenting.
- *The Apprentice* or *Shark Tank* show: using a similar format to these shows, ask teams to pitch new products or business ideas to the business owners.
- Talent shows and competitions: asking teams to showcase any personal talents they have that represent their hobbies and interests.
- Eye gazing: this is a favourite of mine and is inspired by the global eye contact experiment where strangers on the streets of many cities gather on a specific day and randomly sit opposite each other and stare into each other's eyes for at least five minutes. The idea behind this exercise is to allow people to see beyond one's looks, job title, or social status. It can do wonders when desiring a team to bond and dissolve barriers between them.
- Healing and light spiritual activities: these could be group yoga sessions or sound healing meditations using different musical instruments such as the flute or Tibetan bowls.
- Campfire stories: simulating a campfire and asking members to come up with uplifting stories to share.
- Wall of fame: asking each team to create a wall of fame of their collective work achievements.

- Pictionary: Pictionary stimulates the imagination, and either the classic version or a company-related version would be fun to play.
- Old-school sports-day games: it would be fun to go back down memory lane and get a chance to play spoons and balls, and run obstacle races, etc.
- Futuristic style events like VR games and metaverse experiences.

Other ideas that could work wonderfully as entertainment for your corporate events include live painting shows, dance shows, glow in the dark shows, acrobatics, parades, fashion shows, a launch of an NFT, light walkers on stilts, projection mapping on stage, live musicians and stand-up comedians.

Food and beverages

If you are running an event in a hotel, then the selection of food and beverages will rest with the hotel. You can ask for multiple menu options when working with the chef and F&B team. If your event will be serving food once, make sure you have a good selection for the appetisers, main courses, and desserts. If your audience exceeds a 100 persons mark and time for food is limited to a lunch break, then it is best to opt for a buffet style of serving rather than a seated menu. Seated menus often take much longer and require a lot more labour to cook and serve the food. If you do have a large audience but will most likely be seated throughout the event, as is the case with an awards ceremony, then you can opt for a sharing-style menus.

When selecting menus, make sure there is a variety of options. Take into consideration the audience and their dietary needs; for example, gluten-free, pescatarian, vegetarian, vegan, low-carb, low-sugar, kosher, halal, etc.

When your event runs over many days, as, for example, some corporate training courses do, try to introduce more variety to the menu or the venues in which lunch is being served.

When putting together a menu, try to introduce at least two options for each segment of the menu, be it appetiser, main course, or dessert. If you are opting for live food stations during your event, then make sure there are enough stations and chefs to cater to the crowd. Ending up with queues of hungry people will ruin the experience of the event.

If your event is sampling food items, then make sure you have the right licences and permits to do so. Ensure that the caterer handling the food is adhering to the highest standards of food safety, which include hygiene, transport, storage, presentation, and disposal.

If your event includes serving alcoholic beverages, then make sure you have sought the required approvals to do so. Check if your company's policy allows for serving and covering the cost of alcohol.

Dress code

Dress codes for events could be deciphered differently depending on gender and the cultures. What is semi-casual in the US is very different from what is semi-casual in the Far East or Europe. For example, formal attire may require a jacket but not a tie for men. Don't leave room for speculation. In the Middle East and the Gulf region, some events may require the locals to come dressed in their national attire or an attire that is respectful to the cultural and religious norms of the country. These need to be mentioned.

Here is the briefest crash course you can have on dress codes:

Semi-formal, or casual: in some companies, casual means jeans are allowed, and T-shirts and sneakers too. This could also mean linens, khakis, polo shirts, and shorts. If shorts are culturally inappropriate, then please do specify that. For women, casual can also mean floral dresses, day dresses, jacket with shorts or jeans, T-shirts, or other types of tops. If you are hosting an event in a reserved country or at a company that is culturally or religious, then do specify what is acceptable in terms of dress and sleeve length for both men and women. Specify if open shoes are acceptable or appropriate as well.

Business casual: for the male gender, this often means polo shirts or collared shirts are expected with informal pants. Business casual for men almost always indicates closed shoes. Whether jeans are allowed or not differs from one culture to another, so I suggest that you specify that on the invitations. Business casual for female executives can include a skirt, pencil dresses, blouses, blazers and appropriate heels or any shoes that are often found acceptable in the office.

Formal or business attire: this usually means suits, ties, and closed shoes for men. In some regions, this also means the national attire for both genders, and a sophisticated look for women, such as dress pants or a skirt with a matching jacket, or a lady suit.

Other attires would include gala, cocktail, or red carpet.

Seating arrangements

Seating arrangements in corporate events are usually decided based on the type of event, the space available at the venue, and the number of attendees. The most common seating arrangements for corporate events are:

- **Banquet or roundtable seating:** suitable for large groups with each table seating five, eight, or ten individuals. If you require the tables to leave an open end in case the audience is supposed to look in front of them, then this version is called 'cabaret' and is more common in corporate events.
- **A U-shape:** tables and chairs connected to make the shape of the letter U facing the stage or the host of the event. The open end of this structure allows for the presenter to come up close and interact with the audience. This is ideal for business meetings that require long deliberation sessions and is usually ideal for groups below 50 individuals; otherwise, the design becomes ineffective.
- **Theatre:** everyone is seated in parallel lined-up seats facing the front of the hall. This is ideal for large group corporate events that require the audience to pay extra attention to the stage and the material presented.
- **Classroom:** like the theatre style but requires desks or writing support.
- **Hollow square:** as the name implies, the seating is arranged in a square shape. This is ideal for smaller seating capacity and seated menus and outdoor dinners.
- **Boardroom:** usually for senior executive meetings or meetings conducted formally and on a strategic level or when a boardroom

with a table is already installed in the venue. This seating arrangement is ideal for groups of fewer than 30 individuals.

- **Fishbowl style**: common in academia and suitable for medium to large crowds, it is now becoming more common in the corporate world too. The chairs are arranged in a series of circles with a smaller circumference as they draw closer to the centre. The key executives often sit in the inner circle with employees surrounding them in the outer circles.

Floor plans

It is imperative to create a floor plan for your event, especially when you are hosting a big one. Floor plans will show either in 2D or 3D all the elements of your event and how they are sized in relation to the number of crowds expected. Floor plans give you the advantage of envisioning your event, where each function is hosted, and how the audience journey is going to unfold. With a floor plan, you'll be able to see if the space you have is sufficient for the activations you arranged. They also allow you to plan your entries and exits, warehousing, storage, and seating better. A floor plan is very helpful for outdoor events that require large-scale set-ups and stages, parking spaces, and amenities such as toilets and registration booths.

Stage and stand designs

The stage provides the very first impression of an event. It usually is the place where the theme is reflected. Alternatively, if it is a trade show, your stand or exhibition booth would create the first impression. Stage designs are often crucial to the success of an event. The design of the stage can take on many forms and can also follow the specific theme you are hosting.

You need to decide on a proper size for your stage, decided on the design of the screens that it will hold, the backdrops, the lighting, furniture, décor, props and banners it required. They need to stand out, grab attention, and be clearly branded.

Sound and light

Regardless of their size, sound and light are important for every event. They improve the overall experience and add a much-needed element of ambience.

Have a sound and light checklist on hand. This list usually includes the types of mixer boards, microphones, the number of speakers, how many screens are required, and the sizes necessary to be relative to the areas they are placed in. The list could also include further details such as the types of receivers, adapters, and transmitters.

Testing both sound and light is very important and should be done enough in advance to make changes where necessary.

MC (Master of Ceremony)

Large corporate events require a professional MC. In many companies, the CEO or CMO takes on this role. I would advise you to exercise caution in relation to this, and it is often recommended only when these executives have had the right amount of training to be on the stage. Sometimes, the event may be too long for one corporate executive to host.

If you are hosting an awards ceremony for a thousand people, and you expect the stage ceremony to take more than an hour or two, then a talented MC will help you make this part of the event engaging and fun.

When selecting an MC, make sure they fit the theme of the event, and they can host any entertainment segment or team building activities that are planned. A good MC, in general, is well-trained in hosting events, inspiring, entertaining, has stage and has charisma. An MC can be spontaneous on stage when needed, and, most importantly, can engage and energise the crowd.

Making your MC selection is best done when you interview the MC in person and have a long enough briefing and rehearsal sessions with them. Your MC needs to know your audience, the objective of the event, who the key influential people in the crowd are, the background about the brand, the brand persona, and the tonality and flow of the event.

If your MC requires a speech, make sure it is written in simple language and according to the time segments offered on stage. Nothing is more disheartening than a good MC mumbling with long and complicated words and run on sentences on stage.

Photography and videography

Having the right team of photographers and videographers for your event is also important. There are photography teams that specialise in certain types of events. The scope of the event will dictate the size of the team required.

Health and safety

Safeguarding everyone experiencing your event is also one of your responsibilities as an event organiser. Clarify what rules and regulations must be followed and who needs to do what. As I write this book during a global health pandemic, I know well that events in this time require the availability of sanitisation units, social distancing, and mandatory wearing of masks. The pandemic has also affected the way food is served, with a lot of events not allowing sharing platters. Some events now call for a cap on the number of attendees, and in some countries, there is a prerequisite of having everyone show a vaccination certificate or a negative PCR that is valid for as little as 48 hours.

But health and safety are much more than sanitisation and sneezing into a branded mask. Health and safety in events cover many other aspects such as *force majeure* occurrences like the breakout of a fire or a thunderstorm or any natural disaster that prevents the event from taking place.

Having run many events in the Middle East and specifically in a land with a hot climate, I find it funny that I mentioned thunderstorms. Nevertheless, I did have a few unforgettable instances of sudden sandstorms that were strong enough to demolish the build-up of my event onsite.

If you happen to work for a company that has a dedicated health and safety officer, run the event plan by them and note down the health and safety requirements that apply to your company. The health and safety officer can also offer you a risk assessment of the event. All industries have their own, which cover things from food poisoning to animal shows to automotive crashes, and these need to be identified before the event takes place.

You will need to organise first-aid cover for attendees or have a dedicated team onsite. There could be the need for a doctor onsite as well. Familiarise yourself with the emergency exits and who to call in case of one, such as paramedics, and what happens if a medical evacuation is required.

Security

Depending on the type and size of event, you may need police or security officers to look after the welfare of your audience, employees, and the event execution team. They will ensure no outsiders come into the events and will look after valuables, equipment, and important items such as vehicles, décor, branding and any other objects that are necessary for the event to run smoothly. If you are having VIP guests, you may also need to consider hiring dedicated security personnel or vehicles.

Insurance

It is best to provide insurance coverage to everything being constructed or promoted and everyone attending your event, including staff, workers, and vendors. The same goes for the venue, machinery, and equipment. If you are working with third parties, make sure they confirm that they are insured as well.

Weather checks and emergencies

Weather checks are critical to the success of your events, not only the outdoor ones. The weather can affect road traffic and may delay the arrival of people or items to the event. You need to monitor reliable weather-forecast channels, have communication ready, have a back-up plan ready, and be able to move from outdoors to indoors, or vice-versa, when needed.

Now that the world has seen a spike in digital events, internet connectivity has become as important element to an online event. Internet connectivity is important for both the speakers and audience. I will provide a checklist for digital events by the end of this chapter.

Use of radio equipment

Don't underestimate the benefits of having a radio system. These cannot be replaced with mobile phones or WhatsApp messages. If you are using the system or the team is, ensure they understand the communication protocol on these systems and the necessity of having them handy and turned on all throughout the event. Make sure you test your radio equipment and that it is fully charged and if they operate on batteries, that extra ones are available on site. Make sure you identify the radio controller and instruct the team to follow their rules.

Cost tracking and payments

You may need additional seating, food, flowers, microphones, catering requirement, photographers, cameras – you name it – on the day of the event. It is best to track costs carefully and schedule payments on time.

Permits

Make a list of all permits that are required for the event. These could include work permits for stage or kiosk construction, or other permits for hiring promoters, models, actors, DJs, etc.

Sometimes, you may require permits for hiring a specific location, transporting equipment, setting up signage, stage, lights, playing loud sounds after a specific hour, sampling food, etc.

Build a contact list

Make a list of the people who are onsite working with you with everyone's names, phone numbers and addresses. In your contact list, make sure back-up contacts are included. When working with outsourced teams, make sure you know the entire team working on the ground with you.

Clear communication

As a communicator, you need to place your best bets on how to communicate for events. When communicating with attendees, make sure invitations are sent not just in the mail or by email, but also on calendars, and are communicated to administrators of departments. Where necessary, creating WhatsApp groups for events has proven to be very helpful, especially during events that spread over many days.

Sometimes, you also need to follow up on attendance by follow-up phone calls. Assigning points of contact who are readily available to respond to the attendees comes is also needed.

Briefing sessions and rehearsals

Call for briefing sessions with all teams and workers who are taking part in the event before your event begins. The frequency of the briefing sessions depends on the scale of your event. Run a test on sound, music, lighting, photography, and videography. With the photography and videography, identify the locations where interviews will be shot, group photos will be taken.

During the rehearsal session, go over the agenda and sequence of events with the team on the ground. Depending on how lengthy and sophisticated your event is, make sure you rehearse and time the event segments. If this is an awards ceremony, for example, then rehearse it, taking into consideration the time it would take for all winners to be announced, the time required to have them come on stage and receive their award, which could be a trophy or certificate, and where these should be displayed.

Identify which side of the stage the winner needs to come up on and which side or area he or she needs to exit on. If the awards are being handed over by a promoter, make sure they can identify the winners, and if you have many winners, then make sure the trophies with the names marked on them are lined up in the same order as the names are going to be called out.

A similar scenario would be a raffle draws. If you are giving out prizes or gifts on stage, make sure you have the prizes lined up in the same order in which they will be given out.

Working with vendors

The world of events is very broad, and you may hardly find one vendor that can deliver well on all types of events. The choice of vendor needs to reflect the size and scale of your event, and you need to make sure they have the right team and engagement level. The vendor selected needs to have the right type of experience in this specific event, and the teams, both at your end and the vendor's end, are going to have to work well together.

You will need to align with the vendor and agree to a scope of work that is very well-defined and clear. What's important is to study the skillset available with the vendor team to ensure that what they have can build on your concepts and campaign and not restrict them.

Be clear on your budgets as well so as not to exhaust options and to ensure you have the right type of vendor on board.

Request for feedback

Events are a learning process. The more you work in the field, the better you become. Nevertheless, each time you execute an event, you get ideas on how you could have done it better or differently. Knowing that our memories are bound to fail us, it is only fair that you log these in as soon as you can, collectively with the team members that worked with you during the event.

Understanding the attendance and the behaviour of the audience during the event is crucial. Identify when the peak of attendance and excitement was and when the audience experienced fatigue and lost interest. Examine the types of enquires and complaints that were logged in. These should be sought from not just the feedback channels installed but from all staff who interacted with the audience.

The comments you will receive from the feedback surveys that you conduct could also collect ideas and suggestions from the attendees. As they fill you in on their thoughts, try to note these down so you can apply the feedback to upcoming editions of your events.

Post-event reports need to be written with bruising honesty. While events run, many unforeseen glitches or mishaps do take place, and often. These probably go unrecognised by many yet need to be identified on your post-event reports. Additionally, you need to revisit the entire event and see where you could have done things better. Note down the segments of the events that had the lowest and highest engagement and put down ideas to on how these can be improved in the future.

The more improvement ideas you plug in to your report, the better your next event will be. The ideas could range from critical matters like additional scaffolding and lighting structures or better sound systems to perhaps additional directional signage or a different method of distributing giveaways.

No matter how many events you run, you'll find that the crowd is often happy and cheering you on. You will often get many a 'thanks' and 'good jobs' at these. Yet, these should not stop you from asking yourself how else you could have done things better.

Virtual events

We have officially entered the era of virtual events. While some speculate that virtual events are expected to replace many in-person events due to the higher level of convenience and cost efficiencies, I don't think they will ever overtake in-person events. No one can ever discount the importance of face-to-face interactions. Having said that, are most likely going to be running more virtual event.

Here is a list of things to consider when you run a virtual event on an online platform.

- Does it allow an easy and quick registration? Is the platform experience as good from a mobile as it is from a desktop?
- Is it compatible with the technology platforms that are adopted at your company – for example, Microsoft Office, MS Teams, or even the default web browsers that are used in your company?
- How many users can log in at the same time?
- What tracking reports the platform offers?
- What type of attendance reports can you get? For example, how many views per session, or break-out rooms, or on-demand views? Other reports could include matters such as chat engagements, form filling, clicks on links, etc.
- What type of engagement features are offered by the platform, such as raffle draws, polls, votes, chat rooms, etc?
- How can you capture new data from these platforms too, especially if your event is not one for employees, but for customers or the public?

Here are a few considerations when running a virtual event:

Decide if the event requires a secured registration for employees only or if it is open for the public. If this is an event that only employees or a certain group needs to attend, make sure log-in credentials have been sent and shared with everyone ahead of time.

- Decide what options to activate or deactivate; for example, recording the event, turning cameras on, enabling chats and mics for participants.
- Work out a back-up plan in case connectivity is lost and ensure the internet doesn't lag.
- Timing is important to digital events; they don't necessarily follow the same time recommendations as ones held in person.
- The duration of the event is also important to look into. By nature, digital events need to be a lot shorter in duration than in-person ones. Keeping the audience engaged is a lot more difficult, and I know how hard it is to grab someone's attention online for a prolonged period. I have seen that an event for employees needs to not exceed the 40-minute mark while these can run up to three hours in real life.
- Monitor the engagement. As with everything digital, you have the great advantage of having real-time information on the attendees. This means you can see when they are logging on and when are they dropping out.

Hybrid events

Hybrid events, as their name implies, are usually in-person events that include an element of virtuality. This may be a live streaming of the event that audiences other than the attendees can watch, or the inclusion of speakers or presentations through a live broadcast as well.

Hybrid events will require technical preparations.

- What additional cameras, microphones recording support systems and are required, and where will they be placed?

- What additional internet connectivity is required?
- In case some of your audiences are joining from different countries, has the timing of the event been aligned with their time zone?

When audiences are expected to contribute to the event – for example, an online speaker or panel member is joining in – you will need to schedule testing checks with them. You'll need to provide them with advice, such as ensuring their computer's built-in cameras and speakers are working properly, or if a branded virtual background is required.

In both virtual and hybrid events, make sure the team selected has a successful track record in hosting such events, and identify the level of support and support team needed.

Regardless of the nature of the event, this field is so much fun yet requires a lot of organisation and detailed planning. Events are a great propeller for brands and when done right are sure to increase brand love and affinity.

17

BUILDING A MARCOMMS STRATEGY DECK – PART 1

'By failing to prepare, you are preparing to fail.'

— Benjamin Franklin

Jim Rohn's famous quote 'Success is 20% skills and 80% strategy' is awfully true and has stuck with me for years.

The first few chapters of the book provided frameworks that assist in navigating your way into a company and establishing a clear view of where the company is, where it needs to go, and how you can help it get there.

Apart from establishing a marcomms function, be it from scratch or not, putting together a marcomms strategy deck could be daunting. This chapter breaks down a strategy deck into a list of questions that, if answered, can help you articulate your plans through a series of clear actions. It also allows you to channel your thoughts in an organised manner to arrive at a comprehensive strategy that covers the marcomms spectrum, marketing, branding and communication.

This is not a chapter that discusses the many different types of strategies that are out there, nor does it cover strategic thinking philosophies. There is plenty of literature on these out there. I am not here to do the thinking for you, I am here to give you a template that helps you present your thinking in an optimal manner. This chapter follows a guided approach for building a strategy step-by-step through a series of questions.

What you need to get started

If you know what the problem is, you will investigate the right solution. A marcomms strategy deck often includes the following sequence of thoughts:

- A clear understanding of the company's business objectives and future.
- Awareness of the external and internal factors that can either help or hinder the company when it comes to achieving its objectives.
- Knowledge of the competition and the stakeholders.
- The messaging that needs to be rolled out to achieve the company's objectives.

A marcomms strategy deck is broken down into three sections, each focused on the following disciplines:

- Branding.
- Marketing.
- Corporate communication.

Each one of these disciplines contains a remit of channels and mediums. Your job as a marcomms professional is to be a matchmaker and connect the right message to the right channel at the right time. Nothing is set in stone, and like I mentioned in an earlier chapter, sometimes you must go through the process of trial and error. Test, measure, evaluate, and then do it better the next time around.

Questions to ask when building a strategy deck.

Here is a list of questions to answer when building a marcomms strategy deck. These create the foundation of the work. In the next two chapters we will delve into the messaging and channels.

1. What are your company's business objectives?
2. What internal and external factors affect your company?
3. What have you learnt from the past?
4. What role will your department play?
5. Who is your competition?
6. Who is your target audience?

1. What are your company's business objectives?

This question can most likely be answered through the findings from the early chapters, mainly Chapters 3, 4, and 5. This early section of the deck is about how you sell yourself to the management, so don't get lazy and just repeat the company's vision and mission statements. Reiterate your understanding of the company's direction; for example, are they expanding, building awareness, or merely defending their position.

In the case of expansion, explain whether the company is acquiring a horizontal or a vertical approach. That is, if they are acquiring new but related businesses, or new but unrelated types of businesses. Are they launching new sub-products in the same industry or expanding into new customers and different industries?

Business objectives usually fall into the below categories:

Profitability – earning more profits and seeking new growth opportunities or reducing costs.

Growth – business growth in terms of growing market share and size of operations. Depending on the region and the market conditions, be it mature or emerging, companies either strive to maintain their market share or grow it.

Efficiency and effectiveness – optimisation of resources, operations, processes, and organisational structures to allow for optimal efficiencies. This also helps the company react to external and internal changes.

Innovation and technologies – deployment of innovation and technologies to facilitate faster services, accurate reporting, and learning. It could also be to reset a company's position in the market.

Quality improvement – enhancing the quality of products and services through innovation and added value services.

Human development – the company's goals on job creation and employee training.

Community welfare – companies and commercial businesses also play the role of responsible corporate citizens and are expected to increase the welfare of the communities in which they operate. This can be manifested in sustainable initiatives such as reducing emissions or in humanitarian initiatives such as reducing poverty and gender inequality.

2. What internal and external factors affect your company?

There are different ways to answer this question. You may use a generic overview but could unintentionally slip into irrelevancy. Two common management frameworks to use would be the SWOT Analysis or the PESTLE Analysis. The SWOT Analysis covers both internal and external factors, we touched upon it in Chapter 3. The PESTLE Analysis focuses on external factors.

SWOT Analysis

Review your findings from the earlier frameworks in Chapter 3,4,5 and 6 and use a SWOT (Strength, Weakness, Opportunities, Threats) Analysis model to present your findings. Show where the vulnerabilities are, where the business can make more money, and how shareholder value can be increased.

Here is a quick explanation of the elements of a SWOT Analysis:

Strengths – the business capabilities that allow a company to expand and continue growing. These are made available for a variety of reasons; it could be the region you operate in, a first-mover's advantage, a product differentiation, or a territory exclusivity. It can also be the years of experience, the quality of your products and a large market share.

Weaknesses – these are the reasons why a company is not tapping into its fullest potential. This could be due to limitations in the manufacturing operations, a delay caused by imports and exports, lack of a certain skill, growing competition, or changes in customer preferences.

Opportunities – these are factors to utilise in growing your business or allowing it to thrive. Opportunities could be presented in new partnerships, regions, technologies, or innovations.

Threats – these are factors that will threaten the present stance of a company. These could be a change in legislation, a new technology or emerging competition.

PESTLE (Political, Economic, Social, Technological, Legal, Environmental) Analysis

In scanning the external factors, I personally find comfort in the PESTLE model, which was originally created by Harvard University professor Francis Aguilar in 1967. The approach has been refined several times over the years yet remains easy to use and produces amazing results. PESTLE stands for Political, Economic, Social, Technological, Legal, and Environmental factors, all of which constitute the macroeconomic environment that affects your business.

Below are examples of what such factors can be:

Political factors address legislation and policies related to the political environment influencing business operations. For example, an upcoming election may be causing unrest among the people making them less receptive to spending. This can also be presented in sanctions, embargoes, and new policies on recruitment, pricing, and distribution. In the Middle East, political unrest is no stranger to most businesses. The region is known for its political unsteadiness, and in recent years, currency fluctuations, and border situations have greatly affected businesses. Other factors could include changes to foreign trade policies affecting imports and exports, or the addition of value-added tax.

Economic factors could include inflation rates, oil prices for some regions, unemployment rates affecting disposable income, or any other factors related to the supply chain of your company.

Social factors could include the changing demographics of your target audience. You could be competing for the attention of an ageing population, as is the case in Japan, or on the flip side, a very young population as is the case in the Middle East. Wikipedia states that in the Middle East, the median age is 26.8 years. Understanding your demographics will tremendously affect your product development and marketing strategies.

Technological factors will cover what technologies and innovations are going to affect the operations of your company directly or indirectly. To illustrate this point, consider how electrification and autonomous technologies are affecting the automotive sector and how stock trading and FinTech apps are affecting the banking sector.

Legal factors take in matters such as the emergence of new legislation or changes in laws that affect your company or your work as a marketer. These could be changes in data protection laws, trademarks, customer privacy, or internet safety laws. As of late, the e-commerce world is facing an increasingly demanding regulatory system that is always issuing new laws.

Environmental factors include changes in the environment that are leading to scarcity of resources and other supplies that affect a company's access to raw material and good labour. Environmental factors could be related to the harsh weather conditions brought about by climate change. They also take into account demands from world organisations such as the UN for sustainable sources of energy. To learn more about the environment and how it affects a company, read the section on CSR in Chapter 15.

Based on the PESTLE Analysis, you can draw conclusions on how your industry is evolving. You can research and present trends by reading industry publications or downloading market reports. One of the simplest things to do is to read online research and customer feedback surveys.

Technology today pretty much touches all aspects of life. I can't believe there are coffee makers out there that now have voice recognition. The start of every year is an opportunity to spend time researching the latest trends in technology. As communicators, we have never seen a time when technology and marketing have become so intertwined. This does not hold true in sales and advertising only, but in designing seamless customer journeys as well.

3. What have you learnt from the past?

In this section, you are going to touch on what the department delivered in previous years and what lessons were gathered in the process.

The objective of this section is not to show off how good you were or how awful your predecessor was but what can be done to make things better.

It is also in this section that you can show how marcomms budgets were spent and how the spend can be better utilised in the future. This was addressed in Chapter 6.

Below is an example of a summary of marcomms projects delivered and how you can present them. In the table below, the percentage of completion and a summary of learning and setbacks on each key project are presented.

Discipline	Milestones	% of Com-pletion	Setbacks	Learning	Way Forward
Branding	Brand positioning exercise. Brand guide revamp. Environmental branding exercise.	100% 100% 45%	Budget on hold.	Workshop implementation.	Commission a branding agency for environmental branding.
Marketing	Increased lead generation by x%. Improved conversations by x%.	Ongoing	Late briefing from businesses.	Provide additional time for planning.	Closer collaboration with the sales and commercial units.

Discipline	Milestones	% of Com-pletion	Setbacks	Learning	Way Forward
Promotion	Delivered 5 key promotions. Cross-promoted with online commerce.	85%	Legal revisions and contractual agreements required more time than anticipated.	Manage stock and logistics.	Implement an online stock control system. Partner with a more reliable delivery service provider.
Public & Media Relations	Increased PR value by 23%. Increased coverage of interviews.	100%	Increase the brand SOV (Share of Voice). Increase media reach and media value.	Improved media relations strategy contributed to more quality coverage.	Increase the number of round-tables and direct stories pitched to journalists. Find new social media influencers to collaborate with.

Discipline	Milestones	% of Com-pletion	Setbacks	Learning	Way Forward
Customer Relations	Launched a segmented commu-nication campaign.	97%	Imple-mentation of CRM systems required longer inte-gration than anticipated.	Better time predic-tion on the technology implementa-tion side.	Convert internal newsletter to a web-based blog.
Sponsor-ships	Carried out x sponsor-ships suc-cessfully. Introduced smaller-scale community sponsor-ships.	90%	A drop in ROI to previous years due to a drop in footfall.	Re-evaluate long-term sponsorships on yearly basis.	Consider a new platform or launch a spon-sorship-related product promotion.

In this section, you can list any challenges in the present marcomms functions, such as:

- Marketing budgets are below industry average. For example, in your industry, budgets usually range from 5% to 7%, but yours is at 3%.
- In order to meet competition, your company may need to increase spend by at least 2%.
- Marketing budget is heavily dependent on promotions, and moving forward, you need to reduce the percentage of promotions and increase publicity and brand building.

4. What role will your department play?

Now that you have demonstrated your full understanding of where the company stands and what it wants to achieve, your department will be providing the strategic marketing and communication services. Chapters 7 and 8 are designed to help you arrive at an accurate vision of your marcomms function and the type of work it will offer.

5. Who is your competition?

In this section, you can present the competitive landscape of your company and show what your competition has been up to. You may present a comparison that shows the areas in which your competition is winning and the ones in which you are. If you are lagging behind the competition, it is important to explain the consequences of not catching up.

Presenting your competition can also be done in a simple fashion by categorising it into three types:

Direct competition – companies that are offering the same product or solution to the same audience.

Indirect competition – companies that are offering different products and solutions to the same audience and can possibly take them away from you. A power generation company offering gas-fuelled generators can face indirect competition from a renewable energy company offering solar panels.

Replacement competition or phantom competition – companies that offer a very different product or solution to yours yet compete against the same purchasing power your customers hold. Take, for example, a watchmaker facing competition from a holidaymaker because the same audience is choosing lifetime experiences over buying expensive watches. In recent years, multimodal transportation platforms such as Uber have become a replacement form of competition to car makers. These new entrants are trying to convince customers not to buy cars and to shift from an ownership model to a usership model. Replacement competition can sometimes impose a larger threat to a business than its direct competition.

6. Who is your target audience?

In this section, you will identify your target audience. The best way to identify your audience is to list all groups that have two-way relationship with your company. You can also list them in terms of their influence on your business. Here is an example:

- Customers.
- Prospective customers.
- Employees.
- Partners or principal brands.
- Local communities.
- Investors and shareholders.
- Governments.
- Trade associations.
- Political groups.
- Labour unions.

- The media.
- Suppliers.
- Stockholders.
- Society.

Prioritisation is the process of identifying your audience, and it is very important. As Jeroen De Flander said, 'You cannot be everything to everyone. If you decide to go north, you cannot go south at the same time.' As you list the audience groups you are targeting, revisit their influence on your business and list them in the order of their importance.

The next chapter will build more on the target audience analysis and will then move to the messaging house section.

18

BUILDING A MARCOMMS STRATEGY DECK – PART 2

'Get closer than ever to your customers. So close that you tell
them what they need well before they realize it themselves.'

— STEVE JOBS

After you have identified the business objectives, target market and competition, you need to conduct an in-depth assessment of your customers and the brand's customer journey. This is often referred to as customer personas.

Customer personas are a key step to the success of your marcomms campaigns. The framework exercises in chapter 4 and 5 should help you gather some data on your customers.

Today's technology enhancements can assist you in building and documenting an up-to-date collection of customer profiles. If your company is using a customer data platform that then the platform will be able to provide you with a wealth of information on customer behaviour across every touch point on their journey.

The first step in identifying your customer personas is to have a clear understanding of your customer experience. Customer experiences were briefly touched upon in Chapter 3 in the First Impressions Framework.

Customer experience

Understanding your customer experiences begins with building your core customer journey. A customer journey begins once the customer considers the purchase of a product or service until the actual transaction takes place.

A customer journey is often broken down into five stages:

Awareness – this begins with the moment the customers begin their research on a product or service they wish to have.

Consideration – this is when the customers begin to close on their options on which brands to consider.

Conversion – this is a key stage when brands work on converting potential customers to actual ones.

Retention – is when a brand needs to keep their customers locked in by satisfying them and keeping them coming back.

Advocacy – when your customers love your brand and turn into brand custodians promoting the brand to their friends and family.

In analysing your customer journey, you also look at:

- **Points of friction** – these are the painful moments where the customers are unsatisfied be it online or offline. These could be call dropouts, incomplete searches, discrepancies in prices, or delays in delivery.
- **Accountability** – your employees know who is accountable for every stage of the customer journey and the customer feels they know who to contact.
- **Data-driven decisions** – your company has accurate and enough data to make informed business decisions.
- **Training** – you are able to put in place the right types of training programmes for your employees to service your customers better.
- **Optimised conversion** – you can identify what is needed to produce higher quality leads and efficient ways to convert them into actual sales.

Creating customer personas

Based on your mapping of the customer journey, you can now create the profiles of your customers. Customer personas need maintenance and upkeep. The factors we discussed in the PESTLE Analysis in the previous chapter affect customer behaviours and the defined personas that were attributes to them.

You may also need to conduct a research exercise to arrive at your customer personas. In this exercise you will need to map the sales or service journey and conduct a gap analysis. The result of the gap analysis would be a suite of enhancements to your customer's journey, both in the short-term and in the long-term.

The type of research that you do could be a mix of qualitative and quantitative research. Qualitative is simply the non-numerical form of data. It is an outcome of feedback surveys, focus groups, community engagements, and suggestions brought forward by customers or employees. Quantitative research is more of the numeric or econometric data extracted from sales transactions reports, engagement reports and market reports to help you understand the customer attitude towards your brands.

Questions to ask when building a customer persona profile:

- What are the priorities of their lives?
- How is their lifestyle shaped? What are their spending patterns?
- What is their outlook on a career? How do they earn an income?
- What technology do they most frequently use?
- What social media channels do they consume the most?
- What brands do they like?
- What channels of communication do they prefer to use in their interaction with brands?
- Who are the influencers in their purchase decisions?
- How do they search for and buy products?
- How much do they contribute to your profitability?
- What do your products and services offer them? What needs do these products meet?
- What additional products or services would benefit them?

Use a descriptive approach in presenting the profiles of your target audience. You can do so by telling their stories. Here is a sample of a customer persona:

Maya is a 30-year-old expatriate living in Dubai. She works for an advertising agency because she loves the blend of art and science in her career. She loves the fast-paced life, and the glamour of travelling for client's video shoots. She works on a make-up brand and is quite influenced by the beauty products she promotes on her job. She has a morning facial routine and a before-bed one too. She is constantly trying on new eyeshadow and lipstick shades and never leaves the house without some make-up on. She is constantly dressed in colourful, mismatching clothing that resembles high-end street fashion. She rarely visits a store and loves to browse online fashion platforms such as Shein and Namshi. She loves L'Oreal, MAC, Subway and Perrier brands. She orders her clothes, fresh chicken, cheeses, and organic greens online. She spends her weekends at home binge watching Netflix and Apple TV original series with her fiancé.

Maya often wonders if her job will allow her to be an available mother and reads random articles on Medium about parenthood. She herself publishes her writings on poetrysoup.com and drafts random posts on life and personal development on LinkedIn. When she feels conflicted about her career, torn between the euphoria of delivering an award-winning campaign after long nights of work and how much she misses her little niece, she swipes her screen up and randomly orders a meal on Deliveroo. Maya wants to save up and be conscious consumer who can help save the planet. She wishes to have an affordable electric car such as a MG ZS EV and does not wish to spend her income on lavish city brunches. She prefers to travel on smart budgets using Airbnb short-term rentals. Her dream is to be the next Tina Fey, but Arab and curvy.

With the clarity you have gained, you can then create themes for each of the personas you are targeting. Here are a few examples of themes:

- Progressive achievers – family-driven, high achieving corporate executives. They live by the 'work hard play hard' philosophy.

They want to live with smart style and provide for their families at the same time.

- Frugal environmentalists– those who bargain till the last minute, most likely to buy second-hand or lease instead. They consider a minimalist approach to consumerism not for saving money but for contributing to the issue of climate change. They look out for seasonal discounts, and often buy second-hand items online.

- Impulsive glitterati– often rich, famous, and good-looking. They shop for entertainment and therapeutic fulfilment. They spend a lot of time online eye-shopping high-end brands and are out and about reporting their trendsetting behaviour on social media.

- Meticulous researchers – they love to research and ask questions on BuzzFeed and WikiHow. They watch YouTube reviews and DIY tutorials before a purchase. They are frequent contributors to star ratings online and often skip word-of-mouth recommendations and place their trust in Google.

- Young trendsetter – youthful, ambitious, self-motivated, have a lot of hobbies and side-hustles, they want to become online influencers and wish to travel and explore the world.

The theming exercise will help you decide how many campaigns you want to run and what type of messaging you need to reach your audience. These campaigns make up your messaging house and the 'positioning' part of the STP approach.

In presenting your customer personas, you need to cover the customer's demographic, lifestyle, life goals, shopping behaviour, the technologies they use and the brands they like. Here is an example of a brand persona for a car dealership.

Progressive Achievers

Demographic profile:

EMIRATI, MARRIED WITH KIDS, MIDDLE AGED, MULTIPLE CARS (4-5)

Government employee in mid-level role

Key codes:
- Comforting simplicity - ease of usage
- Reliable, trustworthy
- Smart choice
- Image maintenance

KEY DEFINERS
- **Family is priority** and all decisions are made keeping their preferences & comfort in mind
- Leads a **very planned life**, keeps key milestones in mind and works towards it to **always provide better for his family**
- Takes **regular breaks with his family & friends. Seeks novelty** only in terms of travel & going out, **keeping in mind his family's comfort**
- **Evaluates his options thoroughly**, willing to take career risks only for better job prospects/ more income

GOALS
- To make his family proud by achieving **professional success and climbing up in the work hierarchy**
- Aspires to **start a side business in future** that can be additional source of income for his family
- Wants to **provide good education** to his children that can help them have a stable future with changing time putting a lot of challenges

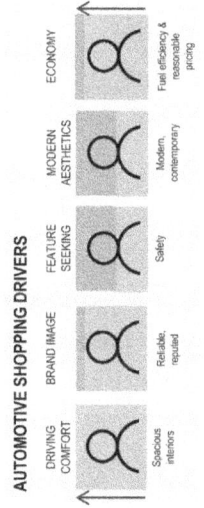

AUTOMOTIVE SHOPPING DRIVERS

DRIVING COMFORT	BRAND IMAGE	FEATURE SEEKING	MODERN AESTHETICS	ECONOMY
Spacious interiors	Reliable, reputed	Safety	Modern, contemporary	Fuel efficiency & reasonable pricing

Brand consideration: Lexus 570, Toyota Land Cruiser, Cadillac escalade, Nissan Patrol

LIFESTYLE
- Weekdays are spent at work, followed by spending time with family. **Relaxing/ Me Time is usually indoors** (TV/ Play Station)
- Weekends are **strictly with family & relatives, occasional outings with friends**
- Checks out **latest information** (work related or general) to keep himself updated
- Takes out time to **work out/ exercise**

TECHNOLOGY
Technology is associated with speed, convenience & efficiency. Stay up to date with new technology basis what they hear from their younger peers

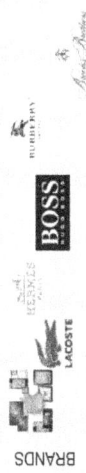

Critical for fast communication, convenience & efficiency

Prefer games and viewing select content

BRANDS

VEHICLE FUNCTIONAL NEEDS
- Spacious & comfortable interiors for family travel
- Safety enhancing features
- Economical choice from a reliable brand

EMOTIONAL NEEDS
- Trusted choice that reflects the family's progression
- Simplicity that is comforting

What messaging will you use to appeal to your customers?

Deciding on your messages is a crucial point that will help you envision the type of frequency and type of messaging that you will cluster in your campaigns addressing your personas. You need robust and compelling messages for your audiences. The framework of your messages needs to be coherent and mapped against different marketing channels. Design the number of campaigns that need to be executed to meet the objectives stated above.

Marketing campaigns usually fall into different categories, and each serves a purpose.

Broadly speaking, the three types of campaigns are:

- **Thematic campaigns.** These carry emotional narratives that can create harmony and bonding with your brand. They speak of the brand's greater purpose. They are effective brand awareness tools that build a relationship beyond fulfilling your need with a brand.
- **Seasonal push campaigns**. Seasonal campaigns are tactical by nature and are designed around the season of high demand or low supply. They are promotional in nature and intended to generate more sales. They focus on value-added or price points to drive instant demand.
- **Product campaigns.** These are product launches or re-launches that are used for new products, product extensions, and sub-products.

Do not fall into a plan driven only by one type of messaging. This will yield results in the short term but not in the long term. Even with the tightest of budgets, I always advocate for thematic campaigns as part of the messaging.

A marcomms messaging house is always focused on the position and the value your brand wants to offer.

Branding

We touched upon branding in Chapter 3. There are different outlooks on the term 'branding', and it is used differently from one company to another. In retail-driven companies, branding is considered part of the marketing remit. In others, it falls under corporate communications. To ease the task of planning for your brand, I've kept it as a stand-alone discipline.

Brands are constantly evolving; a brand grows with the company. The elements that constitute a brand strategy are stipulated in the diagram below.

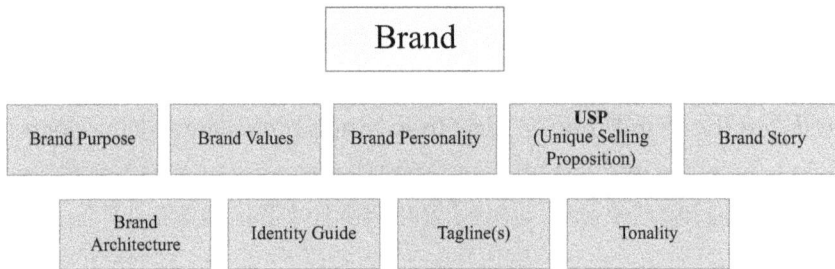

Brand				
Brand Purpose	Brand Values	Brand Personality	USP (Unique Selling Proposition)	Brand Story
Brand Architecture	Identity Guide	Tagline(s)	Tonality	

Brand purpose. A brand purpose is the overarching reason why a company or an institution exists beyond its commercial and profitability objectives. It is the essence that has brought the commercial idea to life. A brand purpose paves the way to a brand vision and mission statement. A company vision is a statement that encapsulates where the company wishes to be in the future. The mission statement is the series of principles and actions the company will adopt to achieve its vision and stay true to its purpose.

Brand values. Brand values are the series of principles that a brand will adopt while it is setting out to achieve its vision and conducting its day-to-day operations. These values can also change with time. They are set in place to align the company to one direction. Brand values were discussed in depth in Chapter 11.

Brand personality. Brand personality or brand persona is the attribution of human traits to a company to facilitate the manifestation of its objectives. The Brand Personality Framework is presented in Chapter 11.

Brand USPs (Unique Selling Propositions). A brand USP is the reason why the brand is different to its counterparts and how it is set apart from its competition. USPs were covered in Chapter 3.

Brand identity. A brand identity is a collection of elements that make up the brand. These range from tangible elements such as logos, colour palettes, and visuals to intangible elements such as brand stories. Brand identity was covered at length in Chapter 12.

Brand Tagline. A brand tagline is a punchy and memorable way to express its USP to its customers throughout its multi-disciplinary campaigns. Brand taglines were also discussed at length in Chapter 12.

Tone of voice. While the tone of voice of a brand is part of its brand identity, it is one of those crucial elements in the formation of a brand, and, as such, it deserves regular review. You can read more on tonality in Chapter 11.

Marketing

The objectives of your annual marketing plans are derived from the fundamental marketing mix of 4Ps. Online businesses can also refer to the 9Ps model, which can be found in books focused on digital marketing. These objectives reflect the company's business objectives.

The marketing 4Ps model is as follows:

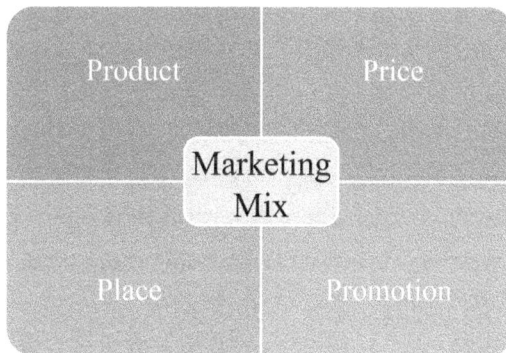

Product: In this section, you list the product strategies and plans, such as:

- New product lines and inventions.
- Product line extensions.

349

- Product line alterations to become more sustainable or suit a specific market.
- New or updated packaging and product design for renewed interest.

Price: the pricing strategy adopted:

- Fixed price in all territories.
- Local pricing targeted at different territories.
- Reduced or increased pricing to address any pricing issues.

Place: Identifying the strategy to be adopted in the distribution of your product or service:

- Expansion geographically.
- Change or upgrade retail channels.
- Addition of new channels like online markets.

Promotion: The marketing messages that will persuade your audience to buy your goods. Promotions are the promises made to your customers, in other words, the advertising messages. These are covered in the Messaging House section of the chapter above.

Marketing channels

Here, you can address how each marketing channel will be utilised, and which ones may not be of service. Here is a reference framework for marketing that can guide you.

The marketing spectrum ranges from digital to traditional channels. The disciplines of marketing are many and will vary depending on the nature of your business and the type of products you sell. The importance of each will be set by you. The effectiveness of your channels is highly affected by the objectives you have set.

Traditional			**Marketing Channels**				Digital
Personal Selling	Cross-Selling	Events/ Roadshows	Advertising	Email Marketing	Social Media	Digital Display	
Direct Selling	Sales Promotion	Social Selling	SEO/SEM	Mobile	Online & Web Commerce		

Digital marketing channels

Google's definition on digital marketing goes like this: 'Digital marketing is the process of building and maintaining customer relationships through online activities to facilitate the exchange of ideas, products and services that satisfy the goals of both parties.' The keyword here is 'online'. Digital marketing is mostly digital advertising taking place over the internet and mobile platforms.

- **Search Engine Optimisation (SEO):** SEO is the process of refining your website using off-page SEO techniques so that it will be indexed and ranked by search engines naturally. This includes organic listing, paid listings, and additional elements such as Google Maps, images, shopping results, and more. SEO allows you, over time and by using the right keywords, to give your brand top-ranking visibility on the search listings.

- **Search Engine Marketing (SEM):** SEM allows you to display your ads via the results produced by search engines. Both SEO and SEM are about getting more visibility and traffic from the search engines for your company or website. Year on year, research shows the increased effectiveness of SEM for brands, both B2C and B2B.
- **Digital display:** Digital displays are the most common form of digital ads and relate to paying for advertising spaces on online channels, such as social media channels or other forms of online and mobile channels. These are highly effective because they allow you to target different segments of viewers with customised messages. They vary in forms and the most common ones are banner ads, programmatic and retargeting. Banner ads come in a variety of placements and direct the view to your page. Retargeting allows the ad to reappear over the digital journey of the targeted customer on the different websites he or she is visiting. Digital display ads are also very popular on social media platforms.
- **Email:** Although it is a rather mature technology, having been around for two decades, email marketing, when done right, is highly effective in terms of engagement and value. It has always proven effective for both B2C and B2B business, when utilised correctly. Modern-day retail, especially the fashion and beauty industries, is highly dependent on email marketing.
- **Online and web commerce:** This section covers the presence of your website and commerce platforms. Websites are the credible way in which companies and brands communicate with customers and mark the success of the customer journey. They require specific customisation to ensure customers are connecting and finding the content that they need. They are also the gateway to

a company's online commerce, where it can sell its products and collect customer insights.

Address any enhancement or changes required on:

- **Site layout and design**. Websites require refinement of the overall aesthetics and appeal every couple of years. Also ensure the latest web technologies are integrated to allow for dynamic content such as video.
- **Commerce**: Brands planning to sell online will need to work on the commerce aspect of their website to create easy and safe purchasing experiences. Commerce sites need to address the element of customisation, where the content is displayed differently depending on the viewer's needs.
- **Media and blogs:** A modern website will require an updated media gallery displaying all the latest news and a blog. I touched upon blogs in Chapter 3, and these are highly effective for both marketing and PR purposes.
- **Careers:** Your website might require an update or the addition of a 'careers' portal. The 'careers' portal can help you build a database of potential new employees and should provide input into the working culture of the company.
- **Content:** Your website's content needs to be updated and rich. It should include interactive elements and forms in addition to the generic suite of photos and videos.
- **Two-way communication**. Present website requirements need to allow for the company to interact with its visitors and interested parties.
- **Mobile:** These will include the types of ads and commerce that are displayed and generated on mobile phones. They usually

accommodate the small screen size and other customisations adapted to a person's use of his or her mobile phone. Mobile marketing includes location-based targeting, text messaging, display ads, brand mobile apps, and in-app ads as well.

- **Social media:** These will include the advertising campaigns you wish to run on the social media channels that are best suited to your audiences and messages. The most popular channels are Facebook, Twitter, Snapchat, LinkedIn, and TikTok among others.

A comprehensive check list for websites was provided in Chapter 3.

Conventional marketing channels

- **Personal selling:** Creating demand for your products and services when your sales team establishes a direct relationship with the customer.
- **Direct selling:** This is achieved by a company's direct sales force or authorised dealers and distributor networks through licensing and franchise agreements.
- **Cross-selling:** This is achieved by bundling the sales of your products or services with others from your portfolio or outside products that complement yours.
- **Sales promotions:** Special deals in the form of discounts or value-added deals and bundles that encourage the customer or consumer to either try the product or repeat its purchase. These usually include coupons, rebates, and multiple purchase offers and deals.

- **Events and roadshows:** Covered in Chapter 16, these range in type and are up-close-and-personal experiences with the customer in a physical or digital setting to encourage product and service trials and purchases. These could include product launches, sampling activities, and demonstrations.
- **Traditional advertising:** There are many different means that fall under this banner by which a brand can disseminate its tactical and thematic messaging. These are often identified as television, cinema, and radio commercials, out of home or outdoor billboards, and newspaper and magazine print advertisements or advertorials. Other traditional forms of advertising can include the distribution of flyers and pamphlets.

Find your ideal mix

In putting together your marketing strategy, map your marketing objectives against the channels that fit best. For example, if your objective is to increase the quality of your leads, you may need to reassess or introduce retargeting techniques or up the delivery in your performance marketing. You could need more display advertising or social media influencer endorsements.

If you are a B2B business, you may need more focus on SEO, and if it is going well, maybe it's time you consider SEM. B2B businesses do benefit from social media as well, if the channels are right. LinkedIn's Sales Navigator solution has proven effective. You may be operating in a market where traditional marketing is still effective.

Despite all the changes in how people consume music, FM radio stations still work in some regions and industries. Your research and findings should help you arrive at the right marketing mix and chan-nel selection and prioritization.

In the next chapter, we will look into corporate communications strategy frameworks and how these get built.

19

BUILDING A MARCOMMS STRATEGY DECK – PART 3

'The art of communication is the language of leadership.'

— JAMES HUMES

Corporate communications strategy

The next part of your department's strategy will cover corporate communication disciplines, and in this chapter, we will focus on PR and internal communication matters. We begin with public relations and media relations at work. Chapter 13 is dedicated to PR, and on the spectrum below, it is closely intertwined with your marketing and messaging house. We then touch upon other disciplines that were also covered in the book – Sponsorships and CSR in Chapter 15, and Corporate Events in Chapter 16.

When planning for corporate communications, you are looking at all or some of the below:

	Corporate Communication	
Internal		External

Brand Archives	Corporate Reports	Corporate Publications	Crisis Management	Investor Relations	Media Relations	Public Relations

Internal Communication	Leadership Communication	Corporate Forums	Sponsorships & Events	News Management

- **Public relations:** The act of sharing stories with the media and publishers to build the trustworthiness and credibility of your brand(s).
- **Media relations:** Developing relationships with journalists, editors and content creators. Media relations is built over a series of tactics that include pitching stories, pitching for interviews, and supplementing the media with opinion pieces and articles of different forms.
- **Investor relations:** This is a specific discipline in PR in which listed publicly listed companies communicate with their investors and shareholders. It includes the many types of communications the company conducts with its community of investors, stakeholders, financial institutions, and governments. These include updates on the company's achievements, organisational structure and leadership, and financial performance.
- **Corporate publications and corporate reports:** The act of producing publications that are created by the company to relay its news to specific audiences. These could be internal and external newsletters, online magazines, and corporate reports such as

annual reports, feasibility studies, financial reports, and sustainability reports.

- **Crisis communication**: This is the planning and preparation of coordinated strategies for disseminating messaging and information required in times of crisis where a company's reputation is at risk. Crisis situations can be operational or reputational in nature.

- **Archives:** Corporate archives contain all types of material, such as reports, press clippings, campaign messaging, photos, videos, bios, and other items that are worth preserving to help the communication in the company remain connected and of value.

- **Leadership communication**: Any type of communication that is disseminated from the leadership of the company. This includes messages from the board, C-suite executives, and managers in the form of memos, announcements, speeches, and business updates. Leadership communication is both internal and external.

- **Internal communication:** As stated in Chapter 14, internal communication is the accumulation of all initiatives that are dedicated to the company's internal audiences. These come in the form of events, activations, and announcements.

- **Community relations:** Referenced in Chapter 15, community relations are undertakings by a company to serve the communities in which they operate with the objective of positioning the company as a responsible corporate citizen. These initiatives come in multiple forms such as diversity and inclusion initiatives, environmental initiatives, sponsorships, and events.

- **Corporate forums:** These are get-together meetings, either virtual or physical, for the stakeholders of a company, either external or internal, to exchange ideas and relay messages. These could range from annual operating plan meetings to press conferences to strategic retreats.

- **Sponsorships and events:** Covered in Chapters 15 and 16 of the book, these include trade shows, exhibitions, congress participations, sponsorships of sporting platforms, and different types of events.

Putting together a PR strategy

When discussing your PR Strategy, be sure of the PR and media objectives. State your long-term publicity goals. These would include matters such as gaining product publicity, securing sponsorships, disseminating news and corporate stories, managing crises, educating your audiences, giving back to the community, training your media spokespersons, and managing governmental affairs and investor relations for larger companies that are public.

Here are examples of broad communication PR objectives:

- Increase your brand reach with crafted news to targeted media outlets. These curated stories can be around the company's solutions for customers, thought leadership messages from the seniors, and how the products are being researched and innovated.
- Develop PR campaigns with key stakeholders and employees to continue the storytelling of your company.
- Develop a PR extension to your marketing campaigns. This is achieved by building on your product and service campaigns. Become the go-to source for media commentary on an issue related to the industries you operate in.
- Create PR stories that are a match to your company's USPs.
- Prioritise the media channels (TV, radio, podcasts, industry titles, and speciality magazines, blogs, and online forums) by creating

an overarching suite of PR stories. What makes a good PR story is covered in Chapter 13.

- Build on the momentum with the existing local and regional news. The continuity of your PR plans will require a PR channel mix, including press releases, press conferences, media gatherings, lining up interviews, testimonial campaigns, sponsorships, CSR initiatives, social media content, branded content, and employee engagement content.
- Expand the company's media coverage and increase traffic to its online and social outlets.
- Encourage further trials of your products through customer testimonies.
- Seek out speaking opportunities and forum participations for the executives of the company.
- Highlight your CSR contributions and turn them into stories that the media wants to follow.
- Profile your leadership team through the delivery of key articles and opinion pieces.
- Use your corporate publications as a means of publicity and positive image building.
- Keep an eye on new and emerging media influencers who have cultivated a community of followers that resemble the company's potential customers. Create plans to engage with them to communicate your messages, thereby creating a sense of authenticity and trust.
- Update and diversify your media lists. When working with a PR agency, make sure you are personally looking at the media lists and that you are aware of the movements of journalists from one news channel to another.
- Prepare a wish list of topics and questions that can be used in pitching for interviews.

- Identify the trends and topical days that you want your company and brand custodians to have specific commentary and insights on.
- Build on existing viral topics and trends by issuing commentary by the company's spokespersons.
- Be ready to address crisis situations such as shortage of stock, resignation of key employees, the impact of your products on the environment, product recalls, and a lot more.

Your PR delivery channels

Corporate PR stories can take on many forms, all of which were discussed in Chapter 13. Here is a list of the most popular channels:

- Press releases.
- Articles.
- Interviews.
- Quotes and commentary.
- Business and market news.
- Sponsored news.

Press Releases

Chapter 13 explained the process of creating a press release and the topics that are usually covered by them. When creating a PR strategy, evaluate your press releases and see how else you can improve on their content and coverage potential.

Corporate press releases cover product launches, corporate announcements and the company's performance and achievements.

Today, there are many ways in which the content of your press releases can gain more leverage and increase your brand's earned media.

In addition to the list of topics covered by press releases in Chapter 13, you can always find ways to talk to the press. Your press releases can cover news about new technology upgrades, such as added features to your commerce site or mobile app. You can also talk about the number of app downloads or increased visits to your side. You can run surveys and polls with your customers on their preferences and shopping behaviour in your industry and share the results as well.

A company's CSR efforts are often picked up by the media. It could be a new charitable contribution to a cause, an internship programme for the youth of a specific minority group, a launch of a diversity and inclusion programme.

Your press releases can also cover stories on your employees. Many companies have employees who have inspirational stories about their personal quests and achievements. These could be about employees who have earned new certifications, written books, completed spartan races or run a local philanthropic quest.

Chapter 13 has a dedicated section on what makes a good press release.

Articles

Your PR strategy will have to include pitching articles to one publisher at a time instead of mass pitching. When pitching your article, explain to the publisher why they would benefit from the content. You can do so by making your company or its spokesperson the expert on the position of a certain industry trend or current situation. You can also pitch an article on an ongoing news story or major upcoming event.

Your articles can include stories on how the company or one of its businesses have launched a new strategy, overcome a major hurdle, or changed its course of action. Your articles can also shed light on the latest market findings on a specific technology or innovation. It could also be a list of useful information on the benefits related to your products and services.

Articles on industry and market topics need to represent two sides of a story. An element of disagreement or opposing view is needed to establish the credibility of the story line.

Interviews

Interviews can be printed, audio or video. They allow your spokespersons to be positioned as authority figures on topics related to their industry. The etiquette of pitching interviews and training your spokespersons on media engagements were covered in Chapter 13.

Quotes and commentary

Although short in nature, the frequency of quotes and commentary allows your company's name to be more present in the media scene. These usually fall under the category of your company's spokespersons commenting on breaking news or industry trends that are making the spotlight. Your quotes could also be linked to major events taking place in your area which in one way or another have an impact on your business. This can also cover social media viral news and trending hashtags.

Business and market news

This is another avenue where the company can share information on the state of affairs in the industry and forecast trends in the market.

Sponsored news

PR is not free and cannot always be picked up by media outlets. Setting aside a budget for your PR is important, this includes buying advertorial space and paying the fees of social media influencers. Benefits include expanded media coverage and better SEO ranking. It increases your brand loyalty and produces higher engagement from your employees.

Internal communication

A major role for the corporate communication function is opening narratives on the inside and fostering cultures driven by values and future outlooks. Like the famous saying goes, never underestimate the value of good communication, and at work, never underestimate the value of corporate communication. If internal communication will fall under the remit of your department, I encourage you to spend time reviewing Chapter 14 of the book.

As in the previous sections, start out by laying out your internal communication objectives. Theoretically speaking, internal communication is part of the public relations cloud and shares the same objectives. For practical purposes, the chapter will dedicate a separate section for internal communications to help you drill down into the initiatives you would like to oversee.

A major outcome that can be created by internal communication is happy employees that are inspired to serve customers. Happy employees make happy customers.

Here are some thought-starters on what your objectives could be:

1. Enrich a performance-driven culture and reward overachievers, thereby reinforcing positive behaviour and enhancing productivity.
2. Encourage open communication and coming forward with new ideas.
3. Improve the communication of customer-centricity through happy, well-trained, and loyal employees.
4. Create channels for two-way communication both from the bottom-up and top-down to allow clarity and alignment.
5. Be able to reach and engage employees of all ranks and locations.
6. Strengthen the position of your company as an employer of choice.
7. Foster transparency and allow relationships to be built on trust and allegiance to the company.
8. Turn employees into brand custodians.

A prerequisite to successful internal communication is your company's tone of voice. I would recommend that your company's brand persona be created by doing the exercise in Chapter 14. In bringing your company's tone of voice to life, you will need to have a general guideline on what to do and what not to do.

Create the themes of your messages that you wish to relay, and, additionally, the activations and the initiatives that pull the internal communities together.

Identifying your internal audiences is as important as identifying customers and external audiences. Companies don't always have a harmonious pool of audiences. Companies in manufacturing would have employees that are white-collar and blue-collar. Each may not have access to the same modes of communication, such as emails and instant messaging. The employee clusters will have different aspirations, needs, and wants as well. You will need to study how best to reach each pool of employees.

Identify your internal communication channels: emails, intranets, blogs, video conferencing, newsletters, and bulletin boards. Podcasting is an effective way to communicate with employees as well. These are great for keeping employees informed.

Internal communication channels

Internal messaged can be communicated through many different channels, and these could include:

- **Intranet.** This is the most popular form to facilitate internal communications for companies.
- **In-person meetings.** Meetings take many forms as well, from small intimate ones to large offsite ones.
- **Virtual meetings.** These could also range from video conferences to online seminars.
- **Phone meetings.** Less used these days but some companies still adopt phone conferences.
- **Written communications.** These come in the form of letters, newsletters, announcements, and memos and are shared digitally or in printed formats.

- **Events.** Employee events range from awarding ceremonies to planning meetings.
- **Research and surveys.** Designed to get feedback from employees.

Internal communication forms

Leadership communication: This provides employees with a sense of ownership and belonging. It instils the feeling of security and safety at the workplace. Effective leadership is all about timely and transparent communication. People love to be informed and acknowledged. In your internal communication planning, create a two-way communication stream for leaders and employees.

To ensure great leadership communication, there needs to be continuity and consistency. For a leader to be perceived as great, he or she needs to have great communication skills. In this part, I urge you to identify any communication and media skills required for the leaders of the company. We touched upon this topic in Chapter 13. Consistency is achieved when the communication of the leader carries the same tone and is humble and friendly. Communication will always carry a clear set of values and beliefs as well. These usually reflect those of the company.

Divisional communication: Divisional communication covers messaging that needs to be communicated by the division leaders to employees of that division or the company. Divisions that often communicate frequently to the internal audiences include Operations, Sales, HR, Service and After-sales, Customer Excellence, Compliance, Legal, Health & Safety, and Audit.

Strategy and performance communication. Other topics that will be covered in your internal communication plan will include the communication of annual plans and future goals. These pieces of communication are usually championed by the C-suite, mainly the CEO and in some organisations, the CFO. Communication of performance and targets is usually done on a monthly, quarterly, and bi-annual basis.

Learning and development. This is run by the HR department and is aimed at enhancing knowledge acquisition and the adoption of new skills for the employees. You could collaborate with the company's L&D team to help develop training material and a training program or just keep the organisation updated.

Topical day activation. Topical days can also be great platforms for internal communication. Communication on topical days is highly effective in bringing up the affinity levels and giving a human tone to your company. Identify the topical days that can be leveraged for internal communication such as Labour Day, World Cultural Diversity Day, and Happiness at Workday in addition to many others such as Mother's Day, Christmas, and New Year. This topic was tackled in more detail in Chapter 14.

Social media. Today, companies are using social media channels such as TikTok and Snapchat for effective employee engagement and communication.

Events. Awards ceremonies and roadshows can be effective in creating a high-performance company culture. Schedule these for the year as part of your internal comms plan.

Complete your plan by listing the initiatives and mapping them against a timeline.

The next section of the Chapter will focus on elements that your plans should cover, and these are:

- Timelines
- Measurement and analytics
- Reports

Timelines

Success certainly doesn't come easy and won't occur without an element of accountability and clarity. Timelines hold you responsible for the delivery of your initiatives. In presenting your plans, add a timeline to each and explain the length of time it will take to complete each.

Measurement and analytics

The next element to consider in your plans is how you are going to measure the completion and success of your projects. Measurement means data, and this will allow for informed decisions. This also helps you in justifying your marketing spend and your overall requested budgets.

Measurement and analytics help you monitor and record the success and progress of your campaigns. These are varied and change from one marketing channel to another. I will share with you a summarised version of what the most common metrics are:

Discipline	Measurement Metrics
Digital Marketing and SEM (Search Engine Marketing)	**Ad Impressions (IMPR).** The total number of times a digital ad is displayed on a viewer's screen whether it is via a platform or social media channels such as Facebook or YouTube. **Ad Views.** The number of times your advertising message was viewed on a specific platform. **Ad Clicks.** Clicks happen when a viewer clicks on the ad and an impression only happens when they see it. **CTR (Click Through Rate).** The number of clicks that your ad receives divided by the number of impressions (IMPR). **Conversion Rates.** When your ad successfully converts into an actual purchase of your product or service. **CPA (Cost per Acquisition).** Most common in digital marketing, it explains the marketing cost required to acquire a new customer. CPA is calculated by dividing your marketing spend (Campaign Cost) by the number of customers acquired (conversion). **PPC (Pay Per Click).** Advertising cost of a paid search on Google; that is, clicking on an ad placed in Google's search engine. **CPC (Cost Per Click).** The amount paid when a viewer clicks on your ads.

Discipline	Measurement Metrics
SEO and Website Analytics	• Page rankings. • Pages crawled per day. • Pages from organic searches. • Location visibility. • Page traffic (total number of visits on a weekly or monthly basis). • Forms completed. • Videos played. • Sign-ups. • Chats. • Uploads/downloads. • Page views and repeated views. • Average pages per session. • Average time on page. • Bounce rates. • Session durations. • Basket abandoners for e-commerce sites. • Bookings and reservations.
Social Media	• Traffic and referrals. • Engagement – the total number of interactions with a platform including the likes, shares, subscriptions, follows, direct messages, comments, and mentions. • Leads. • Conversions rates.
E-commerce	• Order values. • Cart performance. • Modes of payments. • Bookings. • Best performing products. • Conversion rates. • Repeat purchases.

Discipline	Measurement Metrics
Email and SMS marketing	• Open rates. • Bounce rates. • Leads. • Click-through rates.
Public Relations	• Press clippings. • PR value (advertising value multiplied either by 3 or 4). • SOV (Share of Voice) by volume. • SOV (Share of Voice) by reach. • Tonality and sentiment (Positive, Negative and Neutral). • Top articles by reach. • Cover stories. • Top language. • Positive and negative media mentions both online and offline. • Reach by territory.
Events and Road-shows	• Number of visitors or footfall. • Contacts and database collected. • Session analytics. • Surveys and feedback. • Speaker engagements. • Feedback surveys.
Sponsorships	• Value of media and PR coverage. • Notable positive changes in social media following around the period of the sponsorship. • Positive changes in the sales and lead generation during & post any CSR activation. • New customer data collected.

Reports

The delivery of reports that will be generated by your department is part of your strategy deck. Here are examples of reports that are usually generated by the marcomms function:

Report	Description
Department Activity Summary Reports	These summarise your department's activities and are usually issued on a monthly, quarterly, or annual basis. This report may be based on non-financial data where you present a collective list of all work delivered by the marketing and communication teams at the company. The objective of the report is to provide a concise overview of activities taking place across the organisation and the communication verticals.
Budget Reports	These present how the budget is being utilised. Budget reports are usually issued on a monthly, quarterly, and annual basis. Budget reports show the status of the budget, and how much was spent against the plan and previous years and time periods. Budget reports are sometimes presented by campaigns or by channels as well.

Report	Description
PR Reports	PR reports, also issued monthly, by brand or company, within a company show the news that was generated during that period. The report will show the media value generated from the news. Coverage reports segregate the value coming in by type of media channel, such as TV, web, newspaper, and online social channels. Some also integrate the feedback or coverage generated organically from online communities and social media influencers. PR reports also show the share of voice for a brand in its markets. SOV or Share of Voice is not only generated from news but also from online reviews, e-commerce, and search activity on search engines. In simple terms, SOV explains where the voice of the brand ranks amongst its competition in each market.
Campaign Performance Reports	These take on many forms depending on the types of campaigns and promotions run. Performance is measured by the leads generated and conversations into sales made. These include statistics on the behaviour of your target audience with the campaign and on what channels, times, and in what circumstances the campaign had peak performance.

Report	Description
Social Media Reports	These provide a summary on the activity that has been published on your social media platform (posts, stories, and videos). They include information on the type of engagements received both organically and paid (likes, comments, reactions, shares, post link clicks, and other post clicks). Shows the number of total impressions received and benchmarks against previous months to track how well the posts are performing. Showcases the top-performing posts on your different social media platforms.
Web Analytics Reports	These reports explain how your brand's website is performing in terms of visits and other activity. A corporate website analytics report will show how many people visit the site and for how long, and what their journey on the website is. For an e-commerce site, your web analytics will showcase the entire activity taking place on your site, what lead types are bringing in the visitors, and details on the transactions and conversions taking place. Your web analytics can also include many details on the engagements with the sites. These would include who is using discount codes, signing up for emails, downloading brochures, following your social media links, and watching your video content. More details can also be provided on the activities on the search bars and how baskets are being checked out.

Report	Description
Market Research	Market research reports provide a general update on the industry and markets trends and the latest shifts in customer behaviours. They include information about the industry's competitive landscape, industry trends, key competitors and industry size. They also highlight the latest technologies and disruptions in the market.
Retail Analytics and Reports	If you work in a retail-drive environment, retail reports provide analytical data critical for making marketing and procurement decisions. These include inventory levels, supply chain movement, consumer demand and trends in sales and purchasing power.
SEO Reports	SEO reports show what progress has been made on a brand's searchability and ranking status. SEO reports track your website's SEO performance. They document which SEO tactics efforts are working (e.g., identify specific keywords for organic search) and which need revision.
CSR (Corporate Social Responsibility) Reports	CSR reports summarise all CSR initiatives run by the company. The larger an organisation, the more elaborate in form these become, with set measurements such as Global Reporting Initiative reports and ESG. Many businesses striving to be socially responsible use the triple bottom line – an organisation's impact on people and the planet, in addition to its profits – to determine strategic priorities.

Other topics included in your strategy deck

Human skills. This part covers changes to your team structure and new team hires. Propose the team structure or skillsets required for the year. These were covered in Chapter 8.

Vendor requirements. This section addresses any changes in your vendor requirements such as the need for new agencies, added scope to existing agencies, or the need for new vendors in technology, creative, production, media planning, executive branding, etc. Pitching for new agencies was covered in Chapter 8.

Research and development. This section will cover any requirements for updated research done on markets and customers. These may be required for new market-entry strategies, customer behaviour insights, or launch of new products and solutions.

Technology and digital platforms. Investments related to new dashboards, monitoring systems, and other software required to maintain efficient and updated operations.

Departmental costs. Costs related to operating your department. These were included in Chapter 6.

Budgets and calendars. You may present these as outlined and explained in Chapter 9.

Implementing your strategy

Strategies are never set in stone. Even the greatest ones fail because execution is what matters. Your success lies not only in how well you craft your strategy but how well you execute it. The execution of your strategy is the litmus test of your success.

Here are a few tips on how you can ensure your strategy deck gets manifested into real wonderful work:

- Create excitement about your strategy by involving your team. It is important that the members feel a sense of ownership and accountability and understand the role they play in bringing this strategy to life.
- Dissolve the silos between the marketing and communication team members by sharing the comprehensive plans to both of them showing them the roles they will play in the implementation.
- Build your team's KPIs (Key Performance Indicators) based on the actions that were outlined in your strategy. KPIs will allow you to review your team members' performance on a regular basis and help you reinforce the strategy to them.
- Communicate progress on the strategy and use the measurement tool and the metrics suggested to evaluate progress towards the goals. Allow for open and transparent communication. Assess what's working and what's not and reflect on improvements with your team.
- Utilise the Enablers such as the processes, SLAs (Service Level Agreements), and policies discussed in Chapter 10 of the book to assist you in delivering work with minimum hurdles.

- Allow for deviations. There will be changes to your strategy and you need to be agile and receptive to the changes in the environment that will affect the execution of your strategy.
- Report to the leaders of your company how the strategy is coming along throughout its implementation journey.

In closing, I wish to reference author Robin Speculand, who wrote: 'It's better to have excellence in execution than a winning strategy because you then know how good or bad a strategy is. From there, you can adjust as required during the execution phase.'

In the next and final chapter of the book, we will touch upon skills that can help you excel in your career.

20

SKILLS THAT GET YOU THERE

'The key to realising a dream is to focus not on success but significance, and then even the small steps and little victories along your path will take on greater meaning.'

— OPRAH WINFREY

I was lucky to start my career working for some of the world's best advertising agencies. I worked on global brands and high-profile regional ones. I also worked for multinational companies, partnered for start-up for a stint of time, and then went on to work on brands in the public sector and large family businesses. While working on the client-side has its unique lessons, working in account management of an advertising agency during its glory days was a great learning journey that taught me many lessons that I wish to share with you.

Caution! I am not going to preach to you on leadership and management styles. Personally speaking, I still do not believe that I can. I have been diagnosed with the self-indulgent syndrome of 'I'm not there yet.' Perhaps it is this trait that has gotten me to where I am in life. Since this part of the book is an insight into my personal experiences, I will share with you, with my potent honesty, some lessons that shot me forward in my career. I hope that some if not all will help you in one way or another.

Lesson 1: Surrender to your passion.

Unlike other jobs on the corporate spectrum, I do not believe you can survive working in marcomms without having a passion for it. This is a field that requires self-expression and putting your own mark on things to make a difference. It is a litmus test of how well you can tame your ego. Your career in this industry is driven by how well you can embrace empathy. Marcomms requires fighting for budgets, making your point to a non-experienced audience, defending the creativity of the work, and creating harmony for the brand with its internal and external stakeholders. Time and budgets are always against you. Working in this dynamic field means that you are expected to put in a lot of long hours (and sometimes weekend benders), and the only thing that will get you through is really putting a whole lot of heart into what you do. As cliché as it sounds, just like diamonds, the inside process is messy and turbulent, but the outcome is beautiful. My advice to you is simple. If you are not madly in love with this field, choose another one.

Lesson 2: A 'complete' brief is not a utopian dream.

When I worked on the agency side, I gave up on the dream of ever receiving a proper brief that could help prevent rounds of changes and messy conversations, let alone the build-up of resentment and negativity when you keep the team working late. A client's brief is never going to be 'good enough', I declared many years ago. Clients speak a different language from creatives, and this is how it should be. They are focused on sales, product mixes, and extensive data reports and you are supposed to compress it all into a high impact short format campaign. Working on the client-side now, I beg and plead that you realise the importance of putting in proper briefs. And, oh, please respect the timelines required for the process. Learn to help your collaborators and teams, especially agencies and vendors, with the tools that are out there and give them a proper brief.

Lesson 3: Take a look around; get envious but not jealous.

It's easy to get sucked into a vacuum of your own work. Make sure to keep in touch with the outside world and always stay up-to-date with the latest trends and ever-evolving perceptions of this field. Thanks to the internet and social media surge, real-time feedback is now just a Google search away. I admit, I am an envious person; I want to have what the successful ones in the field have. I follow many bright and talented CMOs on LinkedIn. I read their articles and watch their panel talks with excitement and investigative observation. Envy is when you want what others have because you believe you can get it too. If you believe it, you can achieve it. Jealousy, on the other hand, is toxic. It is based on a false belief that you don't have what others do. Everything in life is a muscle; train it well and it will become stronger. I learned so much over the years, and I am proud of this self-improvement quest that I put myself on.

Lesson 4: You don't know what you've got until it's gone.

The grass is truly always greener on the other side. Working in a demanding field like advertising lends itself to making you want to complain about how clients do not understand you and how they have it so much better. I spent many years wanting to jump to the client-side thinking it was much better and perhaps less demanding. There is a whole set of other challenges if you work on the client-side of marcomms. You are among the few who understand your field. Your internal audiences are sometimes administrators, engineers, factory managers and shark salespeople. They often than not, blame their poor performance on marketing and many of them would criticise a campaign or an event you ran with hard work in a dismissive way. Enjoy every stage of your career and the learning curves. The field of marcomms has ample opportunities and a range of jobs, all of which are dynamic and special in their own way.

Lesson 5: All you need is the intention to do something.

I had my fair share of criticism and scepticism at work. I heard enough observations on my career path with investigative probing from HR managers in interviews like, 'You change jobs too much,' 'You don't last long in one place,' 'Do you know what you want?' 'Why move from a great brand to a local one?' 'Why do you think you can do this job?' I know I got myself into matters that I really did not have enough knowledge or experience in, but I knew that I had the intention to learn and excel at them. And, yes, I did.

There are industry acquaintances who look at me and ask, 'Where do you work now?' A question that holds with it a clear judgement: 'You keep changing jobs.' I answer loudly and confidently because I am proud of every milestone in my career, and you should be too. If you are reading this book, it means you are out there trying to better yourself, so kudos to you.

The business world today recognises those with the intention to do something and not those who know how to do it. 'Some people say they have 20 years' experience, when they have 1 years' experience repeated 20 times.' – Stephen M. R. Covey to Richie Norton when Norton asked if he was too young to train older executives for Covey.

Lesson 6: Get started anyway.

Socrates rightly said, 'The only true wisdom is in knowing you know nothing.' Both my parents progressed in their careers by learning through books and on-job training. They read and studied college while they were raising me and my siblings. Today, the world is full of easy and accessible knowledge. I cringe when I compare the price of books to make-up sets and perfume bottles. Knowledge is cheap. In addition, you have masterclasses, free webinars, scholarly articles, great case studies on SlideShare, and Google has your back. You can connect with the best in your field over LinkedIn and meet great marketers through societies and industry forums. The tools are available and some are free. All you need is to get started, without hesitation or procrastination – get started anyway.

Deadlines can be unforgiving, and new requests can keep piling up until you are overwhelmed. Like religious ceremonies that you were taught to respect, pay your courtesy to yourself by developing yourself. Read books, take courses, download white papers and reports, and reach out to others in the field and connect with them. I still believe in books, much more than blogs or online courses.

Lesson 7: Just because you're not in the 'Creative department', that doesn't mean you can't be creative.

In 2018, I attended a high-performance leadership course at work led by the renowned Dr Corrie Block alongside senior colleagues from my company. Individuals in the room were asked to describe each other using one word, write that word on a post-it note, and then hang it on a flip chart notepad. To my surprise, almost all the notes posted about me carried one word: creative. Till then, I really did not know that people perceive me as creative person.

Creativity is the key to problem-solving and a key to successful marketing and PR. Humans in big organisations tend to label and frame themselves into roles. I like to be a change maker. Creativity is not exclusive to our industry, but it is certainly a main ingredient.

How to earn it? Please don't be a cookie-cutter marketer and don't become mechanical in your delivery of campaigns. In other words, don't repeat what was done the year before. I don't believe that creativity requires a heavy exertion of imagination. It requires the belief that there is always a better way or a new way of doing something, even when you have done it before, and you've done it well.

Lesson 8: Apologise and mean it.

A large portion of learning comes from admitting your mistakes. More important, admitting that you do not really know it all. It is easy to get defensive and feel the need to blame others and the circumstances, the infamous ones being time and budgets, for when things are not great. Apology teaches empathy and humility. It tears down walls of the ego and allows team members to focus on achieving goals rather than proving themselves right. Saying to someone 'You are right, I am sorry' brings about nothing but respect and trust.

Lesson 9: Learn to unlearn.

'The future belongs to those who unlearn and relearn.' – Wayne Mansfield. There is so much that I learnt in the field that no longer holds true today. Marketing for mature marketers has changed so much in its approach – similarly, the strategy setting and working with teams. I remember how a campaign idea was pitched in a way that showed how the visual and headline could be adapted to all types of sizes and channels, such as TV, billboard, and ads.

Today, the strength of your campaign lies in its versatility and the ability to carry different copy, imagery, and media selection instantaneously. Similarly, in working with teams, I was taught that the strongest teams are those with the highest areas of speciality. Today, I look for well-rounded, experienced people with the will to work on multiple areas. Finally, while for years I held the flag of pride called multitasking, today, I know how bad it is for maturing at work and producing the greatest ideas. I am now a person who doesn't shy away from focusing on one task at a time and giving it its much-needed attention.

Lesson 10: The ups and downs are part of the joy ride.

You are going to get through situations where you get rejected and turned down. You may carry out amazing work that doesn't meet the approval of some of your peers or management. You may follow every piece of advice in the book and, still, your campaigns might not work. Whatever it is – it is part of the ride. Instability is part of the plan.

'There is so much more to life than what you experience right now. You need to decide who you are for yourself. Become a whole being. Adventure.' – Roy T. Bennett. Don't let the expectations and opinions of other people affect your decisions. It's your life, not theirs. Do what matters most to you; do what makes you feel alive and happy. Don't let the expectations and ideas of others limit who you are. If you let others tell you who you are, you are living their reality – not yours.

Lesson 11: Stay curious.

Curiosity killed the cat but sent man to the moon. There is a reason for everything. Curiosity is the birth of philosophy and innovations. You never get what you want from life from one single job. No one role is going to give you the knowledge and experience that will propel you forward; your curiosity will. Curiosity is the power to your passion and the driving force to your life. The opening of my book touched upon curiosity, and this is what led me to my career. Stay curious.

Books and how I got here

Some say reading is to the mind is what exercise is to the body, and I concur. One of my greatest blessings is that I was raised in a family of devoted readers. When I reminisce back to my childhood, a lot of my memories are like old classic movies where the houses have libraries filled with books.

My father created a dedicated reading room in our home, which had three large libraries carrying hundreds of books stacked on shelves mounted all the way to the ceiling. The collection of books reflected my father's interest in history, politics, and business, while my mother's collection reflected her ambitious quest to venture into the world of journalism and nutrition. My collection today carries a lot of the literature in the field of marketing and self-development. I have often found books comprehensive and handy to go back to. Corporate trainings and certifications are great too, but often can be too condensed or contain only the outer shell of a topic. Books, on the other hand, are lengthy and carry a lot of great examples and references.

I must confess I still prefer reading paper books to digital ones. While technology has enhanced a lot of aspects of our daily human lives, consuming e-books and audiobooks still cannot compare to the feeling of holding a book in your bare hands and flipping through its pages.

Here are the titles that I have referenced in this book. They have greatly helped in enriching my career.

- *Corporate Communication: A Guide to Theory and Practice* written by Joep P. Cornelissen. This is the first read I sought when I moved to the client-side and took on corporate communications duties. It served as textbook material that helped me refresh my mind with the theories and the basics one should attain to succeed in communications. It is Joep's book that inspired me to write mine. I am nowhere close to having Joep's knowledge as he is a well-known university professor, but my intention is to offer the context in a practical and hands-on style whereas he is excellent at providing theory with great case studies for practice.
- *Marketing Management* by Greg W. Marshall and Mark W. Johnston.
- *Marketing Strategy and Research: In the Context of Different Organisations* by Ghazi Mokammel Hossain.
- *The One-Page Content Marketing Blueprint: Step by Step Guide to Launch a Winning Content Marketing Strategy in 90 Days or Less and Double Your Inbound Traffic, Leads and Sales* by Prafull Sharma.
- *Turning It On* and *Bricks to Bridges* by Robin Speculand.
- *The PR Masterclass: How to develop a public relations strategy that works* by Alex Singleton.

- *The PR Strategy Manifesto: 8 Steps to build a PR campaign designed to get massive media coverage by Mickie Kennedy.*
- *The 1-Page Marketing Plan: Get new customers, make more money, and stand out from the crowd* by Allan Dib.
- *Sponsorship Strategy: Practical Approaches to Powerful Sponsorships* by Ken Ungar.
- *Brands and Branding, Second Edition, by The Economist* by Rita Clifton.
- *Business Strategy* by Jeremy Kourdi.
- *Building a Story Brand* by Donald Miller.
- *The Fall of Advertising and the Rise of PR* by Al Ries and Laura Ries.
- *Taking People with You* by David Novak.
- *Book of Branding: A guide to creating brand identity for start-ups and beyond.*
- *The Practice of Adaptive Leadership: Tools and Tactics for Changing Your Organisation and the World* by Ronald A. Heifetz in collaboration with Marty Linsky and Alexander Grashow.
- *The Laws of Brand Storytelling* by Ekaterina Walter and Jessica Gioglio.
- *This is Marketing: You Can't Be Seen Until You Learn to See* by Seth Godin.
- *Verses from Somewhere* by Dean Jackson.
- *Crisis Communication Strategies: How to prepare in advance, respond effectively and recover in full* by Amanda Coleman.
- *Light Their Fire: Using Internal Marketing to Ignite Employee Performance and Wow your Customers* by Susan M. Drake.
- *What the New Breed of CMOs Know That You Don't* by MaryLee Sachs.
- *The Event Manager's Bible 3rd edition: The complete guide to planning and organising Voluntary or Public Event* by D.G. Conway.

- *How to Win Corporate Sponsorship: Helping you win the corporate sponsorship you want!* by Kim J. Harrison.
- *How to Write & Give a Speech* by Joan Detz.
- *Hey, Whipple, Squeeze This: The Classic Guide to Creating Great Ads* by Luke Sullivan and Edward Boches.
- *Purple Cow: Transform Your Business by Being Remarkable* by Seth Godin.
- *Working in Public Relations: How to Gain the Skills and Opportunities for a Career in PR* by Carole Chester.
- *Quantum Marketing* by Raja Rajamannar.
- *A modern guide to public relations including Content Marketing, SEO, Social Media & PR Best Practice* by Amy Rosenberg.
- *Shoe Dog: A Memoir by the Creator of Nike* by Phil Knight.
- *The 22 Immutable Laws of Marketing; Violate them at your own risk* by Al Ries and Jack Trout.

Before I end this book, I'd like to make a few points about the fun you can have in diversifying your career in marcomms. I say that because to date many believe that the best marketers are those with focused career paths in major organisations or single industries.

I truly believe that you have the right to experiment in the field and to get a chance to work in its multi-faceted areas. It is my opinion that you should never bind yourself to one side of the trade. You can also join the field from other fields such as sales or customer service. The plain is wide and welcoming; each one of you has a chance to go in a direction that makes you happy and excited.

The path to a successful marcomms career is not bonded to one industry

I never subscribed to the notion of hyper-specialisation in the fields of marketing and communication. When asked how marketers thrive in the tech era, Raja Rajamannar, Chief Marketing Officer of Mastercard and author of *Quantum Marketing* says, 'Be a know-it-all. Don't limit your understanding to your own industry.'

In this context, I truly share his sentiment. We are not meant to live our marketing and communication journeys bonded to one industry or sector. By diversifying our experience, we might be presented with opportunities to lead teams in new fields and new industries, and we should not miss out on those chances.

The more you know, the better you become

I have worked in advertising, branding, media planning, communication, sales, business development, and public relations.

I worked with and for companies in a myriad of industries such as automotive, airlines, tourism, banking, FMCGs, F&B, automotive, manufacturing, construction, and energy.

Not many agree with this notion. In fact, I have been faced with more criticism than praise when it came to my career choices.

I was in a job interview once, and the recruiter, a young enthusiastic gentleman who sounded like a fresh graduate applying textbook theory front and centre to his judgments, kept staring at me and saying out loud to the meeting, 'She's changed jobs way too many times,' 'She's changed jobs way too many times,' 'She's changed jobs way too many times.' His repetition was about to make me dwindle myself down into a reactive position or perhaps preach a defence, but, luckily, I knew very well that where I stand in life, and it is not for the faint-hearted. I chose to breathe and smiled instead.

Marcomms professionals who work on global brands are not entrepreneurial enough to work for local or homegrown brands

I have come to realise that there are two schools of thought in our industry. There are those who believe that the best marketers out there are those who have been working for the biggest and best global brands. And there are others who believe that marketers who work on local and homegrown brands are more resilient and have been exposed to a wider spectrum of marketing applications.

I have been on both sides of the trade. I have worked for global and fast-growing brands in multinational settings and for small homegrown brands in local settings. The learning opportunities on both sides of the hill are endless.

On the global front, you get access to a wealth of knowledge, and it is up to you to decide how much to gain from it. You get your hands on global reports on how economies are unfolding, what technologies are out there disrupting the sector, as well as amazing reports on the most intimate of insights about the global consumer.

You also work with industry tycoons and get exposed to award-winning work. You get to meet the most professional of executives in the polished corporate world. Yet, you may become highly specialised in the field you are in, and there would be many teams doing other types of work that you may not get exposure to.

If you have an entrepreneurial or intrapreneurial flair, joining an SME or start-up will surely provide you with a rich experience and an opportunity to work on many projects of different natures. You will have to handle strategising, budgeting, media planning, running events, and, probably, sourcing give-aways. You will need resilience and openness to learn. More importantly, you will need to get yourself very knowledgeable about the different fields of marcomms, marketing, branding, PR, and internal communications.

Your budget should not decide how good you are

A marcomms professional is, in my definition, a corporate executive that resembles a chameleon in the woods. They scan their outside environment in 360 views, adapt to the brand and market circumstance, and take up the colour of their environment.

When I left my last job at the agency, I was handling two of its biggest clients in the Middle East. The first was a suite of international F&B brands that translated to over 200 retail outlets, and the second was a world-class airline. I oversaw a budget that exceeded the 150-million-dollar mark. The media was my playground; the brands were splashed across the Middle East and Africa regions. Budgets were never a hurdle at work.

When I joined my first client-side job, the marketing budget was not even close to what I'd had in the past. The company estimated marketing and promotions to be 0.3% of every restaurant's sale. The number of outlets was small, and the principal brands were providing minimal support to the marketing funds. I had to think of new ways to stand out from the crowd. This forced me into exploring marketing beyond the grand approach to spending on media. It wasn't easy, but I learnt that it was doable.

You are backed up by a great agency

Another great myth about marcomms professionals is that they are successful only if backed up by great agencies and a team. No doubt this is often true, but if you, like me, have been there all alone for some time, you can still make it.

There are many marketers who started departments on their own in both local and international firms and eventually created full-fledged teams gradually. You have what it takes to carry out great work, not necessarily with an award-winning agency backing you up.

You can learn anything, but only if you want to

Not having the exposure in marcomms doesn't mean you cannot venture into its many fields. The similarities in the fields are undeniable. Creativity and seamless execution remain at the heart of the entire process. Just like my professor suggested in Chapter 1, if you apply the right tools, you can do it.

Creativity is at the heart of business success

Think outside the box, and you will find a solution to every business problem. I am a true veteran of creativity in business. You can get creative through research, knowledge-seeking, widening your horizons by exploring industry practices, and moving beyond the ordinary thinking of problem-solving to answer needs. My sister holds the best definition of creativity. She says it is intelligence having fun. To me, creativity is honouring an idea and testing it. If you're not scared of failure, you have no reason not to try.

Marketing, PR and Comms are all one

What our industry really needs is unity. Today, we often hear of 'marketing' or 'comms'. You have marketing awards and PR awards. We either sign up to marketing societies or PR societies. But it shouldn't be the case. With data being abundant, the lines have been completely blurred between marketing and communication practices, and the challenge remains how to best utilise the data you have across both functions. Creativity and problem-solving bind us all together.

You don't need to be married to your industry forever

When Steve Jobs lured John Sculley to leave Pepsi and join Apple in selling personal computers, his famous pitch was sealed with the question 'Do you want to sell sugared water for the rest of your life?'

397

If you have spent many years in one field or industry, this should not define you. It's never too late to change. There are plenty of means to allow you to broaden your scope, and the more you know, the more you can offer the world. In this regard, this book will certainly enable you to take on a senior role in the field of marketing and communication, even if you did not get to experience all the avenues of marketing and comms beforehand.

In closing, Marcomms is great fun! And you will be a great marcomms trail blazer. I hope that you found at least some of the content of this book beneficial.

If you have applied any of the frameworks or approaches mentioned in this book, I would love to know how that worked for you and hear your thoughts. Drop me an email on marwa@marwakaabour.com.

MARWA KAABOUR

Marwa Kaabour is a CMO-level executive with 25+ years of experience in establishing and leading strategic marketing communications for global and regional brands in the Middle East. Among her achievements is establishing marketing and communication functions from scratch for companies and government entities. In addition to her strategic 'from scratch' capabilities, she has expertise in developing core functions for large and portfolio businesses, leading cross-functional teams, and creating harmony and efficiencies in both marketing and comms – as well as contributing to organisational transformation.

Marwa is an expert in a diverse range of subjects including specialisations such as business transformation and digitisation, strategic marketing, branding, public relations, brand management, corporate communications, and executive profiling. Her core expertise lies in elevating strategic management, creation and launch of B2C, B2G and B2B brands, media relations, corporate communication, change management, and growth marketing.

Marwa started her career with award-winning international agencies like Leo Burnett and Impact BBDO. She then moved to the client-side, bringing agency-level expertise into solo-firm marketing and communication. Her experience spans multiple industries, including energy, power, manufacturing, automotive, airlines, banking, FMCGs, F&B, construction, and retail businesses. This versatile background has led her to contribute to a broad spectrum of global and regional brands such as Nissan, Infiniti, Renault, Volvo Penta, MTU, Nestle, Emirates Airline, Pizza Hut, and entities that fall under the Government of Abu Dhabi.

Marwa was named *Campaign's* Middle East 2021 'Marketing Game Changer' and was selected as one of LinkedIn's 'Most Engaged Marketers' in 2014. She was also selected to be the UAE's 'Highly Commended Female Marketing Leader' by the Women in Marketing Institution in London in 2018. Marwa was named 'Best CMO in UAE' by the Digital Stallions Community and winner of Al Masaood's 'Best Leader Award' and 'Best Support Department Award'. Marwa frequently lectures on the topics of Marketing, CSR, and Communication at Abu Dhabi universities. She is part of the Advisory Committee for the Abu Dhabi School of Management. She is consistently recognised for exemplary management performance in leading marketing campaigns, driving innovative strategy, and establishing procedures to increase enterprise-wide efficiency.

An advocate of women's empowerment, health, and financial literacy, Marwa often blogs about the topics of CSR and brands' higher purpose. She is a member of the Marketing Society, UAE Chapter, and frequently publishes articles. She holds an MBA from the American University of Sharjah and a Bachelor of Marketing and Management (with honours) from the same university. She is a Certified Sustainability Marketer, with an accreditation from the Center for Sustainability Excellence, and a Certified Digital Marketer, with accreditation from the Institute of Digital Marketing in Ireland.

Currently, Marwa is the Group Head of Marketing and Communication for Al Masaood Group, one of Abu Dhabi's largest conglomerates. She was selected as the 'Best Leader' in the Group in 2019 and 2020.

www.ingramcontent.com/pod-product-compliance
Lightning Source LLC
Chambersburg PA
CBHW020846210326
41597CB00041B/604